Cherish the Love

WRITTEN BY
MILDRED K. SIMPSON

Butterscotch Memoirs

ISBN 978-0-9885227-6-3

Printed in the United States of America

Design: Julián Galván | www.juliangalvan.com.ar

This book is dedicated to God who was my inspiration.

My late mother Mildred Bieard, my sisters, Florence, Rosa and Audrey.

My beloved (late) Marvin C. Peay; and to all those who supported, encouraged and believed in me.

Chapter one

"Will this rain ever let up?" There was a chill in the air, the temperature having drastically dropped. The predicted category three storm was raising its ugly head. Marcus was driving at about five miles per hour, his windshield wipers barely keeping up with the torrential rain. Despite the downpour, cars sped past Marcus as if they were rushing to a fire. Downed tree branches and debris littered the roads making many impassable. Car alarms were being activated, and police sirens could be heard throughout the city. The police had a horrific job trying to remove pedestrians from the streets.

To avoid causing an accident, Marcus decided to pull over to the side of the road. He called the office to inform Mr. Wright, his immediate supervisor of the travel conditions; there was no way he would be able to reach work on time. The phone kept ringing until finally the answering machine came on. He left a recorded message and backed it up with a text message. "Why didn't I call out today? This is crazy; I'll probably be the only person at work if I make it in." Within minutes, Marcus's phone rang. "Hello Mr. Wright, yes it's a nasty day but as you know my contract calls for me to ... yes sir," Marcus sighed with exasperation. "I know it's a weather advisory but, as you know Mr. Wright, I can only be excused because ... yes sir, I understand. Goodbye, have a good day." Wow, he sure gave me an earful, Marcus thought and shook his head.

Why had it taken Mr. Wright to tell him to turn around and go home? He heard the weather report; the storm was just as predicted, but he had underestimated the severity of the storm.

Despite the flooded roads, downed trees, and high winds, Marcus made it home safely. He was disappointed he wouldn't be seeing Tressa, his new love interest. He was a single brother that was going places, and she just might be the woman to go with him. In anticipation of seeing her, he dressed in one of his best suits, one he usually reserved for diplomatic affairs, he was sure to catch her attention.

Marcus was raised by two bachelors, his father and grandfather, both educated with impeccable class and taste. He was taught to treat every woman with the utmost respect; every woman should be treated like a queen, despite their social or economic standing, personal appearance or beliefs.

Marcus was ashamed to think so much about a woman, but she mesmerized him. He wondered how she was making out in the storm and prayed she was safe.

Leaving the car, he hurried into the building, out of the elements. As soon as he was safely inside, all the lights went out. Marcus assumed the generator would kick in, but after an hour of waiting in the dark, he became one of many residents that called management for assistance, to no avail. At least he had enough batteries and canned food to last at least a week. He found some lanterns and placed them around the condo. "That's better; now I can maneuver around the place." Marcus noticed his telephone blinking, "Thank God that still works." He played the message and heard, "Marcus, this is Dad, I've been trying to reach you all morning. Please call me when you receive this message." Marcus did just that; he immediately called his father. "Dad, what's wrong? Why didn't you call me on my cell?" "Son, I tried, I've been calling you all day." "You have?"... Marcus checked his phone, nothing, then checked his BlackBerry. "There it is." He had mistakenly given his father the number of his BlackBerry, which was not working. "Dad, what's wrong?" "Your grandfather's house was hit by that great oak. The front of the house is seriously damaged and the basement is flooded. I have been here all morning. Can you come and help? I know the weather is bad, but I need you." "Dad, what about Pop, is he OK?" "Yes, he's fine. He's sopping up water as we speak. We called several companies to remove the tree, but no one is available." "Dad, I'll be over as soon as I can, and before you tell me, I'll be sure to wear my raincoat and boots."

It took Marcus hours to get to his "Great Pop's" home. He was devastated by what he saw; the tree covered the entire front of the house. "Dad, I am here!" Marcus went around the back and down into the basement where Avery Dallas was happy to see his son. "Son, are we happy to see you." "My God, what a mess!" Marcus was impressed because it looked like the entire neighborhood had come to help. They had several huge water vacuums sucking out water. For insurance purposes, Marcus and Avery took lots of pictures because "Pop" (Les) Dallas was overwhelmed and documenting the disaster was the last thing on his mind.

By the end of the day, the tree had been removed and the busted windows patched up.

They secured the house, and the three of them headed to Avery's until the storm let up.

Marcus was so proud of his grandfather, who he lovingly called "Pop." For Pop, there was no "Lord why me?" he knew he was not exempt from trials. Pop thanked God for his neighbor's help, support from his son and grandson, their love, and most of all that no lives were lost.

Several days later, the community started to come alive. City workers cleared as much debris as possible. The Mayor's office urged citizens to stay off the roads that were flooded because of downed wires, thereby avoiding electrocution. The police patrolled the streets as best they could, diverting people to sections of the city that posed less danger.

As Marcus lay in bed, he thought about the brown beauty. He first noticed Tressa at the law firm where they both worked. He was waiting for the elevator, and when the doors opened, there she was dressed in a white linen suit, wearing a pearl necklace with matching earrings, and her hair pulled back in a ponytail.

She was leaning against the wall of the elevator with her legs crossed, carrying a briefcase that reeked of leather. He took a double look at her and extended his hand. "Good morning, I'm Marcus Dallas, and you are?" Tressa hesitated, making eye contact before extending her hand. "My name is Tressa Bowers." Marcus thought to himself, "Who is this woman?" He could not recall ever feeling this way, he felt like a schoolboy. When the elevator doors opened, they got off on the same floor. Then a light bulb went off in his head as he remembered her picture on one of the brochures in his conference packet.

Marcus hurried to his office and retrieved the packet. "There she is! Tressa Bowers, Attorney at Law. To his surprise, she was the keynote speaker and the host of three workshops throughout the week. He eagerly read her biography, "She earned her degree at Harvard, graduated third in her class and received many awards for academic achievement and community service."

On a whim, he decided to attend the conference. The topic: "The New Laws that Impact Litigations in Real Estate." He hoped his calendar was clear; he hadn't taken the time to review the presentations or register. Hurrying to the conference, he found Mr. Cross, the coordinator and asked if there was room. Mr. Cross checked through his file. "Let's see, yes, you're in luck, I have one space left." Handing him the roster, he said, "Please sign here. It begins in 30 minutes."

Now Marcus had to clear it with his superior, racing from office to office he frantically searched for Mr. Wright, but to no avail. Noticing the secretary, he called out, "Sheila have you seen Mr. Wright?"

With her hands on her hips, she focused on him sharply. "You talking to me, Mr. Dallas? You can't be—I never heard you say, 'Good morning' or 'Hello Ms. Johnson!'" Marcus slowly walked up to her, took her hand and kissed it. "I apologize, Ms. Johnson, firstly I'd like to say Good morning. I would also like to say you look especially nice today, and ask whether you've seen Mr. Wright?" Removing her hand and putting it behind her back, she said, "Yes I have, he went out to get the morning paper and will return directly." Marcus thought, directly, who says that? "Thanks, Ms.

Johnson."

As Marcus was walking away, he saw Tressa and her entourage heading up the hall to the conference room, he thought he saw her cut her eye at him but wasn't sure.

Marcus spotted Mr. Wright singing and thumbing through the paper as he slowly walked into the break room. He didn't want to seem too anxious, so he cautiously followed him. "Good morning, Mr. Wright." "Hi there Dallas, having a good morning are ya?!" Marcus nodded, "Yes sir I am." He began, "Mr. Wright I would like to attend the seminar that's being presented today, I know it's a little out of my field, but it seems like a topic that could benefit the Bureau. This is the kind ..." Mr. Wright abruptly cut him off, "Son, I have you assigned for the seminar on 'Critical Thinking in the Far East,' that's being presented on Thursday," he said, looking over his glasses before adding, "all day." He took a deep breath. "I am not sure this seminar today would be beneficial to you or the Bureau (taking a deep breath), as a matter of fact I ..." "Mr. Wright, I have no objection to attending the seminar," Marcus politely interrupted, pleading his case, "however, remember I'm here to learn all I can about any and all types of laws and procedures. Those include reforms, legislative rulings, and mandates, and keep in mind, any and all information I learn, I will incorporate into my final report to the bureau and ..."

Mr. Wright held up a hand, stopping Marcus short. "If I give you permission to attend the conference, remember your attendance is dependent upon any assignments from the Bureau. Go, Mr. Dallas, never let it be said that I prevented you from learning! And, that was meant to be sarcastic!" "Yes, I know Mr. Wright, and I took it in the spirit in which it was given." Mr. Wright gave Marcus a side-glance, a look of disapproval. Marcus hurried off knowing Mr. Wright was not amused.

In addition to checking his calendar, Marcus hurriedly opened his emails from headquarters to see if there were any assignments, but there was nothing crucial. He informed his supervisor at headquarters, Mr. Parker, that he would be attending the conference and would check in at the conclusion; however, in the case of an emergency, he should contact Sheila Johnson, Mr. Wright's secretary.

Grabbing a notepad and pencil, he hurried to the conference room. It was packed, standing room only, but he didn't care. Tressa was already speaking and displaying all the signs of a professional speaker/presenter. She was poised, she interacted with the audience, her body language was composed, and she injected humor as a way to relax the crowd. She was approachable and very much in charge. To Marcus she glowed, it was a spiritual glow that seemed divine. At the break, chairs were brought in for latecomers, and to his surprise and delight he was ushered to a seat at the front of the room, a few feet from the podium. How did I get so lucky? He watched Tressa's every move, hanging on her every word. The conference was intense. She concluded her session by handing out a survey to be completed and returned at the conclusion of the session. In completing his survey, Marcus remarked that the information provided was invaluable and scored Tressa's presentation one hundred, ten being the highest in each category.

When the conference concluded, Marcus went to his office and closed the door. He had several reports to complete and submit to the main office by close of day. Just when he had started to focus, he heard Tressa's voice. "Why is my heart pounding like this, she's only a woman," he mumbled to himself. He leaned back in his chair and closed his eyes, hearing a still, soft voice say, "For the Lord God is a sun and shield: the Lord will give grace and glory: no good thing will be withheld from them that walk uprightly." He was stunned, never had he heard a voice so loving, calm and reassuring. He had heard this said before. Of course, it was a Bible verse. What did it mean? Was it about Tressa Bowers? Marcus whispered a prayer to God for revelation and direction.

Being the professional, he decided to watch and wait, he did not want to show his hand just in case Tressa was unavailable. He knew he would have to perform the usual spot checks, first the fingers to see if there was a ring (engagement or wedding), next would be the office photos and gossip. Never had he met a woman with so much personality.

Tressa was so absorbed in the conference, she lost track of time and found herself in a flustering predicament. A document for a client that was to be presented at a meeting in less than a half hour was jammed in the copier. "Darn it, why me? I don't know how to open this machine." She hurried to ask the secretary for assistance. "Sheila, could you assist me, please? My document is stuck in the copier—again!"

The secretary shook her head, blatantly bent on ignoring her pleas for help. "I've shown you several times how to operate the copier, Ms. Bowers." Tressa gritted her teeth. "Sheila, I'm in a time crunch, and I don't have time to ..." she stopped before finishing her sentence. She was getting more and more frustrated, her voice starting to rise, her body language becoming more aggressive. Realizing this, Tressa caught herself and stepped back from Sheila's space.

Just as she'd resigned herself to returning to the copier unaided, she heard a familiar voice, "May I be of assistance?" Turning, she saw Marcus standing there, staring down at her. Her first thought was, this man is so fine, who wouldn't want his help? "Yes, if you could, my document is jammed and I ..." before she could complete her sentence, the document was retrieved. "Wow! Thank you! Mr. Dallas isn't it? You saved my life." Like in a storybook, their eyes met, and it was something at first sight. Tressa wasn't sure it was love, but it was something. "I don't know if you noticed me, Ms. Bowers, but I attended your conference this morning." "I couldn't miss you, Mr. Dallas for obvious reasons." Marcus was befuddled, what did that mean? He assumed it was meant to be humorous after he noticed Tressa giving him a sly grin. "I am happy to meet you again, Mr. Dallas, but I'm in a hurry, I have to run." Glancing at her watch, she explained, "I have a meeting in twenty-five minutes."

Tressa hurried to her office to call the Montagues and inform them she would be approximately twenty minutes late; they were not impressed. They gave her twenty minutes and only twenty minutes. Howling with frustration, she grabbed her briefcase, purse, and coat and hurried to get a cab. "God, please help me." This was the firm's premiere client, her testing ground. Mr. Goode would hear about this, and it may not reflect positively on her professionalism. He would be sympathetic, but stern. I can hear him now; don't let this happen again, young lady! She didn't want to hear it!

Tressa ran for the elevator and pressed the down button, nothing happened. "What's going on, is this some kind of conspiracy?" She swept her hands through her hair, wanting to scream, but suddenly the doors opened; there he was again—her hero, Mr. Dallas! "We meet again," he stood aside. Pressing the express button, he asked, "Why are you so rattled?" "I am rattled because I'm late for a meeting. I have to be there by 2:30, and it's 2:10. I have twenty minutes to get across town." "May I be of assistance?" Marcus asked, arching his brows. "Oh no, you've done enough," said Tressa, "I can't impose upon you." "Yes, you can, where are you headed? It can't be that far. I'm sure I can get you there in less than fifteen minutes." "You can, in this traffic?" Marcus nodded. "I promise you I can, I have connections."

The twist of Tressa's lips indicated a smile. "OK! Mr. Connections, I'm in no position to resist your gallant assistance." "Fine, so where are you going?" "I'm on my way to the Great Tower Building on 59th Street." Lord if he can pull this out of the bag, I would forever be grateful. Marcus escorted Tressa outdoors; looking around, he quickly approached a policeman. Extending his hand, he pulled something out of his pocket. It was some sort of legal thing; communicating something to the officer, he beckoned to Tressa to come. The officer ushered her into the police car, put on the siren and sped through the crowded streets. As the car sped away, Tressa turned to look at Marcus through the back window. "He is definitely going to have to explain this!"

In less than five minutes, Tressa was at her destination. Marcus' timely intervention had saved the day for her, and her previously disgruntled clients were now pleased as the meeting drew to a satisfactory conclusion. With the meeting concluded, Tressa was putting away her papers when she found a business card. Written on the back was, "Ms. Bowers, it was my pleasure to serve you. Feel free to need my assistance anytime. Marcus Daye Dallas." Tressa placed the card in her purse and smiled. When did he do this? I hope I will need your services again, Mr. Dallas, I definitely have to thank this guy.

Tressa hurried home from her busy day, reflected on the meeting and the positive outcome. She successfully closed the deal with the Montagues and earned a 20% commission totaling $60,000. She was emotionally drained, but grateful her prayers had been answered. She needed this case to prove to the firm and herself she was worthy. She thanked God over and over, first for the success of the meeting and second for the kind gentleman that assisted her in her hour of need.

Tressa was a goal-driven woman. She knew what she wanted when she graduated from law school after interning at several law firms. She did not want to be a permanent employee, anywhere. She wanted to make her mark and move on. Her dream was to own her own law firm, she was good, and she knew it. Law firms had sought her out before she graduated and offered her top dollar. She was only twenty-three and had already amassed an impressive reputation and bank account. Her contract with Lewis and Benton offered her three years of security with full benefits and bonuses in the thousands. So far, her career choice had afforded her a beautiful home and financial security. Tressa was blessed to have a loving family, loyal, lifelong friends and unyielding faith in God, what more could a girl want?

Looking around the room, she noticed those things that needed her attention like the cobwebs under the bed and dust on the furniture that she had ignored for weeks. How many times was she going to tell herself to put aside a day for cleaning? The house could use a professional touch, but for now it was not a priority. The firm had assigned her numerous cases that demanded all her time. However, unfortunately, the weather would definitely affect meetings. For some clients, it would be a godsend and for others a financial setback and inconvenience.

The next couple of days, the city was plagued with terrible storms. Tressa's rest was broken as she was awakened by the sound of strong winds. The windows shook so hard it seemed as though they might shatter. Today, it was bitterly cold; the temperature had dropped to single digits. It was the kind of day that made you think twice about getting out of bed to attend countless meetings. She was suddenly stunned by a loud crash. Jumping off the floor, she ran to the hallway to investigate.

The wind had blown the window open in the hall, which stood at least six feet out of her reach. Disgusted, she ran to the telephone to call her brother, Devan, but the line was dead. As she turned to go to the kitchen, a flying object flew towards her head, she screamed and ducked. "In God's name what was that?" Lying at her feet was a piece of a tree branch. "Lord have mercy, that could have killed me, what next?" As the rain poured in the window, Tressa made it to the closet to get the ladder and tripped halfway up the stairs.

What am I going to do? Once she positioned the ladder against the wall and climbed it, she discovered she was too short to reach the window. This is frustrating, I can't close the window—the rain is pouring in the house, and I'm soaked. Just then the doorbell rang, and she heard a familiar voice calling. "Tressa, open the door." "Lordy B, it's Devan," Tressa said. "Wait a minute, I'm coming," she called back. Tressa ran downstairs and threw open the door to see Devan standing there soaked; she pulled him into the house with so much force, they both fell and laughed. Devan helped Tressa to her feet and gave her his usual bear hug. "Tressa, once again, big brother Devan has to come to your rescue. Girl, what would you do you without me? I had a feeling you needed my help. The same thing happened the last time there was a storm; girl, you desperately need a man," he said with a wink. "What if I were out of town or indisposed, what would you do?" "Well, Brother," she said, putting her hands on her hips, "I do have friends and other family I can call." Raising a hand and placing it on his muscular arm, she said, "I can depend on you; you see I know you adore me andwant to make sure your favorite sister is safe, right?" "Right," replied Devan. "So let's do that now." He reached the open window, closed and bolted it. "Now for the mopping up process ..." Tressa pointed towards the closet door where the mop and bucket were.

After they cleaned up the mess, Tressa offered to cook breakfast. She hadn't noticed the time, but she heard the chime in the hall strike seven times; it was only 7:00 a.m. "I should be preparing for work. I need to check the forecast for today." When she opened the door, she could not believe her eyes. Tree branches and trashcans covered the entire neighborhood. Rubbing her chin, she said, "I guess no one's going anywhere today."

Soaked, she hurriedly shut the door. She attempted to call the office, but there was no dial tone. Devan watched as Tressa frantically tried to make a call. Realizing the landline was dead, she tried her cell, her jaw dropping as she noted the blank display. "I can't believe I didn't charge this stupid thing, now what?"

Devan bit his lip, trying not to smile. "Big brother comes to the rescue again. Here, Tressa, call before this one dies." She dialed her supervisor's private number, and he answered. It was apparent he was wide-awake. "Goode here, how may I help you, Ms. Bowers?" "Mr. Goode, as you know we are under a tornado watch, my home..." "Dear girl, you really don't think I expect you to come in today, do you?" Mr. Goode's mild rebuke cut across her words. "Let's see what it's like tomorrow, or better yet, since today is Thursday and tomorrow may be just as bad, I'll see you on Monday. I suggest you work on the Addison case. Remember, we need a summary to present at next week's meeting." Tressa looked at the phone as if looking at Mr. Goode with a smirk on her face. "Yes, I know, Mr. Goode, I'll have it prepared." Like I need him to tell me that. Mr. Goode was one of the nicest and most intelligent supervisors she ever had. He was a confident and articulate man. He made senior partner in the firm in less than three years and had been a mainstay for over fifteen years. She considered it an honor to work with him. His only flaw as far as Tressa was concerned was his second guessing himself. He would prepare a brief and read and re-read it, change and edit it until he thought it was perfect; in the end, the final product was an exact copy of the first draft. When she finished talking to Mr. Goode, she walked to the kitchen where Devan was eating. "I was going to fix you a big breakfast, Brother, what are you eating?" Devan flashed her a cheeky smile. "You are going to fix me a big breakfast, this was just a snack, and by the way, what did the boss say?" "He told me to take the next couple of days off and make sure I prepare a summary for next week's meetings." Expanding her chest, she added, "That summary, my man, was completed weeks ago."

Tressa cleared the dishes and asked Devan how he made it to her house. Devan smirked. "Baby girl, I started out three hours ago, and as you know, I only live an hour away. I stopped by Simone's to make sure she and Taylor were safe. Of course, she pretended not to care that I was there, but I could see the look of gratitude on her and Taylor's faces.

Tressa swung round, arched her eyebrows in surprise. "I thought Taylor was at Mom's!" "Simone got her yesterday; she said she missed her daughter. Anyway, they were fine, and I left because I called you and did not get an answer. I thought Gregg might be here, but was hoping he wasn't." Devan despised Gregg, partly because he was so possessive of Tressa. The kind of possessiveness that was scary. Tressa once had to get a restraining order on him, and that was the last straw as far as Devan was concerned.

Devan was the head of the Bower family, and he took his job seriously. He was their protector. When their father died, he made Devan promise to take care of the girls, even though he was only eight years old. This was a huge responsibility for such a little fellow.

He never told his mother about the promise, believing this was his fate. He made a vow to himself at that young age; that he would never marry or have children until his sisters were happily married and secure. His daily prayer was for God's support and direction. His mother Jesse had instilled in them the importance of prayer. As children, they could articulate their problems and ask God to help solve them. They gathered every Sunday for dinner and family prayer.

These family gatherings strengthened and encouraged Devan. He had grown into an upstanding and resolute man. A college education was expected, and he led the pack. He received his undergraduate, graduate, and doctorate, never missing a beat, all the time supporting his family mentally and spiritually. He was a catch that managed not to get caught.

Simone, Devan's twin sister, on the other hand, was a piece of work. She was an "ole me ole my" sort of woman, full of gloom and doom, and three years older than Tressa. They were both very pretty, educated, family-oriented women. Simone, however, had issues no one could identify with. Was it the loss of her husband? Maybe, no one knew for sure.

She had met her husband at work where they

were both scientists. After dating each other for one year, they were married in the preacher's study one week before he was to leave to begin his tour in the military. Two years later, their daughter, Taylor was born. Simone was a high-end woman and loved to brag about her finances, even though she could never hold onto a dime. This, according to her was an issue in her marriage because Simone wanted the best of everything, which Craig didn't mind.

His complaint was that Simone wanted everything right now. Perhaps Craig's drafting into military service and the duties therein had blinkered him from Simone's excessive spending habits. Perhaps, but nevertheless, knowing Craig's salary would be drastically cut when he went into the military, Simone continued her spending. She purchased a new townhouse and used the $10,000 check Jesse gave them as a wedding gift as a down payment on a Jaguar. Craig never knew about the money, and when Jesse found out, she was furious.

To better understand Simone, Craig often called Tressa, hoping she could shed light on his wife's character. Tressa didn't know what to tell him and felt thrown in the middle of a sticky situation. Tressa was shocked and appalled when her mother asked her if she had feelings for Craig. "Feelings for Craig, I hardly know the man, and that's my sister's husband." Tressa was heartbroken by the insinuation and never accepted another call from Craig.

Unfortunately, Craig had been killed by a drunk driver just days after being discharged from the military. Simone was initially distraught on receiving the news, she cried uncontrollably and went through the motions of a grieving widow. She was so distraught, she allowed his family to make the funeral arrangements, and after the funeral she disappeared for weeks. Her family was both concerned and disappointed with her, but she didn't care. Jesse tried communicating with her to no avail and asked her best friend Ciera to talk to her. Simone told Ciera she could never understand her hurt and pain, and to leave her alone. Devan was the person who finally got to the bottom of things; he knew her best. He knew that deep down she was dying, despite her outward demeanor, she was lost without Craig. Simone told Devan she had made herself a promise that when Craig came home she would show him how much she loved him. She knew that everyone assumed she was cold and hard, but she genuinely loved Craig.

Devan discovered that part of Simone's resentment was Craig's confiding in Tressa. Why did he have to involve her in their private life? After all who was Tressa to him? In reality, Devan suspected Simone's resentment of Tressa was her belief that Craig had a crush on Tressa. True, he was always complimenting her on something. If it wasn't her hair, it was her outfit or her most recent promotion. Tressa was the golden child, the success story, the wonder woman or so Simone seemed to think. Devan knew better. He knew that deep down Simone knew Tressa was a loving and kind sister, who adored and respected her, but how could he get her to show her sister love and respect? Tressa had been at a loss when it came to Simone. Simone said she loved Craig but was overheard to say in the aftermath of the funeral, "Now I got my $10,000 back and more." When Tressa questioned her about it, she broke down and cried. "I didn't mean to say that, I'm sorry." However, minutes later, she attacked Tressa. Storming back to Tressa she demanded, "Who told you about the conversation?" "Why is that important Simone? Did you really say such a thing?"

"Yes, yes, I did!" She stood face to face with Tressa. "And so what if I did! I deserve it, every dime! He did nothing for me." Simone attempted to walk away. "You hold it, Sister." Tressa marched after her, took hold of her arm and swung her round. "Craig gave you a beautiful child and tried to give you a wonderful life but you and your stupid folly, greed and pride wouldn't let him. This man, your husband died in a fatal car accident, killed by a drunk driver. Do you blame the drunk driver; no, you blame Craig for being at the wrong place at the wrong time. You are the victim instead of Craig. His family is hurting as well as his child, your daughter, and it's all about you, always all about you!"

Simone rolled her eyes at Tressa and walked away. This was not the Simone Tressa knew. Why was she being so cruel? Perhaps the reason Simone resented Tressa was because of something she couldn't face.

However, after much persistence, it was Devan who convinced Simone to seek medical attention, he knew she needed counseling and time to heal for the sake of her child and the family. Devan sat in Tressa's lounge, he knew he had to ask the question that was bugging him, he also knew it might incur her wrath, buthe had to know, out of concern, after all, he was her brother. "Tressa?" "What?" He could see her hackles were already up, damn. This wasn't going to be easy.

"Gregg," he said as firmly as he was able. "Has he been calling you?" "No Devan, and let's just have a nice day, I don't want to talk about Gregg." Tressa's eyes flashed a warning. "OK Sis! I don't mean to frustrate you or pry, but this is the perfect opportunity for that creep to worm his way into your space." "Let's just check the rest of the house, OK!"

After checking the house, Tressa told Devan she was tired and wanted to go back to bed. "OK Sis, I am going to crash here for a few hours; I am still sleepy." "Great idea, Brother, go lie down." Devan retired in the spare bedroom he called "his room" and slept for hours. When he awoke, it was noon. He arose when his phone rang. Sluggish, he answered, "Hello." "Hello man, this is Gregg." There was silence. "Talk about the Devil." "Devan, I know how you feel about me man; I called because I am concerned about Tressa. I've been calling, but no one answered." "Yea, she's fine – her phones are out." "Yes, both of them." "No, Gregg, she's asleep, and I am not going to wake her. I will tell her you called." "Oh will you?" remarked Gregg. Devan took a deep breath, "I said I would, and I will. I'll leave her a note; it's up to her to respond, good-bye." Devan hung up, looked at the phone, rolled his eyes and preceded to Tressa's room with the note; being careful not to wake her, he taped the note to her door that read, "Gregg called—the bum, I told him you may or may not call him back. I hope you don't! I received a call from one of my coworkers who needed my assistance. If you need me—call. I pray your phone services are back on soon. Love ya!! Bro."

Tressa finally arose around 1:30 p.m. "Whew! Boy did I sleep." She crawled out of bed, made her way to the window to see that the rain had subsided. To her amazement her phone was blinking, which was a sure sign her power was back on. "Who can this be?" She immediately dialed her mother's number. The phone rang, and rang and rang. "Now where is she? She'll call me when she can." She noticed the note, read it and then threw it in the trash. "How am I doing? He doesn't need to know." Tressa went downstairs to the living room. The house was chilly.

Chapter two

Marcus's doorbell rang. Getting up, he looked out the side window of his condo to see who it was. There was a figure standing in the doorway dressed in rain gear, dripping wet. He couldn't tell if it was a man or woman. Putting on his robe, he answered the door. It's you, what are you doing here?" It was his ex lady love, Tia. "How did you manage to make your way to my home in this bad weather? And why?" Tia shrugged, standing in the doorway. "I managed to make it here because you were in the area. A tire blew out about four blocks away, I called AAA and they said they wouldn't be able to make it for at least three hours. I didn't know where else to go and that's when I thought of you. Lord knows I didn't want to think of you, I mean!"

Marcus frowned, "Sure you didn't. Why didn't you call one of your other friends that live just as close?" "I did Marcus dear,' Tia said flatly, "no one answered." "For good reason." "Now, Marcus, that's not nice, and, for the record, they are not as close as you. Marcus met her brown eyes, no warmth in them, never was, but perhaps he was being unkind, the day being what it was. "Come in, Tia, you're letting the heat out. I was fixing breakfast, you'll have to wait." "Aren't you going to offer me some breakfast? I'm starving!"

Marcus directed a finger towards the refrigerator. "You're welcome to fix yourself something; I wouldn't deny anyone a meal." Tia shook her head, "No thanks, second thought, I'm not that hungry." Marcus smirked, hands on hips. "I didn't think so." Tia was happy to see Marcus; he was her one true love. Marcus often reminisced about the two of them, they shared beautiful times together and, in truth, he had fond memories of her. They learned to ride bikes and roller skate, together. She was the first girl he kissed. Those memories were priceless. Their childhood relationship continued in high school. They attended both junior and senior proms together and were voted Senior Prom King and Queen.

However, once in college, Marcus began to see Tia in a new light. The difference in their ideologies, morals and personalities became overwhelming. If it wasn't religion, it was child rearing or money matters. Marcus's religious beliefs and heartfelt concerns about his fellow man put a strain on their relationship. As a young man, he joined the Summer Corps, who gave him the opportunity to travel to different countries, helping to build houses, irrigate land, install plumbing, anything the region needed to make life better for others.

He also dreamed of adopting a child. He saw so many homeless children; he was one man that definitely had room in his heart and home for a forsaken child, but Tia wasn't for it. She didn't feel she could connect with someone else's child. And as for the Summer Corps, she felt "those people" had received enough help. Her question was "When are they going to stand on their own two feet and help themselves?" Marcus tried in vain to enlighten Tia about world affairs and disparity, but she wasn't hearing it, she just didn't care. Tia was quick to condemn and rush to judgment.

She seemed to enjoy pointing out what she considered to be his flaws. Marcus knew he was a perfectionist. He was also conceited; driven, ambitious, and stubborn, but he worked hard to change. Tia, on the other hand, was obsessed with her looks; if she obtained a scratch, she was worried it would leave a scar. She overestimated Marcus's patience with her, and for some reason she was convinced he would never meet a woman as pretty or as smart as her. Eventually, Tia walked away. She started dating other people and so did he. No one was as happy when they broke up as Avery Dallas, Marcus's father. He once adored Tia. Their families often enjoyed Sunday and midweek dinners together and vacationed together, but, then she became the woman of the family, making all the family decisions. Avery began to resent that, and eventually, he started missing meals and distancing himself from Tia and Marcus. In his senior year of college, he was asked to join a program that trained journalists and business majors to specialize in the field of protocol and diplomacy. Marcus loved the idea; it was different. He would be able to travel extensively, and the salary was good. The initial training was held in Virginia, which was perfect because he wouldn't be far from home yet far enough from Tia.

Marcus assisted Tia the best he could; once they reached her car, he realized she needed a flat tire changed and some oil. While he struggled to repair her car, she questioned him about his love life and future plans. She informed him that she was happy, and her business was going quite well. Marcus listened, never saying a word. "What's wrong with you Mr. Dallas, why so silent? Scared you're going to reveal a secret or are you just trying your best to ignore me?"

Marcus straightened his back. "Ignore you Tia, who can ignore you? You never shut up! Now if you'll just let me finish." When he was done, he opened the car door and waved his hand as if ushering her inside. "I would suggest you take your car to a repair shop to make sure it's safe, I wouldn't want anything to happen to you." Tia walked up to Marcus and stood gazing at him. "Really Marcus, I'm happy to know you don't want anything to happen to me so ... you don't hate me?"

Marcus backed away, "Tia, in the past year you have had more mishaps than the average person, and somehow you always happen to be near me, and for the record, we are JUST FRIENDS. I have moved on, and I thought you had too." Now angry and frustrated, Tia howled, "Fine Marcus, I won't be bothering you anymore. Maybe one day you'll need me. I thought I meant something to you, why are you dismissing me like I'm nothing? I'm going through some things right now, and I turned to you. You promised me when we broke up you would always be there for me, now you talk to me like I am nothing". "Tia, it's pouring down raining, get in your car and leave; this isn't the place, and I'm not in the mood for your blabbering. Find someone else to lean on, I'm through, and that's final."

Marcus ushered Tia in the car and slammed the door. He proceeded to walk back towards his condo when out of the corner of his eye, he saw a car approaching him at high speed. He ran to a nearby garage for safety, narrowly avoiding a collision and peeped around the corner to see if it was safe. What is wrong with that woman, is she trying to kill me? Tia abruptly stopped the car and waited for Marcus to exit. Unbeknown to her, Marcus had called the police. As proof of her antics, he took pictures of Tia sitting in her car with his cell phone. Minutes later, he heard the sound of sirens, but when he exited the garage to wave down the police, Tia put her foot on the gas and drove straight in Marcus's direction. Fortunately, the police interceded, blocking her; she was just inches from the garage where Marcus was standing. The police exited their car and yelled for Tia to cut the ignition and disembark. She sat there frozen, not believing her eyes. Then, in a fit of panic, she began to scream, "He tried to abuse me, I got away and when I saw him I just lost my nerve. I am afraid of him officer, please don't make me get out my car." "Lady, get out of the car!" a cop instructed with severity. The policemen tried to open the door, but it was locked. The officer who'd shouted raised his baton. "Miss, open the door, or I will break the glass."

Tia rolled down the window and began to sob. "Officer, please, believe me, I was trying to protect myself." Realizing the officers were losing their patience, she reluctantly unlocked the door and slowly exited the car. "Sir, for our safety, we are going to handcuff you and the young lady as well." They pulled out the handcuffs, and when Tia heard the sound of the cuffs, she really performed. "Is this necessary? You have me on a corner looking like a common criminal?" "Yes, mam, it's necessary," the officer said, then addressing Marcus, "Now sir, what's your story?" With no shelter, standing in the cold shivering, Marcus told his side of the story. "Officer, my name is Dallas, Marcus Dallas. The long and short of it is that I used to date this woman. She appeared at my home today saying she had car trouble and needed my help. I fixed her flat tire and changed her oil. She came onto me,

I refused her advances, and she became angry, and you saw for yourselves how she tried to run me down." "Mr. Dallas, can we see some ID?" "Of course," Marcus nodded, removed his wallet and handed the officer his license. Turning to Tia, the officer said, "Miss, can we see your driver's license?" Tia grumbled, rummaging through her purse, she found her license and showed them a copy of her registration. "Now, mam, let's hear it, what's your story?"

Never in Tia's wildest dream did she think Marcus would call the police on her. "Well, officer," she said between sobs, "My name is Tia Brooks. I did go to Mr. Dallas's home because he is an old friend, and I asked him for assistance like I've done many times before. And he agreed to fix my tire, but when he finished he ..." Tia couldn't finish when she saw Marcus staring at her; she lowered her head in shame. "Tia, tell the truth, this is beneath you."

The first officer asked the officer in the second car to watch both Tia and Marcus. He ran their information and found that neither one of them had priors. He uncuffed Marcus but left the cuffs on Tia. Marcus was in a quandary; he didn't know what to do. He didn't want her to get away with trying to hurt him, but he didn't want her to go to jail.

The incident had drawn a crowd though when questioned by the officers; initially, no one saw anything. But from out of nowhere a man came running, yelling and waving to get the officers' attention. "I am a witness, I saw this lady try to run this man down ..." pointing at Marcus, he added, "... this man ran in the garage for safety."

"Your name sir," an officer asked. "My name is

Jonas Point Dexter." The witness went on to describe how aggressively Tia had been driving and said, "It seemed to me she was intent on running the gentleman down." Point Dexter approached Marcus and patted him on the back. "Yes sir, I saw the whole thing, I'm a witness and will testify to this man's innocence." He reached into his wallet and handed Marcus and the officers a business card. "Thanks, sir, I appreciate your assistance," the officer remarked as the police took down his statements and then placed Tia back in the police car. Marcus was amazed at the sudden appearance of Mr. Point Dexter. Looking at him, he was thinking to himself, who do this man remind me of? It came to him in a flash; he reminded him of Barney Fife, minus the glasses.

He had the same build and personality. He was wispy, of average height and smelled like an old cigar. He was wearing a suit at least twenty years old and large, black glasses. "Praise the Lord, as I said, my name is Point Dexter, Jonas Point Dexter. I must do the Lord's will, take a stand, do what's right," he said earnestly, gently pulling Marcus aside to let him know that he expected no pay or praise for his testimony. "I am doing my job as a citizen and Christian."

Giving Point Dexter his undivided attention, Marcus said, "Mr. Point Dexter, that's admirable, and I do appreciate your willingness to serve. I am sure the police will contact you, and the Lord will bless you." Point Dexter gave a thin smile and bit his lip before he said, "Well, as I said, I am not looking for praise, but I wonder sir, do you think this is going to be in the paper? I sure hope not, I am not wearing my best suit." Marcus frowned, he wasn't sure, but he doubted it, somehow. "I don't think so, Mr. Point Dexter, but if it did, I assure you that you look great, actually you look super!" "You really think so?" Point Dexter asked, his eyebrows raised in surprise. "This suit is well over fifteen, no sixteen years old and I ..." The officer interrupted him, "Sir, you can go now, we'll get in touch." Point Dexter shook the officer's and Marcus's hands but didn't budge. I am not going anywhere until this fine young man has been released." "Suit yourself," the officer snapped, walked over to Marcus and said, "I'm sorry, Mr. Dallas, we have to take her in. This is serious; her charges could be severe." "Sir, I don't think she was trying to kill me, merely to frighten me," Marcus protested. The officer studied Marcus for a moment. "Were you frightened?" Marcus nodded, "Yes, I was frightened," he had to admit. "Then, she accomplished her goal," said the officer. "I know sir; however, she has never done anything like this before," Marcus said, his arms outstretched, appealing to the officer. "We have a statement from Mr. Point Dexter that he witnessed Ms. Brooks trying to run you down," the policeman replied, unmoved. "I know officer; however, I refuse to press charges, please, let her go!"

Tia was crying uncontrollably; this was a night-mare. Never in her wildest dream had she imagined she would be handcuffed like a common criminal and thrown in jail. She realized she had lost it and snapped, "Yes, that's what I'll tell them, and it's the truth. I know Marcus will back me up. My God, I hope this doesn't appear in the police blogger, I will be mortified! My father, if he gets wind of this, he will hit the fan and Mother will probably tell them to keep me in jail and throw away the key." Tia's father was a circuit court judge, and her mother was on the city council. Her mother was not as sympathetic or forgiving as her dad. Tia had a history of trouble, and it was never her fault. This was serious; they could say she was committing vehicular homicide or something like that. But her father would get her out of this mess, at least that's what Marcus hoped for. She'll get the usual speech and slap on the wrist, and since I am not pressing charges, she'll be fine.

Marcus's hands were tied; the police gave him some information and sent him and Mr. Point Dexter on their way. Once home dried and comfortable, Marcus called Tia's parents and informed them what had happened. He told them what precinct she would be at and the possible charges, impressing upon them that he did not intend to press charges. Mrs. Brooks thanked Marcus. Marcus then called his father and gave him the lowdown. Avery hit the roof, "Why did you help that crazy woman? She's a fatal attraction waiting to happen." Marcus sighed, he'd been expecting this. "Yes, I know Dad, but all is well, and I am fine." Marcus tried to rest, but he couldn't. He took a shower and went to bed, replaying what happened over and over again. How could she do this to me? Had Tia really lost it?

After much prayer, Marcus had to be honest; he was more worried about Tressa finding out about the incident than his concern for Tia. He did not want her to be stalked by some crazy ex or bothered by the idea that he was still interested in Tia. He promised himself he would tell Tressa about the incident if they hooked up. Before drifting off to sleep, Marcus prayed for a resolution and the kindness of Mr. Point Dexter. The weekend came and went; though he often worked from home, he made it his business to go to the office on Monday, hoping to accidentally run into Tressa. It was a cold morning, and he was low on gas and dreading the commute into the city center. The office was located in the heart of the city with limited parking. Only permanent executives had assigned parking. Marcus had to gas up and get to the office in order to find a parking spot.

He made his way to the gas station and had started to fill up his tank when he noticed a familiar black BMW with the scripture John 3:16 written on the driver's door.

"That's Tressa's car, what is she doing on this side of town?" he asked himself. As he was about to get out of his car, he saw a man putting gas in her BMW. Instantly, he felt jealous. Who is this guy? Is he the boyfriend or ex-boyfriend? He knew that was Tressa's car, but where was she? Then he heard his name being called, "Marcus, Marcus Dallas."

Marcus turned to see Tressa waving at him from the store; she waved him over. "How are you? Fancy meeting you here." "Hi," he responded. "This is indeed a pleasure. I thought that was your car, but I ..." "Yea, that's my car, and that's my brother, Devan," she said gesturing toward the young man. "He's taking me to work today, his old jalopy died.

Devan ambled across and introduced himself. "I heard that Tressa," he said with mock annoyance. "I do not have a jalopy." Forming quotes with his fingers, he added, "The old high-end car is in the shop. Anyway, hi, I'm Devan Bowers, Tressa's brother."

Exchanging handshakes, Marcus was relieved and happy. Thinking quickly, he turned to Tressa and said, "I'm going to the office, can I give you a lift? Perhaps, it could save some time, and I'll be happy to see you home." "Really, are you sure that would not be an imposition?" asked Devan. Marcus shook his head emphatically. "No, not at all." Tressa, seizing the moment, responded "Yes, OK, I'll get my things from the car, be right back."

Marcus felt a howl coming on, but he knew he had to contain himself. He smiled, gathered up his courage, and whispered in Devan's ear, "Please brother man, let this happen! I'm crazy about your sister. I know she mentioned me; I'm the nice guy who rescued her earlier this week. I saved her from a fate worse than death, did she tell you?" Devan replied instantly. "Yes, she told me." Tressa returned and handed her keys to Devan. "I'll call you, I'm in good hands." Devan switched his gaze between Marcus and Tressa. "Yea, sure Tressa, call me in case you change your mind." "I will, I promise, but I won't change my mind." Tressa drove in with Marcus on cloud nine. This was confirmation of her prayers. I know this is the one, I have no doubt, she thought; this is the man I've been dreaming of.

Marcus felt the same way; he was smitten and determined this one would not get away. It was at least a twenty-minute ride to the office, and Marcus savored every minute. They rode for about five minutes without saying a word; finally, Marcus complimented Tressa on her outfit. "That's a classy outfit, meeting today?" Tressa looked at him, her gaze lingering. "This old thing?" she laughed. "No, I just wanted to kick it up a notch today, I just felt like it. I had a miserable weekend. What about you, how was your weekend?" Marcus thought if only you knew. After a second, he said, "My weekend was interesting, very restful; of course, the weather contributed to that."

Sitting back in her seat, arms crossed, Tressa said, "Yea, what a storm, that weather was brutal. Thank God for my brother; he appeared just in the nick of time. I was losing the battle of the water and the mop. And, by the way, Marcus Dallas, you look good every day."

Marcus smiled. "Thanks, Tressa. If you're complimenting my fashion sense, I do like nice clothes, but men don't need things as much as women. They need stockings, purses, hats, caps, suits, dresses, pants ..."

Tressa lightly tapped Marcus on the shoulder, "Stop, Marcus, you are so funny, but that's true. That's just the way we're made. Guys only need their undies, a couple suits, a couple pair of pants, a few shirts and sporty outfits, and they're finished. Women, we need ensembles! I mean, what's an outfit without a matching bag?" They glanced at each other in approval.

Marcus turned up the radio; one of his favorite songs was playing. He was quiet as the tune played while Tressa sat as still as possible, looking at Marcus from the corner of her eye as he drove. She thought how peaceful and happy she was at that moment. Marcus couldn't express to Tressa how he felt; it was too soon, but, his heart was full of joy. He loved this, the girl of his dreams.

As they approached the garage, he was lucky to find a parking space. "See, you brought me luck." Turning off the engine, he locked the doors. You don't think I'm going to let you out without asking for a ..." he paused ... "date for dinner." Tressa was taken aback for a moment; she thought he was going to ask for a kiss, and Marcus knew it. He laughed, "Girl, I'm not that forward, so what about it, how about dinner?" "Can I let you know a little later, I'm not sure of my workload? I'll call you about 11:30, is that all right?" Smiling, Marcus nodded. "That's fine. I'll be waiting with bated breath, and remember, I'm your ride home. What time will you be leaving today madam?" Tressa cupped her chin, replying, "Let's say 4ish." Marcus thought before saying, "Let's say 4:30 my love. My last briefing is 4 p.m and I must freshen up before I see you again." "You're so vain, Mr. Dallas," Tressa teased. "Yes, Tressa Bowers; yes, I am."

Per her word, Tressa contacted Marcus to inform him that she would not be available for dinner. She was loaded down researching and brainstorming for a meeting that Friday. Marcus was disappointed but did look forward to the ride home. On the ride home, he told her he understood, but he wasn't convincing. Tressa, seeing his disappointment, said with a side smile, "If you're really interested in feeding me, how about Saturday? I'm free Saturday." Marcus, pretending to pout, replied, "Sure, if I have to wait until then." He smiled and nudged her jokingly. The ride to Tressa's home was scenic; Marcus listened patiently as Tressa gave him directions. "Make a right at the light, and make another right at the corner and there's my home." As Marcus pulled up to Tressa's home, he was flabbergasted. "Is this yours?" Tressa smiled, took a deep breath and happily responded, "Yes, it's all mine, like it?" "Do I like it? Who wouldn't, this is fabulous! I don't think I can afford you, girl! What a beaut!" "You can afford me," said Tressa, getting out of the car. "I hear you undercover agents or spies or whatever you are usually make hundreds of thousands, not to mention the escrow accounts, offshore accounts and money in Swiss banks, and ..." "OK, OK, so you think I got it like that, maybe I do, and maybe I don't," he said with a wink. I don't know where you could have gotten such crazy information, but one thing I do know, I might have to sell one of my kidneys to take you to dinner." Tressa laughed. "Yea, McDonald's is not my thing. Mr. Dallas just keep in mind, you're dealing with a classy woman; nothing but the best will do. Anyways, I had McDonalds' for lunch. However, if you can't sell a kidney, I do like KFC." Marcus couldn't help but smile. "Now that's my kind of girl, one that will accept a ten-dollar meal." "I beg your pardon Dallas, a meal at KFC will cost you at least $17.00." "That, I can handle." Marcus helped Tressa with her briefcase and escorted her to the front door. "I'll see you on Saturday," he shouted, walking backwards, "and wear something pretty; no jeans, see you about seven." Getting in the car, he yelled out the window, "I'll call to confirm." Tressa waved as he pulled off.

Tressa was on cloud nine. She dropped her briefcase and purse on the hall table and sat on the lounger in the entrance hall. She couldn't believe her day. With her hands covering her face, she let out a loud yell. Just then the doorbell rang, which quieted her enthusiasm. "Who is it?" she called. "It's Marcus," came the now familiar voice. Tressa opened the door and sarcastically said, "Really, Mr. Dallas, is the date cancelled already?" "No sweet lady, I don't have your phone number." Tressa gave Marcus her number, playfully repeating it very slowly; perhaps I should write it down." "Yes, as a matter of fact, that would be nice." "Would you like my personal email address and my cell number and my ..." "Yes," Marcus affirmed, his gaze fixed on hers, "I would. I would like to be able to get in touch no matter where you are!"

Tressa obliged him, and Marcus surprised her by handing her his personal information as well. "Included are my work number, my cell number, my home number, my email address at home and work, and my address. Contact me anytime, and I mean anytime."

Marcus stood in the hallway for what seemed like an eternity. Tressa took the information and clasped it tightly in her hands. "I'll be talking to you, call me if you need a ride to the office tomorrow." "Yes, I sure will." "But call me by 7:00 a.m. so I can get you to work on time." "Yes, I will, I promise." "If you don't need a ride, I'll see you on Saturday about seven, but like I said I'll call." Marcus was blabbering; he didn't want to leave and didn't know what to say. He thought for a moment and said, "That may have sounded a little creepy, I just meant..." "I know what you meant Marcus...its ok" "We'll keep in touch." Tressa ushered Marcus out the door while he was still talking, and they were both laughing. "Yes, Dallas we will be communicating." As she shut the door, she heard Marcus say, "And by the way, I love your home."

As he drove, off Tressa sat staring at all the numbers "Man, oh man, this is pure gold. Wow, I can't wait until Saturday. Lord, please let this happen. She lowered her head and asked for forgiveness. "Lord forgive me if it's your will!"

On his drive home, Marcus marveled at Tressa's home. He couldn't figure out why he was so impressed. Thinking to himself, she's a professional woman with a lucrative job. Why shouldn't she have a nice home? But that house has to be worth a mint. It's none of my business; perhaps I am feeling intimidated. As Marcus pulled into his driveway, he saw the messenger service pulling off. He stopped his car and flagged down the driver. "Looking for me?" "If you're Marcus Dallas?" "Yes, I am Marcus." "Please sign here." Marcus signed and headed to his condo. Once inside, he took a deep breath and opened the package. Several items fell from a large brown envelope. He instantly knew where it was from, "The Office of International Services." Included were a bankcard and a letter of instructions. Oh no! Why now? The contents contained information regarding his next assignment. He should have expected it; after all, he had received notification earlier in the week. He was instructed to report to Virginia in three days. That meant he had to leave on Monday, and he was now disappointed; he thought he had another week. Lord, why now? Today is Friday; I get to be with Tressa tomorrow, and maybe she will have time to spend with me on Sunday for a little while.

Marcus took the bull by the horns and did something that was rare and not usually accepted. He decided to call his manager and inform him of the situation with Tia. Sometimes they will grant you leave for personal situations. Then he thought this is silly, what happens when I really need the time? No, I'll re port and keep in touch with Tressa the best I can. He would be out of the country anywhere from two weeks to two months.

His prayer was she didn't lose interest in him. Marcus slowly walked to his kitchen, put on a pot of coffee, and changed his clothes. His thoughts were on Tressa, now that he finally had her attention, he had to leave. "Boy, just my luck," and as he was feeling sorry for himself, these thoughts came to him—count it all joy, no good thing will he withhold from you; trust in the Lord with all your heart. No matter what—the best will come out of this situation. Thankyou, Lord! I'll leave it all in your capable hands. Marcus suddenly felt at peace; I'll have Saturday. "Lord," he prayed, "I believe Tressa is the one. Please bless me with patience and help me to trust in you and your promises."

He knew he had planted a seed with Tressa and hoped she was the type of woman that would understand his situation; if not, nothing ventured, nothing gained. Marcus's biggest concern was his not knowing Tressa's dating status. Surely, she wouldn't accept a date with him if she had a friend, a steady, a bow, of course not. Nonetheless, he had to focus on his upcoming assignment. He went to check his emails when the phone rang. "Yes, this is Marcus; hello, Mr. Parker. Yes, I did receive the package, it just arrived. I was just going to email you to confirm." Mr. Parker updated Marcus on the clients he would be training and the paperwork he would need. "Yes, Mr. Parker got it. I'll be there on Monday." "Monday?" Mr. Parker queried, "Your assignment doesn't begin until next Thursday." "Sir, my previous email states that I have three days to report." "Yes Marcus," Mr. Parker said patiently, "three days from the date of the training, which does not begin until Monday after next. You received your bank payment card, I assume?" "Yes, I did. Mr. Parker, can you give me a date for the training so I can confirm them with you?" "Let's see, let me look." Marcus heard

Mr. Parker fumbling through some papers. "Yes, here it is, your reporting date is March 10th; today is Friday, February 28." "OK, I understand, I'll be there on the 10th." Marcus was barely able to contain his glee. "Yahoo!" He got a reprieve, an extra week to court Tressa. "Things are looking up, thank you, Jesus!"

Marcus was so happy he went to his closet and started pulling out clothes. After all, he was the fashion king. What would he wear? An hour later Marcus had pulled ten outfits; then it dawned on him he would need reservations. Where should I take her? "Not Shamrocks," that was his and Tia's restaurant. "How about a dinner cruise? No, what if she's afraid of water? I know, the Governor's Place, it's beautiful and romantic." He called to make reservations and finally decided on his outfit. Taking a deep breath, he called Tressa. "Hello." "Hi, Tressa, this is Marcus." "Yea, I recognize your voice." "I'm calling to say I made reservations for the Governor's Place for 7 p.m. Is that acceptable?" "Of course, I love that restaurant! That's a great choice." Hearing Tressa's enthusiastic reply, Marcus said, "You've been there before?" "Yes, several times, the food is good, and it's ..." Marcus interrupted Tressa, "OK, but don't spoil it for me; let's pretend you've never been there. I thought I was taking you to an unfamiliar place." "I'm afraid not, Mr. Dallas; us A-listers travel in the same circles." Marcus traced a hand across his forehead. "I know now! Anyway, see you tomorrow at 7 p.m." "That's a date, tomorrow at seven." Marcus hung up thinking ... this is going to be a long night!

Before turning in, he called his father to update him on his assignment, Tia and his date with Tressa. "Marcus, you be careful," his father warned. Tia's mother called to inform me she has been released; her father posted her bail." "Dad, how can I be happy one moment and discouraged the next?" He heard his father sigh. "Son, that's life. All things work out for the good; in the meantime, watch your back."

As Tressa prepared for bed, she wanted to call Marcus but changed her mind; he might think she was being forward, so she called her mom. Jesse was fast asleep. "Hello?" came the drowsy voice. "Hi, Mom; sorry to wake you, you're not usually sleeping at this hour." "I know baby, those clients wore me out today. I am truly thinking about changing jobs." "That's nice, Mom. I called to tell you I am going on a date with Marcus tomorrow; he asked me today." Tressa gave her a blow-by-blow of the events leading up to the ride home and the date. "I am really happy for you darling. You make sure you get in early enough for church, no excuses!" "Yes, Mom. I'll be at church; I love you, take care."

Once Tressa showered, she prayed and lay across the bed, falling asleep only to awaken because of a haunting dream. She sat up in the bed shaking, confused and frightened. It was a familiar dream, one she had dreamt since her early teens. She looked at the clock; it was 12:30 a.m. Mom is going to kill me, but I must talk to her. Tressa expected her mother to blast her for waking her, but she didn't. "Tressa what's wrong? I know you wouldn't call me at this ungodly hour unless there was a problem." "Yes, Mom there is. I had that dream again." "What dream, or should I say, which dream Tressa?" Tressa sat up in bed in a resting position. "The one about the big wash basin full of dolls. I've asked God to reveal the meaning to me so many times, but no answer comes." "Tressa, perhaps these are your children and based on your concrete decision to only have one or two children, perhaps the Lord is showing you that you will be blessed with a whole tub full of children. Perhaps the Lord has shown you, and you can't accept the answer. In any case, you will make an awesome mother." "Do you think that's the answer Mom? God wouldn't do that to me, would he?" "Then you tell me the meaning, Tressa, because I'm clueless." Tressa sighed. "I'm sorry to wake you Mom; go back to sleep. I really needed to hear your voice." "Good night Tressa, I love you very much." Tressa snuggled in bed and took her mother's advice. For the first time since having these dreams, she gave thanks to God for his perfect will in her life, even if it meant having a tub full of children. However, she still needed and wanted confirmation. "I do believe the Lord will answer me—but when?"

Tressa decided to stay in bed as long as she could. Tonight, she would be with Marcus, their first date. She wanted to be well rested; there would be no housework today, no errands, no cooking, nothing. About noon, the doorbell rang; she peeped out the door to see Devan, her mother, and sister. "What are you all doing here? What a surprise." In a jubilant voice Simone answered, "We decided we needed to spend some time with you today. Devan wants to know about the new man in your life; I want to know if you have an outfit I can wear tonight, and Mom wants to know if you're OK. Honestly, she wanted to see her baby." "Well that's a lot; let's see. First, Devan, I have a date with Marcus tonight; Simone, wear one of those outfits you already have that you borrowed and never returned, and Mom, I am fine. I took your advice and prayed, and I slept like a baby. So there, now we can go in the living room, sit down, and I can elaborate about Marcus Daye Dallas." Marcus awoke feeling anxious, already thinking of the date with Tressa. When the phone rang, he hoped it would be her. "Hello?" "Hello Son, its your father" "Oh..." "Son, you sound disappointed." "No, Dad, not at all. I am always happy to hear your voice." "Sure you are! Son, do you have time to come past the house? I need you to help me tweak some parts on the car?"

Marcus paused before answering. "Dad, can we do it tomorrow? I don't want to get all that grease under my nails today; any other time." "So you are ditching me already, for a girl! 'I'm wounded." Marcus instantly felt guilty. He said, "That's selfish of me; of course, I'll be over—I'll wear gloves." "Good idea, that way you can dirty up my sink like you always have and update me on this new girl in your life." "Yea Dad, I'll be over in about an hour." "OK, Son."

When Marcus arrived, he told his father everything he could about Tressa. He talked nonstop and had to be reminded why he had come over in the first place. The day passed quickly for both Marcus and Tressa, both spending time with their families and both anticipating their first date. Marcus called Tressa exactly at 3:00 to confirm their date, but there was no answer. He left a message stating he would pick her up about 6:15 and, if anything had changed, to please give him a call. When the doorbell rang, he was surprised. Who could that be? He had just left his father's. "Who is it?" "It's Brad, the doorman; I have a package for you. It was left at the counter this morning. I called, but there was no answer, and I was told to give it to you as soon as you arrived." Marcus opened the door. "Who gave it to you?" "A young woman, very pretty, about ..." Marcus ignored him and accepted the box. "Yes man thanks, have a good day."

Not Tia, I can't be bothered. However, he anxiously opened the box. Brad failed to say she was from UPS, and the box turned out to be a set of pots he ordered. "Gee, I forgot I ordered these things, something else for me to burn up." He put the pots away, and as he was preparing to take out the trash, he noticed his phone blinking. "Hi Marcus, sorry I missed your call. All is well; I was bidding goodbye to my family, who paid me a surprise visit. I'm looking forward to tonight. If possible, could you make it 6:00 rather than 6:15? I would appreciate it." Marcus called her; there was no answer, so he left a message. "Of course; see you at six." Hot damn, it's on now.

At exactly 6:00, Marcus was at Tressa's door. She answered and invited him in. "You're very prompt." "Indeed, I am," he said, stepping inside. "It's how my daddy raised me." "Have a seat; I'll be ready in a few minutes." Tressa reappeared, dressed in a different pair of slacks and jacket. "I'm sorry I wasn't ready. The forecast calls for a chilly night. The outfit I had on was too thin." Marcus cast his eyes over her. "I like it," he said, "you look very pretty." "Thank you ..." came the reply as Tressa eyed him from top to bottom "... and might I say you're not shabby! I would love to see your closet." "And I would love for you to see it." Tressa gave him a side glance, a smile playing on her lips. "Are you getting fresh with me Marcus?" "No, it's too soon for that my lady; that will come after our third, maybe fourth date." That long, thought Tressa.

When they arrived at the restaurant, Marcus's table was ready. In the middle of the table was a vase of long stem red roses with a card attached. Tressa was taken aback; most men bring the flowers to the house, he had them waiting for me, and they are beautiful. Two dozen long stem roses. Tressa opened the card and quietly read it. "Tressa: I am so happy to be in your company. This is a long awaited date. I hoped the roses would be as beautiful as you. Affectionately, Marcus."

Tressa gently grabbed Marcus's hand and gave him a kiss on the cheek. "They are beautiful, the most beautiful roses I've ever received." Marcus smiled, glad at her gesture of appreciation. "The maître d will box those before we leave. Are you hungry?" Tressa nodded, pulling her chair closer to the table. "Yes, starving."

They ordered and surprisingly ate from each other's plates. Ordinarily, Marcus hated when anyone asked for his food, but somehow tonight he didn't care. Tressa had a good appetite, and after dinner she had desert and asked for a slice of pie to take home (which she insisted she pay for). Marcus glanced at her and paid the bill, which included the pie. "Do you really think I would allow you to pay for a piece of pie? Come now, sweet lady!" He made sure her roses were boxed, took her hand and left.

On the way to the car, he thought he saw a familiar vehicle. Is that Tia? No, that cannot be her. How would she know where I was or about this date? Once in the car, he circled the block a couple of times, just in case. No one was following him. He relaxed as he drove Tressa home. On the way home, they talked about the office and all the quirky characters that worked there. Marcus purposely did not talk about his personal life; he would reveal all that information at a later date, not tonight. Tressa asked Marcus to explain his connection with the officer that took her to her meeting. He hesitated before finally replying, "He's a family friend that has been on the force for years. Once I explained the situation, he volunteered to help. Thanks for reminding me, I owe him a six pack for that gallant deed." "That was kind of him, but, couldn't he have gotten in trouble for doing that?" Marcus shrugged. "Not really, what did he do wrong? He's paid to protect and serve." "Dallas, you are really smooth, really smooth that was good!"

He smiled and winked at Tressa. I got you, girl!" He played romantic music, his favorite Luther Vandross, and Tressa laid her head back with her eyes closed, humming the tunes. Just before they reached Tressa's, he took her hand and squeezed it passionately; she responded by gently grabbing and holding onto his arm. When they arrived, Tressa invited Marcus in but told him she had to get up early for church. Marcus walked Tressa to the door but declined the invitation. "It's late, and I too must prepare for services as well; however, I would like to see you tomorrow if possible." Tressa thought for a moment. "I should be home around 3:00. How about four? In that way, I can change and fix dinner for you." "That sounds great," Marcus paused. "One question, will you have other company or will it just be you and I?" Tressa frowned. "I'm not sure about that Marcus; is there a problem?" "No, no." Marcus shook his head. "But I would like to talk to you without other ears if that's OK." "I can work that out."

She gave him a hug and said, "See you tomorrow at four."

Marcus was beat; he sat on his sofa and stretched out. What a date, he thought, Tressa never disappoints. She looked fabulous, and that million-dollar smile, it took him to a place that was fascinating, bewildering and fulfilling.

Just as he was about to undress, he heard the beep on his computer, which usually meant an important message. He turned it on and scrolled down to see a message that said, "I hope you enjoyed the date; it will be your last one with my girl! WATCH OUT—I am after you." "Yea sure, then come after me, 'cause this woman is mine! Whoever you are, you have a fight on your hands."

Marcus printed out the email for future reference; he was hoping to have it traced. He was on a mission. The emails didn't bother him too much; he slept like a baby. The next day, he prepared for his assignment. He was never sure how long he would be gone. His job required him to be available until the end of his assignment, no matter the length. So far it had not been an issue, but for the first time Marcus wished he worked nine to five at home.

Chapter three

Tressa arose early to prepare for church. She wanted to talk to Ma or Mother Lizzy, the mother of the church, who, in Baptist churches is the oldest female member. Ma Lizzy was somewhat of a character, who had been a member of Second Baptist Church all her life. This was her family's church; her father was the assistant pastor until his death over twenty years ago. Ma Lizzy was somewhat of a prophetess; she was gifted in the area, but her eccentricities made it hard to rely on and/or sometimes trust her. Tressa liked her and believed in her. She did, however, find her a bit scary but tried not to show it.

Lately, Ma Lizzy's behavior was quite bizarre. Tressa didn't know what the problem was; perhaps it was dementia? Ma Lizzy was middle-aged and had two daughters that she only saw on holidays. She lived alone and often asked members of the church to dinner. Most members declined the offer and those that did accepted because they were lonely and had no one to talk too. Tressa called Ma Lizzy so she could talk to her about her recurring dreams. If anyone could help her, it would be Ma Lizzy if only she could stay focused. Tressa admired herself in the hall mirror before leaving and threw herself a kiss as she headed out. No, you have got to be kidding—a flat tire! I must be at church by 8:30 for Sunday school and to give the church announcements. It was now 7:40 a.m. She called Devan, but he didn't answer. They both attended the same church; Devan drove the church van, and his pickups begun at 7:30. "If I reach Devan, he can come get me," she said aloud. Tressa called until 7:50. "He's not answering, who else, my mom." She then called Jesse and Simone, but their voice mail came on. "Is this some kind of conspiracy? I can't wait around." She called the church to let someone know she would be late. Sister Brown answered and said she would tell the pastor; Tressa was relieved, at least they knew she was on the way.

Tressa decided to catch the local bus downtown to the subway, which luckily was only a few blocks from the church. She changed her shoes and headed to the bus stop, which was three blocks away. According to the schedule, one was due in about five minutes. Panting, she thought, good, I made it in time with one minute to spare. Just then the bus turned the corner. It slowed down and then sped up, going past Tressa's stop. Tressa started yelling, "Hey, bus driver, wait. What the ... I don't believe this." She was irate.

"I'll call MTA as soon as I get to church. They can't do this to us citizens, how many others did he drive past this morning?" She called Devan again, no answer. Seconds later a car pulled up beside her. "Miss, miss, you need a ride?" It was an elderly lady driving a vintage car. It looked to be at least 40 years old. She had blue rinse in her hair, was wearing lots of makeup and fur that looked just as old as the car. She looked harmless, but Tressa was hesitant. "Which way are you going?" She yelled out the window, "Honey, it's cold out, get in! I don't bite." "I am going to Bay Street to catch the subway," said Tressa."

The woman nodded. "I'm going that way, hop in." Bay

Street was about seven blocks away, and Tressa was desperate. The lady made a U-turn while beckoning to Tressa, "Come, come; child." Tressa opened the door and awkwardly got in. She heard voices in the back and noticed three children sitting in the back seat. They were well-dressed and spoke softly amongst themselves; this made her feel more comfortable."

Turning around, she said, "Hello, kids," they nodded, and waved slightly. Tressa, looking around the car and noticed it was well-kept and smelled like a flower garden. After just a few minutes in the car, the woman introduced herself as Madam Keys. "Yes honey, I am a prophet, and I was led to this street; I didn't know why. Young lady, I'm not going to beat around the bush, I saw a pretty girl like you in a vision last night, she was wearing a light blue coat and flats and carrying a bag and Bible. I instantly knew it was you. Please don't be alarmed, I came to set your mind free and to warn you of impending troubles and danger."

Madam Keys continued, "You're struggling with an ongoing dream are you not?" Tressa looked at the woman stunned and numb; she had not bargained for this. What should she do? Tressa sat in silence. She could feel Madam Keys staring at her. Tressa closed her eyes and prayed, and then she felt Madam Keys pat her hand and say, "Dear girl, don't be afraid of me and listen to what I have to say. We only have a few blocks," she pulled over to the curb. Tressa became unbelievably calm, looking Madam Keys straight in the eyes. "Now," said Madam Keys, "you're struggling with a recurring dream, don't be fooled or confused by what you are going to hear. Your dreams will greatly impact your future.

God is trying to prepare you for happiness beyond your wildest dream! However, there will be many highs and lows. You will experience more joy than the average person, but the lows will be excruciating. Your relationship with God, especially your prayer life, will be your salvation. You are surrounded by many— hear me —many enemies.

"You have been singled out by God as 'one in a million.' You will be resented and persecuted; loved and cherished beyond your wildest dreams, don't be afraid, trust in God, trust your instincts; be strong and steadfast. The Lord will guide you; let him lead you. Love your family. Anoint your home and confide in your future husband, hear me, there should be no secrets between the two of you. But more importantly, accept God's will for your life."

Madam Keys started the car and proceeded to the subway; it seemed as though she had arrived with just minutes to spare. Tressa looked at the lady and smiled. "Madam Keys, that is a lot to take in. I'm so grateful to you. This was meant to be, may you be blessed for being obedient. She surprised herself by giving Madam Keys a hug and a kiss on the cheek. Tressa thanked her for the ride, and as she opened the door, one of her bags dropped in the gutter. She exited the car and knelt to pick it up and as she stood to wave, the car had disappeared, vanished. "Lord, where did it go? I didn't even shut the door. What just happened?"

This frightened Tressa, she held her chest for a few minutes as she regrouped. Checking her watch, she was on time for the next train but had to hurry. Looking around, she noticed a woman with two children standing in the bus shelter. Tressa approached the woman and asked, "Miss, did you see a red vintage car leave about a minute ago?"

The woman, acting a little annoyed responded, "No, I am sorry, my children and I have been standing here ten maybe fifteen minutes waiting for the bus, which is late. We saw no car, and I was just wondering where you came from!" "I ..." Tressa froze, "you didn't see me get out of a car seconds ago?" "No, no, I definitely did not."

Tressa looked at the children for some type of confirmation, but they simply stared at her leaning against their mom. Tressa tried to explain but decided it was hopeless.

As she sat in church, she could not get the events of the day out of her head. After the morning service (which Tressa could not recall), Rev. Rayford approached Tressa, "Miss lady, you seemed kind of distant today, is anything wrong?"

Shaking her head, Tressa said, "No Pastor, I need to go home and unwind. I need ..." Just then, Ma Lizzy grabbed her, she was more energized today than usual. Tressa trusted Ma Lizzy until today, but meeting Madam Keys and hearing her warnings were a game changer. Was this fair? Tressa wasn't sure, but she did heed Madam Keys' warning and decided to be cautious. She hugged Ma Lizzy and told her how beautiful she looked. For a woman of her age, she had beautiful skin and the figure of a much younger woman. She demanded attention all the time. Despite her sometimes bizarre behavior, Ma Lizzy was very kind and giving and regarded as a great lady of faith. She made time for everyone that came to her with their problems. Yet, she was somewhat of a mystery. She never talked about her personal life. Her family didn't attend the Second Baptist Church. It was rumored Ma Lizzy created a rift in her family that traumatized her daughters, and they put distance between her, it was sad.

Rev. Rayford grabbed Ma Lizzy and gave her a kiss on the cheek, "Momma, you look like a million bucks! I declare if I weren't a happily married man, I would sweep you right off your feet." Cozying up to the pastor, Ma Lizzy said, "Happily married or not, Pastor, you can sweep me off my feet anytime!" They all laughed, and the pastor said, "On that note, I better leave and join Mrs. Rayford." "Well now, Tressa, do you still need to talk to me? I hope so, I cooked us a lovely meal. I know you don't eat much but ..." Tressa interrupted, "I'm sorry, Ma; I do need to talk, but I won't have time for dinner. I feel bad that you went to all that trouble. Ma, I had car trouble this morning, can I hitch a ride with you? Devan will pick me up from your home?" "No problem," Ma said smiling. "I'll enjoy the company." Tressa gave Ma Lizzy a squeeze. "Thanks a lot, just let me talk to Devan and Mom, and I'll join you in about fifteen minutes at the front." "That's fine Tressa, but keep in mind I also have a deadline, my time is ..." then Ma Lizzy caught herself, "I'm sorry, there's no problem." "It will take me at least fifteen minutes to gather my things." Tressa saw Devan and Jesse and ran to give them a hug. Devan grabbed Tressa and gave her a big brother hug, "Hi Sis, you look beautiful as usual." "Thanks, big brother you look dapper as well." Meanwhile, her mom Jesse wasn't so impressed. She took one look at her and said, "Baby, why do you look so troubled? What's wrong?" Tressa narrowed her eyes.

"Mom, how do you always know? I am going to talk to Ma Lizzy for a while." Turning to Devan, she said, "I need you to pick me up at Ma Lizzie's, my car wouldn't start this morning. I want to be home by 3 o'clock. I'm expecting company at 4 p.m., and I need to prepare dinner." "Let's see, it's now 1:15; Tressa, I have a bus load of people to take home, just call me when you're ready." "I called you and Mom all morning, and neither one of you responded, please turn on your phones," Tressa playfully reprimanded them. Devan and Jesse looked at each other, puzzling expressions on their faces. "Babe, our phones have been on, we actually called you, and you did not answer." Shaking her head, Tressa said, "That is really strange, so strange. I'll tell you about my mystery Mom, you will be amazed. Actually, in light of what happened this morning, I hesitate to go to Ma Lizzie's, but I promised her." Jesse frowned. "Just watch what you say to her Tressa, that woman is acting stranger and stranger." "I will Mom, I promise."

Ma Lizzy was sitting patiently waiting for Tressa. As Tressa walked towards the car, she experienced a sharp pain in her stomach. She stopped and took a deep breath. Minutes later the pain subsided, but Ma had noticed. "Tressa, you look terrible, are you alright?" "Yes, a stomach pain, but I feel much better now." "Are you sure you want to do this, we can always talk ..." "No, no, no! I need to talk about this and get it off my mind if it's alright with you?" "It certainly is. I'll get you a glass of cold ginger ale as soon as we get to the house." "Thanks, Ma."

Because the traffic was so dense, Ma Lizzy drove about twenty miles per hour in a forty mph zone.

Tressa thought she would never get to the house. Ma Lizzy turned on the radio to some dreaded new-age music; this was definitely not what she expected. "Do you like this type of music Tressa? I find it most enjoyable, it soothes the soul."

Without making apologies, Tressa replied, "Well, not really; it sounds rather dreary, sorry to say." Tressa waited for a reply, but Ma Lizzy just shook her head and smiled. As they pulled into the driveway, Ma Lizzy warned Tressa about her barking dog. When she opened the door, a dog the size of a cat started barking. "Shut that noise up, Dolly, you see it's me dog!" Dolly ran around the living room barking until Ma Lizzy picked her up. "He's excitable but harmless. Tressa give me a few minutes to change, and I'll be right with you."

Dolly came over and sat at Tressa's feet. Tressa waved her hand at the dog. "Move dog, get away from me." Dolly ran into the back room and came back with a rag doll, laying it at Tressa's feet. "Thank you Dolly, and here I was so mean to you." She reached down to pick up the doll and Dolly snapped at her hand. "You conniving pooch, I knew I shouldn't have trusted you." Just then, Ma Lizzy entered the room. She picked up Dolly, put her in another room and shut the door. "Sorry about that, she can be a bit feisty sometimes."

Tressa was stunned when Ma Lizzy returned; she was wearing a long white caftan with a matching head wrap; she wore rhinestone kitten heels and about fifteen rhinestone bracelets that jingled to the point of being annoying. Her face was made up with tons of makeup. She was wearing hot red lipstick, false eyelashes that were at least one inch long, and her cheeks had loud orange blush. Tressa was stunned, "Gee, you look ... different!" she wanted to say "like a floozy" but held her tongue.

"Yes, hon, one of my greatest pleasures is dolling up, you never know who's going to stop by or when the Lord is going to call you home." "That's true, that's very true."

Ma Lizzy stretched out on the sofa as if she were being interviewed. Tressa could not believe her eyes, she thought, is this woman crazy?

To break the ice, Tressa complimented her on her home and asked if she had decorated it herself. "No dear, I'm not into that, I have someone to come in every five years or so to update my home. I don't like antiques or outdated furnishings; I make sure my home is tastefully decorated."

Ma Lizzie's house was beautiful; it looked like a museum with modern furnishings. There were pictures of her children and grandchildren on a grand piano in the living room. Over the fireplace hung an abstract picture that looked very expensive. What she found disturbing was a picture of Ma Lizzy on the end table that resembled a picture of her face on someone else's body. It was by no means flattering and whose body was that? Ma Lizzy leaned over to Tressa crossing her legs. "Now dear, let's talk—what's troubling you?"

Tressa leaned forward in the big white chair composing herself. She said "Ma Lizzy, I wanted to talk to you about a reoccurring dream." Just then the phone rang, "Hold it, dear, I must get that, it could be a client."

Looking absolutely puzzled, Tressa thought clients, what kind of clients could Ma Lizzy have? Is she charging people for some type of service? As Tressa listened, Ma Lizzy told someone about some pepper and herbs, what in the world ... what is she giving ingredients for? Tressa began to feel uncomfortable and got up and walked out on the deck. I don't understand what's going on. Does Ma Lizzy think of herself as a medium or clairvoyant? Tressa always thought of her as a spiritually gifted woman, but this? Tressa regrouped and said a silent prayer. She felt she was in the lion's den. Did she dare share her dreams with Ma Lizzy? Lord, please direct me! Her mind went back to the mystery woman she encountered that morning. Suddenly she felt like Ma Lizzy was not someone she wanted to share her thoughts or dreams with. Tressa heard the phone click and saw Ma Lizzy scuffling through the house. "Tressa, Tressa, where are you?" "I'm here on the deck. I didn't want to listen to your call."

"That's OK, my dear, it was nothing. People call me all day for advice and prayers, and I'm always willing to listen and be of service." Ma Lizzy grabbed Tressa's arm and ushered her back in the living room, "Sit down, I can see you're getting more frustrated by the minute. I am here to help. But before you say anything, let me tell you what I've seen since you've entered my home."

Ma Lizzy took Tressa's hands, closed her eyes and began to moan and rock back and forwards. She suddenly opened her eyes and leaned in close to Tressa. "My dear, the dreams that you've been having will greatly impact your future. You will be happily married with a devoted husband, but it will come at a great price. Your sorrows will not be many, but they will be deeply felt. You will have many extraordinary children. Listen to what the Lord tells you even if it seems bizarre. Remember, God works in mysterious ways. You've been chosen. In conclusion, let me say, do not reveal your visions to anyone but me! I'm the appointed one."

Ma Lizzy released Tressa's hands. Tressa lay back on the sofa full of amazement; Ma Lizzy repeated the same things Madam Keys said except for the advice not to tell anyone but her. Tressa felt uneasy about that. She knew she would share this bizarre experience with her family and eventually Marcus. Well, Lord, I asked for confirmation, and you revealed it to me twice in one day, and I must say, it's a lot to take in. Tressa's phone rang; it was Devan. "Hey Bro, yes I am ready. Ma I have to go, Devan will be here in about ten minutes." "May I offer you some nice cold water before you go?" Ma asked. "Sure, why not?" Tressa followed her to the kitchen. When she opened the refrigerator door, she noticed bottles and bottles of water. Ma Lizzy reached in and took out a bottle and poured Tressa a tall glass. Tressa swallowed a small amount and stopped, it tasted bitter. She placed the glass on the table and commented that the water tasted odd. "What do you mean odd? Let me taste it."

Ma Lizzy drank some and smiled. "Oh that, that's just an additive I add to my water as a cleanser and to cut my appetite. I am sorry; I should have given you bottled water."

Tressa began to walk back into the living room, and Ma Lizzy followed her throwing her hands up in the air, mumbling something crazy. She walked up to Tressa, eyeball to eyeball with her white head wrap and caftan now looking like a weird cape. "Tressa when I tell you something, you can bet on it, you don't have to pray, question my truth or prophecies."

Ma Lizzy had started to pace up and down the room. "This was revealed to me, and you can bet it will all come true; don't question me. I'm the chosen one; ask anyone in church." Ma Lizzy was acting irrational, Tressa didn't know what to do or say. "Yes, Ma Lizzy, calm down, I believe you." Tressa was so shocked; she trembled. As Ma Lizzy was pacing, Tressa noticed a weird insignia on the back of the caftan, it had some kind of foreign writing on it. Tressa was going to ask her what it meant but decided she had had enough. "Thanks for the revelation and your hospitality, it was appreciated. I will take everything that has been revealed to me to heart." Tressa walked to the door hoping to see Devan. He had just pulled up; she couldn't get out of there quickly enough. "My brother has arrived, hope to see you at the clothes drive at church, Saturday." She hugged Ma Lizzy and flew out the door. Tressa was in no mood to discuss the events of the day with Devan; she would discuss it later. Right now, all she wanted to do was find the nearest grocer and purchase an acceptable meal for her and Marcus. Thinking about Marcus was like a breath of fresh air. One thing she knew for sure, this incident would be tabled for the night. When Devan dropped Tressa home, she was grateful he didn't ask her why she was at Ma Lizzie's. She was barely in the door when the phone rang. "Hello." "Hello, are you just getting in?" "Yes, this is Marcus, am I still invited to dinner?" "Of course, is it still at 4 p.m.?" "Yes, it is," Tressa affirmed." "Can I come over now and help fix dinner?" Tressa paused, "Yes you can; I would actually appreciate it." Tressa surprised herself; any other time, she would have said no, I got this, but considering her day, she was ready to see Marcus and appreciated the help. "Great. I'll be over in ten to fifteen minutes." "Hurry over, you can peel these potatoes!" Marcus paused, and Tressa laughed. "Well, you said you wanted to help, see ya!" She quickly changed and hurried to the kitchen to start dinner.

When Marcus arrived, the table was royally set and Tressa was ready to eat. "This is nice, I thought I had to help," said Marcus. Tressa smiled. "I was just joking. I can whip up a three-course meal in seconds." Marcus nodded. "I see you can, but how will it taste?" "You'll see smarty pants."

They sat to eat; Marcus held Tressa's hand and said grace. She was impressed and delighted to see that Marcus was a man of prayer. They made small talk at dinner, but Marcus knew he had to discuss Tia and his job assignment with her as soon as possible. After dinner, Marcus helped Tressa clean the kitchen and proceeded to the living room to relax. With the lights dim and the fire roaring, Marcus felt this was the appropriate time to jump in. "Well, my dear, I need to talk, there are some things I need to discuss with you—important things. I don't know where this is going, but I need to be open and above board." "Okay," Tressa said, folding her arms. I'm ready." "Yea, where do I begin?" They were sitting face to face on the long sofa; Marcus took a deep breath and shared his history between him and Tia, including the most recent incident. Tressa did not flinch; she sat listening, nodding and searching his face, thinking, this poor man, he must be in torment. "Tressa, do you have any questions?" Marcus said once he'd finished. "No, I think

I got it. Let me summarize if I may. You and Tia have been together since you were teenagers; you stayed together until college. In time you both discovered you were different, incompatible and went your separate ways. Even though you parted, you still had strong feelings for each other. You both dated other people but nothing serious; she still depends on you because she knows she can. You, on the other hand, would prefer to be left alone, especially since meeting me. Is that about it?" "Yes, that's it in a nutshell."

Marcus took a deep breath and said, "And now the other thing, which is my job. As you know, I'm a government employee. I teach protocol and diplomacy to government and foreign officials, diplomats, private citizens, basically anyone that's interested and can afford to pay. I'm paid quite well, and I love my job. The main office is in Virginia; that's where I report for briefings and assignments." Marcus stood clasping his hands behind his back like a scared child, "My job sometimes requires extensive traveling. I'm often assigned to many high-profile meetings. I work year round often with no break for holidays." He stopped and sat on the arm of the sofa. "I'm explaining all this to say I have to leave on Friday for my next assignment. I won't know where I'm going until I get to the office and meet with my supervisor. These assignments take me around the world. Tressa, I've met many interesting people, and I have always looked forward to these assignments, but now, after meeting you, not so much. Technically, we have four days before I leave, and I would like to spend as much time with you as possible." Tressa was impressed, what an interesting job. Never had she met someone with such a position. She thought he was some type of government secret agent. "Marcus, I hope you know that I look forward to spending time with you, especially since you're leaving soon." She asked to be excused so she could get her day planner. She had two meetings that could not be cancelled, one on Tuesday morning and the other Friday evening; this was great. "Dallas, we have three days to enjoy, that's the best I can do. And they are ... they are Monday, Wednesday, and Thursday."

"That's great"! A giant smile came across his face. In his excitement, he grabbed Tressa and gave her a big hug. He was a little embarrassed but played it off since Tressa did not return the embrace. "Sorry, I got carried away." "Don't be sorry, I liked it, I just didn't know how to respond."

Marcus leaned closer. "Let me give you a hint, how about like this ..." Marcus grabbed her and hugged her again, and this time Tressa threw her arms around him and hugged him back and then they gave each other a passionate kiss. Marcus drew his head back with his eyes closed. "I've been waiting for that kiss, our first kiss, and it was well worth it." For Tressa, it was likewise. She knew she would relive that kiss over and over again.

It was like in those love stories when the woman says her heart fluttered, and her knees went weak. This was a date she would never forget.

It was now about seven, and Tressa had yawned about six times. "I think I better leave so you can get some rest," Marcus said. Tressa walked Marcus to the door. "What about tomorrow? How about brunch?" "Brunch sounds great I can sleep late." "See you about 11 a.m."

"You have a date." Marcus kissed Tressa on the forehead, gave her a warm embrace and said goodnight. Tressa was tired; she almost dreaded tomorrow because she knew she had to tell Marcus about Gregg. She hoped Marcus would be as understanding as she had been. In actuality, their stories mirrored each other. She took a shower, went to bed and immediately fell asleep.

Early that morning, a loud knock came at the door. Tressa jumped up, "Who is it?" She grabbed her robe, unable to imagine who would be banging on her door this early. She had a doorbell, why didn't they ring the bell? She heard a man yell, "Flower Delivery for Tressa Bowers."

"Wait a minute," Tressa peeped out her side window, to see the truck. "Leave them, please!" She slid a five-dollar bill through the mail slot, and when she saw the delivery man pull off, she opened the door and retrieved the flowers. "My, these are beautiful." She hurriedly opened the card, and to her surprise they were not from Marcus. "You have been on my mind, miss you terribly, love Gregg." Tressa was so disappointed; she threw the flowers and the card in the trash and went back to bed. "I should feel bad, but I don't. I told him it was over and not to send any flowers, don't call and don't stop by, what part doesn't he get?"

Just as she was nestled in the bed, the doorbell rang, again. "Now who can that be? It's probably Devan looking for a meal." She looked out the side window to see none other than Gregg. He noticed her at the window and beckoned for her to open the door. "What do you want Gregg? I don't want any company, just go," Tressa shouted. "Tressa please, I have some news, some important news, it's about the property!" "You can send them by registered mail." A hand caressing her forehead, Tressa reconsidered and hesitantly opened the door, waving her hand to usher him in. "What? What is the reason for this visit Gregory Montgomery?" "You still remember my name, at least that's something. Did you get the flowers?" "Yes, there they are," Tressa said flatly, "in the trash." "Really Tressa!" "Cut the crap Gregg, I'm in no mood for your foolishness again. What do you want?" "I finally heard from the realtor; they drew up the papers to sell the property, our property, remember? I brought them over because we both must sign and have them notarized." Tressa reached for the folder, "Give them here." She opened the folder and papers flew everywhere. "I'll get them," remarked Gregg. "No please, please I got this." Gregg could see the frustration on Tressa's face. "I meant no harm Tressa; do you really resent seeing me that much?" "I don't resent you," Tressa stormed. "I just don't want to see you. We always fight, and I'm tired of it. It's just best we don't communicate." Gregg made himself comfortable sitting on the living room sofa, "How is that possible?"

It's possible because I'm a permanent member of this family. Remember my mother and your mother are best friends and we have history." "Yes, and we closed the book."

Gregg directed his forefinger at Tressa. "No, you closed the book; I don't believe we've written the final chapter. What is this about really Tressa? Our different religious views? It can't be! People have a right to have different views, and it shouldn't tear them apart. I believe you're being narrow-minded."

Tressa sighed, fingering her brow. "It's more than that Gregg, and you know it. It's about my right to choose what I believe versus what you want me to believe, that's the problem." Tressa's mind went back to when they met. They lived next to each other until Gregg's father moved the family across town to a "better neighborhood." Yet, Gregg would meet Tressa every day after school, walk her home and then catch the bus home. Their mothers were best friends, and the families attended the same church. Everyone assumed Gregg and Tressa would be the "forever couple." Gregg loved Tressa deeply; he had planned his life around her, which included the grand proposal, lavish wedding, romantic honeymoon and their fabulous "life ever after." To remain close, he wanted them to attend the same college, but Tressa knew she needed to break away from Gregg and his controlling nature. He was awarded a four-year athletic scholarship at a local Maryland college and was disappointed that Tressa accepted a scholarship at Yale. She did love Gregg, but as far as she was concerned they were over, they had grown apart. Gregg was a catch, he was handsome, had no children, and had a promising career. What was not to love?

The fact that Tressa did love Gregg meant she often found herself with conflicting feelings. She was jealous when she saw him with other women, but reasoned to herself that this was normal after being with a man so long. She wanted to maintain a friendship; she could not imagine him as her husband. Each year, Gregg's religious and fundamental beliefs radically changed. Tressa snapped back to reality, "Boy, where was I?" "Probably trying to make up your mind if you wanted me or not. I know we still got it." Getting on the couch and sliding closer to Tressa, he added, "Why don't you give in?" "Give in to what Gregg?" Tressa snapped.

To Gregg this was not a joke, he was tired. He wanted to commit. He felt they could work out their differences. "Tressa, I've given you my heart, I've never cheated on you, and I adore you," he said walking away. "Gregg, the thrill is gone! Let it go." "Tressa what's wrong with me?" Gregg asked, turning back to face her. "I've told you over and over again; I'm tired of repeating myself." Gregg followed her to the living room, "Then tell me once more." "It's no mystery, what does it take to get through to you?" Tapping her index finger into her left palm, Tressa said, "Let me reiterate; you're controlling, egotistical, and most importantly, we share neither political nor religious views, that's life, get over it. And yes, our families share a history, so what? Ours have ended. I don't want to go through this again with you. I'm not interested in you. Don't come around and don't call." Gregg stood there hurt; he threw the papers on the floor and stomped on them. "This is what you do to my heart, Tressa, stomp on it."

He reached out to her to grab her; she thought he was going to force himself on her, and she screamed. "For real Tressa, you think I want you that much? You have got to be kidding. Do you know how many women are attracted to me? Do you know how many I reject? And you think I have to force myself on you? Please!"

Tressa did not apologize. "We seem to be going around in circles, and I am tired." Suddenly Gregg stormed up to her face, "Alright! Alright! Miss goody-two-shoes; strong and fierce, so holy; I don't want to hear any more."

"Gregg this is not about me being good, it's about being a God-fearing Christian. That's who I am, and who I've been practically all my life, and I love who I am. I want to get married and have children, but I want to marry someone who shares my beliefs; I don't want or won't compromise on that. We have no future, that's why we broke it off," she said distancing herself from him. "Do you remember that?" "I have a right to my views."

"Yes, I know Gregg, but you're brutish when expressing them. I don't have to accept your views, and I don't want to live with them either!" Tressa took a deep breath, aware that her voice had risen in pitch and that her face was flushed.

"Let me say this to you, Tressa Bowers, so you'll never have to wonder again. First, I do believe in the Lord my God, and I consider myself a Christian; however, maybe not as orthodox. I believe we have a right to live our lives as we please without all these manmade laws and deep-seated beliefs that pit one nation and one man against another."

Tressa slid a hand across tired eyes. "Give me an example Gregg; I'm not quite sure I know what you're talking about."

"OK; you say that it's only one way to heaven, that if you don't believe in or accept Jesus you're going to hell; well, I don't believe that. There are kind and loving people that are of other faiths, the Buddhists for example, share similar beliefs as Christians except for their belief in Jesus; you're telling me all of those people are going to hell?"

Tressa could only stare at him. "Gregg you are crazy! You call yourself a Christian and put such little value in God's holy word. And, for the record, read John 14:6, Jesus says 'I am the way, the truth, and the life, no man cometh unto the Father but by me,' that's the word of God. And if I'm correct, what you're really telling me is you don't believe Jesus is the Son of God, and that's your right! But I do. And there're our political views. They are so far and different it's ridiculous."

"You know Tressa, you're so important! You're really on a pedestal; I don't want to be around when you fall off." Gregg became angrier and started banging his fists on the cocktail table, "Tressa shut up! Just shut the hell up! The Bible was written by men – who are fallible; the Bible has been written and rewritten so many times, who knows what it really means? I believe all we have to do is trust our own hearts and live by the laws of the land and we will be fine, heaven and all."

Tressa could see Gregg was becoming unhinged. She turned her back and walked towards the kitchen. Gregg grabbed her, swung her around and looked at her for several seconds, "I'm not a fool Tressa. I am a man with his own views that wants to be respected for what he believes." "Gregg, I've heard enough, please leave!"

The doorbell rang; she had forgotten all about Marcus, dear God! She hurried to the door and before she could open it, she heard the door opening. It was Devan. "Devan, I'm so happy to see you," she said retrieving the documents. "Gregg is here, and I want him to leave."

Devan walked past Tressa to the hallway where Gregg was standing. "Hey man what's going on?" Gregg took a deep breath and slowly responded, "It's our norm man, you know us; she never wants to hear me out. I came over because I missed her, see I even sent her flowers. I don't know what's wrong with her; she acts like I'm some kind of ogre." "Just leave, Gregg, just leave," Tressa shouted from behind Devan. "OK I'm leaving," Gregg mumbled. "Your big detective brother has arrived on the scene, and I don't want to be arrested. However, missy, we will meet again, and for the record, I wish you your worst nightmare."

"And that coming from a man who just tried to convince me that we still had a future." Tressa shook her head. Devan; knowing their history was very protective of his sister. He followed Gregg to the door. "Let's go man; she doesn't want to see you."

As Gregg marched down the path towards his car, Devan reminded Tressa why he stopped by. "Oh Tressa, I forgot what I came for; I need the tickets for the fashion show and dance." "Okay." Tressa gave Devan the tickets, and as he was leaving, he saw a man mounting the front steps. Gregg had not pulled off, and when he saw the man get out of his car he got out and approached him. "May I help you?"

It was Marcus. Marcus looked at Gregg and said, "I could ask you the same question." Tressa heard Marcus's voice, pushed past Gregg and ushered him in the house. "Hi babe, come in. I apologize, it's been a hectic morning, and I'm not ready."

Gregg forced his way back into the house. Confronting Marcus, he again asked, "And you are?" Marcus gave Gregg the once over and said, "None of your damn business." "Well, 'none of your damn business,' I'm Gregory Montgomery. I'm sure you've heard about me."

Just then, Devan reappeared, walking in front of Tressa as a gesture of protection. "Gregg let's go, you're finished here." Gregg found his way around to Tressa, "Tell this bozo who I am; if you don't, I will." Tressa looked puzzled, and Gregg said, "Buddy boy, I'm Tressa's husband! Didn't she tell you?"

Marcus was stunned and taken aback. Devan shook his head, walked over to Gregg, grabbed him by the arm and forcibly threw him out the door. "And this time stay out!" "Tressa I'll call you." She could hear them argue as they left while Marcus stood leaning against the kitchen counter with his legs crossed and a look of anticipation, waiting for an explanation.

Tressa was somewhat amused though she didn't want to show it. Taking a deep breath, she began explaining as if she was in court delivering a summation, pleading her case. "Mr. Dallas: I know your work experience will help me in this situation. Your occupation, which I'm sure includes thought and reason will help me navigate through this awkward and necessary summation." Ever so lightly, banging her hand on the counter, "I'm innocent; I have been accused of a heinous crime, lying to someone that I'm crazy about. Someone I barely know but already admire and adore. Please bear with me and be patient. "This is my story: "Mr. Dallas I'm not married to Gregory Montgomery."

Marcus was getting tired; normally he had the patience of Job, but not now. "Tressa, I don't find this a bit humorous." Tressa lifted her hand to Marcus's lips and hushed him. Now being very serious, she said, "Marcus, I'm not married to Gregg. We were married when I was nineteen, five years ago. It was impulsive and stupid. Gregg was controlling and manipulative. In the first week he had demanded my credit cards, he needed to manage my spending; he wanted to know how much WE had in MY savings account, but I was not privileged to his information. No way was I going to live like that. I did love him, or at least I thought I did. I called my mom, and with her support, I filed for an annulment, and it was granted. I have the papers if you would like to see them. Gregg was furious, but I did what I thought was best for me. I'm sorry for the scene; I tried to get rid of Gregg before you came but he ..." Tressa couldn't say any more.

Marcus took a deep breath. "OK Tressa, I believe you. I shared my story with you, and you didn't run." Throwing up his hands and leaning into Tressa without kissing her, he said, "So who am I not to understand?"

Raising her eyebrows, Tressa asked, "So Mr. Dallas, are we OK? Because I remember, you promised me breakfast." Looking at her watch, she added, "Relax, I'll be ready soon."

The remainder of the day was enjoyable. They discussed personal issues and made future plans. Marcus took Tressa's hands and pulled her close. "Now, pretty lady, I hope we're off to a better start. It has already been challenging, and I pray things will only get better." Tressa nodded. "I believe with prayer and our faith in each other, it will."

Tressa made it clear that she was looking for someone to share her life with. Someone goal-oriented, but most of all someone that loved the Lord. She wanted a God fearing man, someone she could talk to and depend on; someone that shared her faith, hopes, and dreams. And, he had to be fun-loving, trustworthy and family oriented. "But for now, a friendly relationship if that's possible."

"Ms. Bowers, I think I am the man for you. I've been waiting for someone like you, the same type of friendship relationship, and who knows what our friend relationship will blossom into? Anyways, let's try. Do you want to shake on it or can we seal it with a kiss?" "Now which is that, the friendship or the relationship?" Marcus winked at Tressa, "I'll let you know."

Marcus and Tressa spent every minute they could together. He was sad to see Thursday because he knew he had to leave Friday evening. They spent a lot of time talking about their past, clearing the air so to speak. Tressa asked him about the outcome of Tia's arrest, and he informed her that she had been released, no charges were filed, and she's probably back to her shenanigans. But he reassured her that Tia was not the stalker type. She feared too much publicity because she had a reputation to protect, not hers so much as her families. Her father would not stand for negative publicity, and Marcus was sure this incident had been swept under the rug.

On Friday, Tressa and Marcus said their goodbyes and promised to stay in touch either by phone, email, and/or text. Tressa hoped he would be home in time for the spring dance and fashion show at her church, which was approximately five weeks away. Of course, he could not promise but said he would try. They kept their word and talked almost every day. Marcus was so happy his supervisor commented on his glow! "Glow, man, men don't glow! What's wrong with you? But things are looking up." Jesse called Tressa Friday night.

"Hello?" "Hello, is this my daughter? I feel abandoned, what have you been up too?" "Mom, I'm sure Devan has filled you in." "Yes he has, but I've been waiting on your version, and as I asked before, what's up?" Tressa was happy to hear from her mother; she told her all about the last three weeks and their mind-blowing events, including the incident with the mystery woman and Ma Lizzy.

As she was telling her about the mystery woman, "Madam Keys," Jesse became very quiet. "What did you say she looked like? Describe her to me again." "She was a real mystery. She had blue hair, a medium brown complexion and talked with a foreign accent; that's funny Mom, I didn't remember that until now." "What type of accent Tressa?" Tressa frowned; it was difficult to place. "I don't know, maybe like Jamaican, an island accent." "Could you tell if she was short or tall?" "No, she didn't get out of the car; however, she looked to be average height." "And these children, what can you tell me about them?" "I vaguely remember them. They were little children, about four or five years of age." "Tressa, during this incident did you feel threatened, frightened or perhaps protected?" "No, I felt bewildered. I couldn't understand why this was happening to me. I assumed by the end of the day that God had answered my prayers. But whose version was correct? Or was either one true. I feel that God had spoken, but the psychic made me feel more at peace." "Tressa, you go to sleep. Know that I love you very much. We'll talk about this again tomorrow." "Mom, Mom, do you want to go shopping tomorrow? I could use some girl time." "Yes, you bet," came her enthusiastic reply. I'll come by tomorrow after 1:00." "Can we get an earlier start? I need to get out, please!" "Yes

Tressa, see you at 11 a.m. sharp, then." This troubled Tressa, she knew her mother and the two accounts of the women were troubling to her. What had she said? She started to drift off to sleep when she heard the computer email send through a message. Getting up, she turned it on to see a message from Marcus. "Good night, sleep tight, talk again in the morning light. MDD." "That's what I'm talking about." Tressa said her prayers and fell asleep. "What in the world?" "Open the door sleepy head, it's your family." "Mom please, have mercy, what time is it?" "9:00." "Wait, I am coming." Tressa scuffled out of bed, robed and answered the door. "Hello, hello, hello!" Simone jumped from behind Jesse, "I got you, Sis." Simone hugged Tressa like she had not seen her in years. "Wow! This is a surprise." "Well, I have another one for you; someone else ..." "Hello, Auntie ..." "Oh, my goodness it's Taylor." "Yes, she's home for two weeks." "How is that possible, I thought all schools had resumed." "Their water heater broke, and they're out for at least two weeks; don't worry, they were given plenty of homework."

Hugging Tressa and giving her a sloppy kiss, Taylor said, "Aunt Tressa, I'm so happy to see you." "Girl, you are growing, you're taller than your momma." "Not only taller, but prettier." Taylor winked at Tressa. "Tressa, hurry, shower and get dressed; remember we're going to breakfast, and no, we don't want to eat in," her mother cut in. "Gee Mom, you took the words right out of my mouth." "I know, now hurry."

After breakfast, Jesse dropped Simone and Taylor home and returned to Tressa's. Tressa could see by the look on her mom's face that something was troubling her. "Momma what's wrong?"

"I want to talk to you about your incident on Sunday. I'm going to show you something." Jesse retrieved a large photo album from her bag and thumbed through some pictures and suddenly stopped. "Now Tressa, look at this picture, does it favor anyone?" Tressa sat staring at her mom before looking at the picture. She closed her eyes and took a deep breath; OK, now she opened her eyes and gasped. "Oh my God, that is the woman that was in the car! This is her Momma, who is she?" "Tressa, that's a picture of my mother, your grandmother, just before she passed away. She had begun to rinse her hair blue, and she used to ride the three of you in her red car. That was before you had to have car seats." "My God, Mom, why do you think she appeared to me like that?" "Probably to protect you. She knew you were seeking an answer to your dream, and I guess the Lord used her to answer it." "Why did she call herself "Madam Keys the prophet?" "Actually, she was a prophet; she could interpret dreams and signs like none other."

Jesse sat on the edge of her chair, "For example, one Saturday, we were all sitting around the kitchen table, just before your father passed, and Dad placed this huge towel on Mother's head. He pretended to be someone with a dream to be interpreted and introduced Mom as Madam Keys, the psychic, and it stuck. Whenever we were in trouble, Dad would say, I'll tell "Madam Keys" on you, she knows what you did, and we would confess our troubles because nine out of ten, Mom did know what we had done. We later found out, however that sometimes it was because the teacher had called, or the neighbors had told on us, but other times it was because she just knew! So she identified herself with a name that we could easily identify." Tressa looked at the picture again. "Yes, ma, that's her. Gracious, the Lord was listening to my cries."

Mom, the strangest thing is the interpretations of Madam Keys or Grandmother and Ma Lizzie's were that they were eerily the same, except granny encouraged me to tell my mate everything, and not to keep secrets. I felt that last week when Gregg revealed to Marcus that we had been married, and that's only because I had not had the opportunity to tell him. However, once I talked to Marcus, I felt a sense of redemption like I had made things right and listened to the spirit...Mom, does that make any sense? Marcus was hurt and disappointed. I never want that to happen again." "And what did Ma Lizzy say?" "She told me to only confide in her; she was the 'chosen one."

"Chosen, my foot, she is a natural born nut!" "But Mom, she revealed all the things Granny said. Where did that come from?" "Probably some dark place, Tressa. I told you to leave that crazy woman alone." Tressa frowned. "But Mom, is she crazy or psychic?" "Read your Bible baby," Jesse said firmly. "There are all kinds of revealers in the word. Some are fortune tellers, some sorcerers, etc., they are interpreters of dreams, and they're not of God."

Tressa could see where her mom was coming from. "Yea, you're right, what was I thinking? You know she's going to keep after me, what shall I do?"

"Avoid her as much as possible, and for heaven's sake, do not tell her any more of your dreams or problems. I think that woman is some kind of devil worshipper." Tressa wanted to believe her mom, but she couldn't believe Ma Lizzy was that out of touch.

Chapter four

Weeks passed, and the church fashion show and dinner was a week away. Ma Lizzy cornered Tressa on several occasions offering her words of encouragement and questioning her about any current issues in her life, but Tressa heeded her mother's warnings. She was not rude or impolite, just polite enough to make sure they were not enemies.

Marcus and Tressa grew closer. They kept their word, and via electronic technology they stayed in touch; she loved hearing his voice. He kept her up to date on the people he had met and the places he had been and was going. He could not promise her he would be home for the show, but promised he would try. Virginia was only a couple hours from Baltimore; perhaps he could drive up and stay one night and drive back early Monday morning if he were in town.

Preparation was underway for the annual dinner and fashion show. The show usually drew hundreds of people. The show was sold out, all five hundred seats. Tressa reserved one seat for Marcus just in case. He said he would call by 4 p.m to let her know if he could make it, but she had not heard from him. This was the one time she yearned for a call; she wanted to present her new guy to everyone. Time was flying, and she had to focus on the show. If he could not make it, she knew he tried his best.

When the clock struck six, it was time for all the models to get ready. The guests were enjoying a lavish meal, and dessert would be served at intermission. Tressa reserved a seat at her table and informed the ushers to escort Mr. Dallas to her table if he showed. Tressa was the MC; she was dressed to the nines. All of the Bowers participated in the affair in one capacity or another. Devan was a model and escort, Simone, Taylor and Jesse were models. At exactly 7:00, the show began. Rev. Rayford opened the show with prayer and Tressa welcomed all guests. She introduced dignitaries and guests that had traveled from across the globe to be in attendance. Once Tressa introduced the announcer for the show, she took her seat; minutes later, an usher informed her that she had guests at the door.

Could it be? Yes, it was Marcus and another gentleman, taller and older than Marcus and just as handsome. Marcus gently leaned down and kissed Tressa on the cheek, "Hi honey, I'm so happy to see you. Tressa this is my dad, I hope it's alright that I brought him." "Of course, it's a pleasure to meet you Mr. Dallas." "Come, follow me." Tressa seated Marcus and found another seat for Marcus's dad. The ushers, anticipating Tressa's request, served Marcus and his dad a meal. They said very little during the show, but Tressa felt Marcus's dad's eyes on her. When any of the family appeared on stage, Marcus pointed them out to his father. At intermission, Tressa had the opportunity to actually talk to Mr. Dallas. "Well, young lady, you're the woman that has mesmerized my son. I can see why, you're very pretty. However, he did say it wasn't just your looks that captivated him."

"I'm happy to hear that Mr. Dallas; I do know how to add, subtract and spell." They laughed, and Marcus looked at Tressa, pleased. Tressa had the chance to introduce Marcus to Simone, Taylor and who else, nosey Ma Lizzy. Sashaying up to Marcus, she said, "So this is the new guy. What a hunk, no wonder you've been hiding him." Turning to Mr. Dallas, she asked, "And who's this gentleman with him, his brother?"

Mr. Dallas laughed, "Hardly! I'm his father, call me Avery." He stood and shook Ma Lizzy's hand and told her how nice she looked. Avery knew the score, he was just being polite but already felt bad vibes from this woman. Ma Lizzy pulled up a chair to sit next to Avery when one of the ushers beckoned her to the front. "Thank God, what a relief, that woman is a nightmare," Tressa said. The second half of the show began, and the first model was Jesse; Tressa saw Avery lean over and whisper something in Marcus's ear. Marcus said something to his dad and pointed at Tressa and then winked. The show was a success! There were two standing ovations as Tressa tried to calm the crowd.

Once Marcus heard that the clothes modeled in the show were available for purchase, he placed an order for three designer suits for him and his dad and his grandfather; he also ordered a dress he liked for Tressa, which would be a surprise for her later.

Avery Dallas was introduced to Jesse after the show. He was quite taken with the mother of his son's girl. As Jesse approached the table, Avery stood and extended his hand to her. He didn't wait for Marcus to introduce them. "I see where your daughter gets her looks. "And you are?" "I'm Avery Dallas, Marcus's father. Is this your home church? It's beautiful." "Yes, we've been members here since I was a little girl." "Oh, I see; my son invited me at the spur of the moment; at first, I refused, but he insisted. You know how my son is very persistent." Jesse shook her head. "Well no, I don't really know your son; I've just met him, but if Tressa likes him, I'm sure he's a nice guy." "He's more than a nice guy," Avery enthused, "he's a great catch, like his dad." Jesse raised her brow, "Oh my, say so ..." Marcus, ever the gentleman, tried to pay Tressa for two tickets, she refused. "I already paid for your ticket and several folks didn't show, so your father is fine. You can, however, donate the money to our missionary fund if you must get rid of sixty dollars." Marcus nodded. "Sure, that sound like a good idea it would be my pleasure." "Well, well, well, here is, Mr. Glamourpuss, how are ya? What was, no, is your name...?" Scratching his head and pointing his finger, "Was it Marcus?" It was Gregg. "Gregory I know you have no regard for the church, but I would appreciate it if you would knock it off and take your meanness somewhere else."

Marcus shook his head, looking at Gregg like he was a fool. He knew Gregg wanted to intimidate him, but that wasn't happening. "Hi Gregory, I hope you enjoyed the show, I did." "I did not! I saw you sittin' with Tressa, and despite what people say, I'm a gentleman; if I weren't, I would have come and sat at that table and caused all kinds of confusion." Marcus looked at Gregg and scowled. "No, you wouldn't because I would not have let you." Gregg looked Marcus up and down, invading his space, ready to attack. "You Johnny come lately." "Hey, what's the ruckus about?" the pastor came across, alarmed by the commotion. "Hi Pastor," Gregg said, "I was introducing myself to Tressa's new beau, he's not the friendliest lad, but since I'm not wanted, I will bid you all a goodnight. So, goodnight and go to hell!"

The pastor was shocked; he had never seen Gregg in this light and never heard him utter a curse word. Rev. Rayford reassured Tressa not to worry, he would handle Gregg later. "No, I'll handle him later," said Devan. Tressa was embarrassed at Gregg's behavior. She apologized for him and asked everyone to forgive the fool.

Rev. Rayford, in an effort to bring peace to the situation, complimented Tressa. "You did an amazing job, and Jesse wow, outstanding my lady," he said, placing a kiss on her cheek. "Thanks, Pastor, and now that that mess is over, I think I'll head home, and Marcus, don't let Gregg deter you; believe me, his bark has no bite."

On the way home, Avery had a thousand questions, but he was really interested in Jesse. "Now, Dad, you better get a grip; Ms. Becky is waiting for you at home, and I'm trying to date her daughter; she may even be your future daughter-in-law. I can't have my father smitten with my mother-in-law, can I?" "Why not, we won't be related. OK Son, I won't pursue Jesse; I'll just admire her from afar, how's that." Marcus tapped his father on the shoulder. "That's just about right my man, just about right." "Now, what's with this Gregg creature." "He's Tressa's previous boyfriend, who's never gotten over her. I feel sorry for him because I think he really loves her. I didn't break them up; they were through when we met. She made it clear to him they had no future, but I guess since she wasn't seeing anyone; he thought he could win her back, who knows. All I know is she's mine." "You know that for a fact!" Marcus answered his father with a sense of certainty, "I'm pretty sure." "Son, sure it up, get it sealed with a kiss and a firm yes, know for sure." "I guess you have a point, those two do have a history. Perhaps I'll do the old "will you be my girl? Check yes or no!" "Whatever works," Avery said, "just do it."

Sunday morning, the Dallas men fellowshipped at their family church and Marcus persuaded them to swing past Tressa's church to say goodbye. Marcus had to leave earlier than proposed and wanted to tell her in person. When he saw her leaving the church, he honked, and she crossed the street to greet him. As he opened the car door, a car raced by and barely missed Tressa. She screamed and fell backwards on Marcus's car.

"Oh, Lord." They all jumped out of the car and ran to Tressa. "My dear, are you alright?" Marcus was dumbfounded, "What in the world just happened?" Was it that crazy Gregg? If it were, Marcus would have to confront him and maybe try to convince Tressa to press charges. Avery moved Tressa to the curb, and Marcus came to comfort her. Jesse, after seeing what happened, ran to her daughter's aid. "Is my baby all right?" "Yes, Momma," Tressa said a little shakily, "I'm fine."

Someone must have told Devan and Simon what had happened, and soon the entire Bower family was at Tressa's side. "Devan, do you think that was Gregg?" "No, Momma, Gregg is in the basement of the church assisting the pastor, I know it wasn't him." "Then who could that have been? Who were they aiming for? Was it Tressa or Marcus?" Devan asked if any of the Dallas men could describe the car? Marcus said, "It was a green late model Ford, but he did not see the driver." Les and Avery said the same. He couldn't tell if it were a man or woman, which seemed odd. Marcus held Tressa until she calmed down. "Tressa, I came by to tell you that I have to leave, but if you need me to stay, I will." Shaking her head, Tressa said, "No, I'll be fine; my family is here—I feel safe. I appreciate your desire to stay, but it's OK. Do call me; let me know you have arrived safely." Marcus reassured her he would call, and they left. "What a close call. You don't think it was that Lizzy woman do you?" Avery Dallas asked. "I don't know, Dad, that's a good question. I don't think she would pull something that crazy in front of the church, and how did she know I was coming?" "She obviously wasn't trying to hit you. I didn't want to say anything, but whoever was driving was aiming for Tressa." With a worried expression, Marcus asked, "Dad, do you think I should leave?" "That, my son, is your decision; you know you have a press conference to prepare for." "Yes, but Tressa means the world to me, and I need to know that she's safe." "Call her brother; he's in law enforcement, a certified, bona fide detective. I'm sure he will follow up and keep you updated if you ask him." "Good idea, Dad, I will." "By the way, did you ever find out who 'watch out' is?" "No Dad, I haven't had time to thoroughly investigate. I did ask the guys in the computer lab as a favor to trace the IP address, but they haven't gotten back to me. I should hear something next week."

Avery looked grim. "Tressa seems worth it Son, but watch yourself. Despite what Devan thinks, I feel this dude could be a danger not only to Tressa, but to you as well." "You know Dad, I feel like Devan; I think the guy is just hurting. I won't give him an opportunity to hurt me or Tressa, but I also think he doesn't want to be seen as a fool. Remember this guy is a professor, albeit an unstable one. Like Tia and her family said, image is everything. You know what? Bad publicity will get him fired!" "Just be careful, just saying."

Les had been quiet throughout this ordeal but finally spoke. "I know you like this girl Marcus, but this seems like a lot of foolishness; do you really think you want to involve yourself in this mess? She has a crazy ex and so do you." "Pop, believe me when I say she's worth it," said Marcus. "That being said, we'll keep this situation in prayer. We need to pray for God's divine intervention, protection, and revelation. I don't want to lose my only grandson over some foolishness. You're both in the same boat, past relationships with two nuts!"

Avery asked Marcus again if he would mind if he asked for Jesse's number, and again Marcus flatly refused. He had never seen his father in this light; a Romeo, who would have thought. Avery took a deep breath as he relayed a message to Marcus. "By the way, Son, your mother called; she asked if you're coming over this summer." "Why would I?" Marcus asked, puzzled. "I have no desire to visit her. If she wants to see me, let her come to the States." Avery sighed. "I'll let her know, and you definitely don't want her to have your phone number?" "No Dad! I gave her my email address; that's just as good. I don't want to hear her voice, and I mean it!" "You've made your position clear, Marcus. I get it, and she gets it. By the way, she sent you a gift." Marcus looked at his father and sighed. "Feel free to send it back unopened; I don't want it."

It would seem unlikely that a man with so much class, a man who taught diplomacy and protocol would hold such a grudge. Marcus was a kind man, a forgiving man, but he resented his mother, maybe even hated her. He could not forgive her for abandoning him. She never offered a reasonable explanation, and as far as he was concerned, he had no mother. As a matter of fact, he couldn't understand why his father was so forgiving.

Avery met his mother (Desiree) at the University of Fine Arts in Italy. Avery Marcus Dallas was raised in a small town in Hagerstown, Maryland by his father, Les Avery Dallas. He was of average intelligence but a quick student.

He worked in law enforcement in the division of Fraud and Security Prevention. He eventually perfected his skills and was promoted to head detective, which landed him a job with the feds. After ten years, he was promoted to an instructor in forensic science. His field was identifying stolen art and other documents. When asked to train law enforcements abroad, he jumped at the chance. Desiree was appointed his associate. She was a detective who decided to go back to school to study forensic science. She was vibrant, intelligent and a looker. The first thing Avery noticed about her was her short, jet black hair. She was a little thin for his taste, but at the end of the day, he decided it was not a deal breaker; she really impressed him. Finding a woman and falling in love was not part of his plans. His goal was to teach and gain as much knowledge in his field as possible. Desiree often asked Avery out, but he refused. In his mind, he wasn't there to date, and he wasn't sure dating a colleague was such a good idea, but Desiree eventually wore him down. She invited him to the university's Valentine's Day celebrations, of all things, and he finally gave in. They sat at the table making small talk and exchanging glances; finally, one of Avery's favorite songs played "Strangers in the Night." They danced the night away, and the rest is history.

They dated for about three years, and when Avery's assignment was up, to Desiree's surprise, he decided to return to the States. Desiree soon followed, they were married a year later, and Marcus Daye Dallas was born nine months later.

Desiree never seemed to bond with her new baby boy. Avery thought this was natural for some women, he figured it might be postpartum depression, and she would soon change; but she didn't. She was short tempered and had no patience with Marcus. It got so bad, against Desiree's wishes Avery hired a full-time nanny. In addition to the nanny, Les also babysat Marcus when Avery worked; this formed a warm, long and trusting relationship between Marcus and his grandfather. Marcus was a beautiful baby, always happy, but when his mother picked him up, he would cry uncontrollably. Desiree would lay him down and send for either his father, grandfather or the nanny.

Avery didn't see this coming. How could a woman so kind, gentle and loving not care for her child? This was a constant sense of contention. Avery loved Desiree and tried to work things out, even recommending therapy. Desiree refused, and without discussing it, she filed for divorce and flew back to Italy leaving Marcus with his father. Avery was shocked and hurt, but relieved. This was not the life he had envisioned for him and his child. It was during this period of his life that his faith in God grew. Marcus was often found kneeling beside his dad praying. He remembered the talks he had with his father about believing and trusting in God. Les was a praying man, and just as Les taught Avery to pray and trust in God, Avery taught Marcus. Avery consistently talked to Marcus about putting his trust in God. Desiree never asked for custody but remembered every birthday. She would send cards and toys, and at the beginning of every school season send new clothes and supplies.

At first, Marcus looked forward to the gifts and calls. When his mother called, they talked for at least an hour. But whenever he asked her when she was coming home, she would never answer. "Mom, don't you love me? When are you coming home?" Her response was always, "Of course, I do; what mother don't love her child!" Marcus found this puzzling and eventually he gave up. Eventually, whenever she called, he refused to talk to her. He was dismayed; she was never present at any of his graduations, or school plays. She wasn't there to see him dressed for his junior and senior prom, what kind of mother behaved like that? Yes, in time he hated her, hated to hear her voice, and when those packages arrived, he immediately threw them in the trash. He often asked his dad what was so wrong with him that his mother would give him up, reject him and abandon him, but Avery couldn't answer, he didn't know, and he wasn't sure Desiree knew. Avery met and enjoyed a long and lasting relationship with his beloved Lexie. Ms. Lexie had been through thick and thin with Avery Dallas and longed to wear his last name; however, marriage was not a part of his plans. He had made that clear to her over and over again, but she never gave up hope.

Marcus's maternal grandparents (Mary and Franco Rossi) loved and adored Marcus. He was their first grandchild. And, Avery was the son-in-law they prayed for; they shared a warm and loving relationship throughout the years. The Rossi's never understood Desiree's rejection of Marcus; they were ashamed of her and often told her so. Avery promised them that despite Desiree's attitude, he would bring Marcus to Italy as often as he could, and they promised to visit Marcus. However, they were very old, and their finances were limited. The visits between them were few and far between, but whenever they met it was heartfelt. His grandparents were faithful. Every birthday, holiday and special occasion they either called or sent a gift; always apologizing for Desiree who had remarried and had two more children. Marcus's first memory of meeting Mary and Franco was when he was five years old. This was the first time Avery returned to Italy since leaving. They smothered Marcus with love. His mother may not have loved or wanted him, but he knew he was loved by his grandparents. They held nothing back, hugs and kisses all day, bragging about his intelligence. Of course, Pop Franco said he got his smarts from him. They showed him off to the neighbors and his other relatives, and Pop Franco brought him soccer balls and uniforms. He declared Marcus would be a great soccer star. However, with the pride came the shame of trying to explain Desiree's abandonment of Marcus. Unfortunately for Avery, he carried a load of guilt because he always felt he had done something to cause her detachment and abandonment.

One of Marcus's precious memories was when he graduated from college, graduating summa cum laude. His father and grandfather were so proud when he walked across the stage, despite a warning from the MC for the audience to remain quiet, he heard them yell, "Go Marcus!" and then another familiar voice in a strong Italian accent, "I am proud of you, Marcus!" He recognized the voice, my God, that's my Grandma Mary, and then he heard, "You honor us, Grandson!" that was Grandpa Franco. He welled up with pride. His grandparents had traveled from Italy to see him graduate. When the ceremony was over, he ran like greased lightning to greet them. "Grandma and Grandpa, my God, this is truly a gift from God! I am so happy." He couldn't stop hugging them. It had been at least eight years since he had last seen them. He took them around town like they were celebrities, introducing them to everyone. They felt so much love and pride, they couldn't stop crying. When it was time for them to leave, Marcus promised them he would come and visit soon.

One year later he did, he kept his word and surprised them. Grandpa Franco was sick and unable to celebrate like he wanted to, and Grandma Mary did her best to entertain him, but it wasn't necessary. He became their blessing. He cooked for them, repaired some fixtures in the house, bought Grandma Mary a beautiful new dress and Grandpa Franco a new suit. Before leaving, he placed one thousand dollars and a lovely note under the scarf on the bedroom dresser and arranged for home care three days a week. Marcus assumed this obligation until the passing of both grandparents five years later. Upon their deaths, they left a will leaving everything they owned to Marcus Daye Dallas, which caused an uproar. At the reading of the will, he finally met his brothers, and after many years, his mother. Marcus did not want the house and furnishings, but he wanted to honor his grandparents' wishes. So after a long discussion with his dad, he decided to keep the house and certain mementos, and divided the cash between the three grandchildren. Marcus was surprised how warm and loving his brothers were. They welcomed him with open arms and told him they were led to believe he wanted nothing to do with them; they were afraid of his rejection.

It was Mary and Franco's desire that Marcus bond with his brothers, but they didn't push it, just in case the union turned out badly. They were young men now according to his grandparents, married with a house full of kids and doing very well.

Marcus was raised with a woman's influence; his father's lady friend, as he called her. As far as he was concerned, Ms. Becky was his mom. She attended parent meetings with his dad, cooked meals and accompanied the family on outings. To show respect, she never slept overnight, and he always saw her in the role of a lady. Becky had no children; she smothered all her love on him and his dad.

For the first time since he was a child, he was able to confront his mother. At first sight, he did not recognize her, but he remembered her voice. "Hello, Marcus." He looked at her for what seemed like an eternity and softly responded, "Hi, Desiree, long time no see." She nodded her head and said in a heavy Italian accent, "That's true my Son."

With a look of disdain, he said, "Let's be mature about this, and please do not call me Son. It is not a pleasure to see you; however, I'm happy to know that my brothers welcomed me. I am puzzled to hear that I would not have wanted to know them; did you tell them that, Desiree?"

"I did discourage it, but I have my reasons, which I'm not going to share with you." Marcus looked at her and smirked. "I don't care, lady! You probably don't know or understand yourself." He walked away from her, and to his surprise, his brother Sean approached him. Extending his hand, he said, "Marcus, I have a desire to be closer to you. I'm sorry about the division our mother has caused. I pray you will one day accept us in your heart as brothers." Marcus welled up and gave Sean a hug. "I too pray this is the beginning of a long and lasting brotherhood." Zack was a little more reserved, Sean explained he was a man with a double mind, he was a pleaser. Sean said he knew in Zack's heart he wanted to embrace Marcus but feared the ire of his mother; he, on the other hand, knew he had to do the right thing.

Chapter five

Marcus and Tressa's relationship grew by leaps and bounds. Despite their busy schedules, they managed to talk at least four times a week. Marcus's work assignments kept him busy. He prayed that Tressa understood his commitment to his job and that she wasn't too lonely. He came home as often as possible; the visits were short but memorable.

Marcus reminisced about the first time they exchanged the words, "I love you." It was on a rainy night. Tressa called him as he was snuggled in bed after a weeklong conference. When he answered the phone, he heard Tressa sing a short version of "Distant Lover" that ended with "I love you very much." "What Tressa? Did you say you love me?" "Yes, I did Marcus Daye Dallas, don't you think it's about time?" Marcus longed to hear those words. He was happy. "Tressa, I wanted to be the first one to utter those words; of course, you know I love you too!" "I know now," Tressa, answered softly. "I've loved you, forever; I don't believe in love at first sight, but I tell you, girl, it sure felt like it." "I know Marcus, I felt the same way. I prayed day and night, asking God to reveal to me if you were the one. Time after time, we endured every hurdle and never strayed from our love." "Marcus," Tressa said earnestly, "promise me you will be faithful to me, and I promise the same." Marcus was silent for a moment and said, "I think that goes without saying, Tressa, but with all my heart I promise." "OK, Dallas; I'm going to sleep now, dream about me." "I will, I promise, and Tressa, I really do love you." "Back at cha, good night, we'll talk tomorrow."

The winter was coming to an end, and the Bower and Dallas families had endured more than they had ever imagined. Devan was determined to find out who had attempted to run down his sister. He had all his cop buddies and friends on the lookout for the car. It seemed to have just disappeared, and Marcus thought he had a lead on the emails that were constantly being sent, warning him to stay away from Tressa.

After an intense investigation, Devan was notified that a car fitting the description of the car that almost ran down Tressa was found abandoned and stripped. He and some fellow officers raced to the location to gather as much information as possible. He knew the tags and other identifying information would be gone but was hoping for fingerprints. They hit pay dirt; Devan could not believe it when they opened the glove compartment, and there was the registration, tattered but readable, and after hours of calls and research they located the owner. He could not believe what they had discovered. That evening, he called a family meeting. After everyone had assembled, he pulled Simone aside and told her to brace herself.

Simone, Tressa, Jesse, and Taylor sat motionless waiting for Devan to speak. "Everyone, what I'm about to reveal may be hard to digest, but the facts have been thoroughly investigated." He looked at Tressa, and slowly approaching her leaned over and sat on the corner of the sofa. "Tressa, the car that almost ran you down was found and has been linked to a student at Brookfield High, the school Taylor attends." Devan looked at Taylor and then at Simone. "Taylor, do you have anything to tell us?" Simone interjected, "I know you're not accusing Taylor of this; she loves her aunt dearly." "Simone, let Taylor talk," said Jesse. Taylor looked down on the floor and would not answer. "Talk to us Taylor. I know you know something about it; do you want me to call Detective Davis?" Devan paused, "Maybe I should have asked him to be here in the first place." Devan got up to go to the phone when Taylor screamed, "No! Don't call him, I'll tell, I'll tell." "Taylor what did you do?" Simone was bewildered; she couldn't wrap her brain around her daughter having anything to do with harming her aunt. Taylor began to cry uncontrollably. "Aunt Tressa, I love you, and I wouldn't do anything to harm you but you...you hurt Gregg, and I love him!" Tressa couldn't believe what she was hearing. "Taylor, have you lost your mind, you tried to hurt me because of Gregory Montgomery?" "Yes, and do you know why? Because you treated him like he was nothing, embarrassing him in front of people and choosing him over that other man." Taylor stormed over to Tressa, shaking her fist in her face, shouting and crying. "I hate you for that! Gregg is kind and loving, and he deserves more that. He has stuck by this family through thick and thin, and how do you repay him? You repay him by humiliating him."

Tressa and Jesse were stunned; Tressa suddenly saw Taylor in a different light. Her niece had been taken in by Gregg. She was hurt but sympathetic; she started towards Taylor, but Jesse stopped her.

Devan strode over to Taylor and took her hands, comforting her as much as possible. He asked her in a kind and comforting voice, "Taylor what did you do? What part did you play in this?" Taylor responded with a mixture of arrogance and boldness. "Well, as you know, Evelyn and I are very close. Gregg ..." "Hold it, young lady, that's Mr. Gregg to you."

Taylor took a deep breath. "Well, then, Mr. Gregg! Anyway, Evelyn agreed with me that Mr. Gregg was being mistreated. He has been a friend to us; whenever we needed something he was there." Her voice rising, she continued, "More than Uncle Devan and the new man, we can depend on him. Mr. Gregg loves Aunt Tressa so much. I heard him say no matter what he did for her she was never satisfied, and now she was seeking love and comfort from another man. You should hear him, his heart is broken." Taylor broke off for a second, struggling to contain her emotions, and then continued, "So, Elizabeth and I, she asked her brother to just scare Aunt Tressa; just pretend. We never intended for her to be hurt.

We figured Gregg, Mr. Gregg would run to her side and then Aunt Tressa would realize that she missed him and wanted him and not Mr. Marcus. But that didn't happen; she still wouldn't give Mr. Gregg a chance! And, when Mr. Marcus's dad jumped out of the car and ran to her, and then Mr. Marcus held Aunt Tressa, I was glad Mr. Gregg did not see that. We ran to church to tell Gregg what happened, but he had left the dining hall; perhaps he went to the sanctuary, I don't know. We planned all that for nothing. Later we thought we should have planned things better. We thought perhaps Mr. Gregg should have been waiting outside. Then he would have rescued Aunt Tressa, and she would have realized ..." "Taylor," said Jesse furiously, "stop talking. I don't want to hear any more. You had no right to interfere in an adult situation!" "The three of you are children and obviously do not understand the severity of your actions," Devan broke in. "What if Tressa was killed? For your information, Carlos and Elizabeth are being held downtown as we speak, and you, young lady will be taken downtown as well."

Taylor stepped backward, shaking her head. "No, Uncle Devan, I didn't do anything! Aunt Tressa is fine; look at her. It's been months since this happened. Why are you doing this to me?" "Simone," Devan said, turning to his sister. "I must take her downtown for further questioning." "I know, I'll get my jacket and purse."

They knew the children would be turned over to their parents; after all, Taylor was only ten, Evelyn was nine, and the driver Cedric was fifteen. They had never been in any trouble and were good students. How did these children allow themselves to become so involved in an adult situation? This was what they wanted to find out. The other question was did Gregg encourage the situation in any way? For his sake, Devan hoped not. "Mommy, please listen to me," begged Taylor. "I know you don't understand why I did this, but Gregg, I mean Mr. Gregg is my friend; I love him, and I saw him hurting. After it all happened, I realized we made a horrible mistake, and we couldn't take it back." Then, from out of nowhere, she emitted a sound like a deep-throated growl. "Mommy, you are to blame for all this! You persuaded me to do this to Aunt Tressa. All the things she has done to you, don't act like you love her so much now. You would have been happy if she was killed, and I know it! I did what you couldn't do Mommy! All I heard all my life was that damned Tressa, why her? I heard you say that on many occasions,

I wish she was dead."

"Taylor, that's a horrible thing to say," said Jesse, horrified. Everyone was stunned. Jesse approached Taylor and grabbed her by the shoulders. "Look, little missy, I know you're going through some kind of juvenile crush or whatever, but you're not going to bring my family down." Taylor jerked away from her. "Get off of me Granny, you're the one who planted these ideas in Mommy's head, I heard you!" "Child, are you crazy? Perhaps you need an exorcism. When did you hear me talk against either of my children?" "When you were angry with my mommy, you use to say, 'Why can't you be like Tressa? she has never given me a day of trouble,' and I heard you, are you going to deny it?" Jesse didn't know what to say. She was saddened by these allegations, but more importantly, she had to search within herself. Was she responsible for this awful situation? Devan was losing his temper and patience, "Explain yourself, Taylor, be specific. Let's get this on the table now!" "I would love to explain ..." Taylor went on to talk about times when she felt Jesse favored Tressa over her mother. "Taylor calm down, what's wrong with you? You're acting like you're possessed or something. I want to understand, but you're making it hard." "Maybe I am possessed; I've been in the company of serpents and demons." Simone slapped Taylor as hard as she could. "That's enough; I will knock the hell out of you! You apologize to your grandmother and aunt right now!"

But Taylor would not apologize; she continued her rampage about the past and what she heard about Gregg until Simone couldn't stand it anymore. She interrupted, "Taylor I'm afraid you took my words and misinterpreted them." She pulled her to the sofa and told her to sit down; Taylor was truly out of control. Jesse stepped away from the group and went to the kitchen and prayed. There was something wicked about Taylor; Jesse had seen this before. She prayed until she heard the Lord utter, "Be still and know that I am God." A sense of relief came over her; now she could carry on. Taylor's memories of events were remarkable and misguided. Most of the situations she remembered were taken out of context. Simone never knew Taylor was carrying this resentment in her heart. She felt guilty, and her motherly instincts kicked in. Simone approached Taylor, hugged and kissed her. "Taylor, I know you must be frightened; I'm here for you, and we will get through this together." "You promise Mommy?" Taylor asked, rubbing her eyes. "Yes, I promise."

Taylor looked back at Tressa and rolled her eyes. Tressa and Jesse exchanged looks of disapproval and shook their heads. "Mom, what do you think is going to happen to her?" "Tressa, that child is troubled, and if she doesn't receive counseling, I'm not sure what's going to happen to her. Simone is guilt ridden; she's not ready for any advice or direction from us." "Mom you're a psychologist, one of the best, can't you talk to Taylor?" Jesse shook her head. "Honey, right now, I'm just a grandmother and she won't listen to me. I do, however, have a couple of colleagues that would be willing to talk to her."

Simone turned to Tressa and confessed that in the past she had said things that were cruel and unkind. She admitted, with some shame, that despite the same privileges and opportunities, she was jealous of her.

She said she both admired and despised her. The reason being, she admitted, "Tressa has a sense of style; she's independent and has a love of self and is an overachiever." Simone admitted she wanted to be like her little sister. She also admitted that at times she verbally said things in front of Taylor that may have been inappropriate and inadvertently brought on resentment towards her aunt. "I'm deeply sorry Tressa, please forgive me!" Tressa stood to hug Simone, but she stopped her. "Tressa, I'm not finished. Before you say those golden words, I need you to know something. Before we can heal completely, I need to disclose a secret that I've kept from you. I know this is not the perfect time, but ..." "No! Not now," said Jesse, intervening. "This is not the time and place Simone. Let's complete one situation before trying to resolve another."

This evening had turned into a real nightmare. Tressa was scared, angry and felt betrayed. What did her mother know and never share with her? Was this some deep dark family secret? "Mom, I need to know what's going on," Jesse waved a hand dismissively. "You will Tressa, let's get this over with first." Tressa looked at Devan; his face was ashen. She knew at that moment this was big.

The three perpetrators were released to their parents and placed on probation for four years. They also had to pay for the stolen car. Carlos and Elizabeth's parents, Mr. and Mrs. Paige, apologized to Tressa. They told her they were ashamed of their role in the accident and assured her they would be punished and thought it best Carlos and Elizabeth no longer had contact with Taylor, but they did not blame Taylor exclusively for the incident.

Weeks later, after things had cooled down, it was time to discuss the elephant in the room. Tressa was tense and anxious. Marcus asked Tressa not to jump to any conclusions; he tried to assure her that it may not be as bad as she thought. Despite his words of encouragement, this was one time Marcus felt it necessary to find his way home, just in case she needed him. The family met at Simone's home after church. She prepared a light meal and asked for prayer before the discussion was underway. Tressa postured herself, waiting to hear this mystery. Jesse seemed very nervous, quite jittery, and just before Simone started to talk, she told Tressa not to take what she was about to hear to heart. Tressa looked at her and Simone. Devan grabbed Tressa's hand and leaned back on the sofa in preparation for the great revelation.

Simone surprised everyone and just jumped in. "Tressa, I once had an affair with Gregg." "What?" Tressa was not expecting this; she was dumbfounded. She felt her body go through some type of metamorphosis. There would be no tenderness, no hand holding. "You did what?! Simone tell me that is a lie. You deceived me like that? Why? No, don't tell me." Tressa got off the sofa and in Simone's face. "Don't tell me this was about your being jealous of me; that you wished you were me and, therefore, wanted to be with the man I loved. Well, Sis, you got what you wanted," she said, tears streaming down her face. "I'm hurt and surprised. I didn't expect this of you and I damn sure didn't expect it from Gregg, the man who loved me with all his heart, the man who loved me and only me. So tell me, who does Taylor belong to? Is Taylor Gregg's daughter?"

Tressa couldn't control herself; she slapped

Simone and shoved her as hard as she could. Simone went flying across the room, hitting her head on the corner of the end table. Devan rushed to help Simone to her feet and sat her down in the nearest chair. Blood had drained from Devan's face. Jesse tried to intervene, telling them to remember they were sisters and that this happened long ago. "Long ago, I was married to Gregg, short-lived, of course, but nevertheless he was my husband. Was it before or after the annulment? Answer me you slut!" Simone didn't answer; she simply held her head down and sobbed. "Mom, when, or how did you find out?"

Jesse had decided earlier that she was going to give Tressa time to calm down before talking to her. But, maybe this was the right time. "Simone didn't tell me; Ms. Vye told me." "Ms. Vye! Gregg's mother?" "Yes, Gregg's mother." Simone hadn't known this; she sat up on the sofa at full attention. "She overheard the two of them on the house phone making plans to meet. She confronted Gregg, and he admitted he and Simone were seeing each other. She laid him out, told him she would tell me, and she did. She left it up to me to tell you." "And you decided I didn't need to know? Wow, Mom! You're really a piece of work. Oh, did you let Simone know that you knew?" Jesse nodded. "Yes, and I also let her know that I disapproved of what she was doing and asked her to put a stop to the affair." "Gee, Mom, that was really big of you!" Tressa couldn't believe her ears; it was as if she were in a bad dream. "You're all traitors."

Just then she heard the voice of Madam Keys, "Never keep secrets from one another and forgive." Lord knows she knew that was the right thing to do, but, she wasn't feeling it. She gathered her belongings and started to leave, but Devan stopped her. "No Sis, don't leave like this; I'll take you home." She wasn't sure if Devan knew "the secret," he didn't act surprised, and she had to know. "Devan did you know about this?" Devan hung his head. "Yes, Tressa, I knew." Tressa went cold, "Get off of me Devan; you stay here with your "special deceitful family."

Tressa loved and trusted Gregg, and to have had a relationship with her sister right under her nose was unforgivable. No wonder Taylor loved him so much. She hurried home crying all the way; her heart broken. Tressa lay on the sofa and tried to force sleep, but it didn't come. When the phone rang, she ignored it until she heard Marcus voice, "Tressa if you're there, please pick up!" "My honey!" She ran and stumbled to get to the phone before he hung up. "Hello Marcus, Marcus are you there?" "Hey babe, what's wrong? You sound distraught. I'm on my way, see you in a few." When Marcus arrived, he didn't have to knock. Tressa was standing at the door waiting, sobbing. "Oh, babe! It can't be that bad, come sit."

Tressa followed Marcus to the living room, and he laid her across his lap. She didn't have the nerve to tell him at first; instead, she told him about the car and her niece; then, after regrouping, she told him about Simone and Gregg.

Marcus told Tressa he was sorry, and he hoped in time she could forgive Simone and Gregg. Shaking her head, she said, "No Marcus, not just Simone and Gregg; Simone, Gregg, Devan and my sweet mom." Tressa was crying so hard that Marcus cradled her in his arms and started to rock her. "Please Tressa, you're going to make yourself sick; please stop crying."

Tressa's tears slowly became whimpers. She became more relaxed as Marcus wiped away her tears. Laying on Marcus's chest and wiping her eyes, she said, "It's situations like this that cause people to drink." Marcus chuckled, "Do you want a glass of wine?" "No, babe, I want a fifth of something." "No, you don't," Marcus corrected, "You really want peace." "You're exactly right. I want peace because now I'll have to ask painful questions I don't want to ask. Like were they still fooling around when we were married? Or, exactly how long had it been going on and had it ever ceased? Marcus, what I don't understand is why Simone would want Gregg, knowing he was still pursuing me. He made his feelings clear in front of everyone all the time, so what was that about? Marcus, I want you to know that I feel betrayed, and I'm angry." She stroked his face with her fingers. "But know this—I haven't had feelings for Gregg in years. He was always around, and I was always discouraging him. This is so crazy, that dog! I hope he rots in hell!"

Marcus held Tressa until she fell asleep. He laid her on her bed and called Devan. He was honest and told Marcus he had known about the indiscretion and thought he had convinced Gregg to leave both his sisters alone.

"When I confronted Gregg, he claimed he and Simone found themselves physically attracted to each other, despite his feeling for Tressa, and they took things to the next level. He never apologized for his actions or for betraying Tressa, and at that point we fought. Despite his being a foot and a half taller and at least thirty pounds heavier, I beat him to a stump."

Devan knew if Gregg reported the fight he would be in a lot of trouble; he never did, probably because he felt he deserved his butt being whipped. Afterwards, he went back to college, and the situation was shoved under the carpet, so I decided to keep my mouth shut to protect myself and Tressa. The affair happened when Simone was having marital problems. Gregg was always skulking around Simone and Tressa; he couldn't make up his mind which one he wanted, and he did a great job hiding this from the family until Simone confided in me that they had had a brief sexual relationship. She begged me not to tell Tressa because she knew she wanted nothing else to do with Gregg; besides, Tressa really loved him, and so I said nothing. I later found out that Simone had shared the incident with our mom, not knowing Mom already knew." "And what about Taylor, is he the father?" Devan sighed with relief. "No, it's Craig's child."

Marcus's heart went out to Tressa. He felt he needed to do something to ease her pain. Perhaps giving her a change of environment would help. Fortunately, his next assignment was in Europe; he was scheduled to leave the following week. He asked Tressa to come with him. He convinced her she could do her job from the hotel and put some distance between her and the family. The idea sounded great to Tressa. She asked Mr. Goode for three weeks leave from the office, guaranteeing him that all of her assigned cases would be completed upon her return and reassured him he could contact her via email, phone or text at any time. She was grateful when the leave was granted. She did not tell any member of the family she was going, she just left.

Marcus shared what had happened to Tressa with Les and Avery. They were concerned; they had become quite fond and protective of Tressa and now leery of the Bowers. Marcus wondered what was to become of the Dallas/Bowers clan.

It was months before Tressa had any contact with her family; she was not in the forgiving spirit. It took days and nights of prayer. Marcus was her rock; he was kind and patient; every time she brought up the subject, he would listen and let her talk and cry. After a while, it was as if she had cried out. Marcus assured her that time did heal wounds, and in time he felt confident that she and Simone would reconcile. They were a loving family; he knew only time and prayer could heal Tressa's pain.

Her constant prayer was 1 Corinthians 13. Marcus told her healing and forgiveness was a process and only possible by the grace of God. Tressa knew two things for sure, one: She had to seek forgiveness, and two: Marcus was a precious gift from God.

When Tressa returned, she was surprised to learn that her best friend Detra was home. Detra was a nurse and seasonal stewardess. In the summer months, she took a break from nursing and indulged her love of travel. Her job as a stewardess with a private airline was always available. Detra knew nothing about the situation with Tressa; she chose not to burden Detra with the details of the situation. She wanted her to enjoy her vacation in the Orient. Detra had a large family that lived all around the world; her parents were professional drifters, nomads so to speak. Her father was an archaeologist who took the family wherever there was a dig, and her mother was a willing-unwilling participant. She longed for a stable life with her five children but lacked the nerve to make a stand with her father. So the seven of them traveled from one country to another in hopes of finding Father's great discovery!

Was he successful? Yes in a way. He and another of his colleagues discovered bones of small dinosaurs, which made the front page in the science journals. Their success and popularity lasted for about a year. The discovery earned more money than they had earned their entire careers. Her father invested in new equipment that cost thousands, and pretty soon all the money was gone. Detra's mother had enough; she left her father and moved the family back to Maryland, where she borrowed money from a family friend, purchased a small house and found a job as a secretary at a local library. Through grants and scholarships, all five of her children managed to get an education. They slowly drifted to other parts of the States to pursue their dreams. "Hello?" "Hi doll, I'm home," "Detra! Girl, I'm so happy to hear your voice. I missed you so much! How long are you going to be home? We need to catch up." "Tressa, slow down, you sound like someone who's had too much caffeine!" Tressa laughed. "I know, I know, but wait until you hear what happened. When are you coming over?" After a brief pause, Detra said, "I have to put my laundry away; let's say in about an hour." "An hour it is."

Tressa was so happy; her best friend was home. They had been friends since high school. Tressa's mind drifted back to their youth, recalling the time their mothers entered them in a beauty contest; neither girl wanted anything to do with it, but the grand prize was $1000 and a modeling contract when they finished school with a reputable modeling agency. It was a tie, both girls stood dumbfounded, not caring who won. The judges never experiencing this before asked the girls how they wanted to decide who the winner would be. Tressa suggested tossing a coin. The judges agreed, Tressa choosing tails and Detra heads. They announced the winner, "Detra Graham." Tressa was relieved, but her mother was disappointed and swore it was a miscount. Detra surprised them all and offered the prize to the next runner-up. The thoughts of makeup and fancy dresses and profiling were too much; her dream was to be a nurse. She finished college but could not find her direction. She and her boyfriend (Devan Bowers) had parted ways, and she decided to put distance between him and Maryland, so she became a stewardess.

When the doorbell rang, Tressa raced downstairs, grabbed Detra and flung her around. "I'm so happy; now my life is complete. My best friend, Detra you look fabulous! Girl, you never change, you are a knockout!" "Tressa, you always know what to say. And look at you, you're glowing; what's going on?" Tressa offered to fix dinner, but Detra held up a large bag, "Chinese, yippee." As they ate, Tressa brought Detra up to speed. She told her about the mysterious Madam Keys and Ma Lizzy; Gregg and Simone; Taylor and the kids, and last but not least, Marcus, purposely not discussing Devan. "Wow, you have been through it. Are you OK? Am I going to have to send you to a therapist?" "No, my therapist is Jesus Christ." "I know that's right Tressa. So how is your new beau taking all this?" Tressa couldn't help smiling. "He has been my rock, Detra. I just returned from Europe with him, and he was so comforting." "I bet." Turning to see a framed photo, Detra asked, "Is that a picture of him?" "Yes, that's Marcus Daye Dallas, isn't he fine?" Detra giggled. "I would say no, but I'd be lying; he is gorgeous. So when am I going to meet this hunk?" Tressa shrugged. "I don't know. He told me last night he'd be home in two to three weeks. Considering the time we just spent together, I think I'll survive. Grabbing her hand and squeezing it, she smiled and said, "Plus, my buddy is home; I know I'll be OK!" Detra watched Tressa as she cleaned the dishes; she seemed very happy and at peace.

The next few months were healing times for Tressa. She knew God had sent Detra home for a good reason; she needed her. She had a hard time communicating with her family. But, she did feel time would bridge the gap. Detra kept her busy with movies, theater, shopping, anything to keep up her spirits. Detra returned to church and assisted Tressa with her church duties, and she also made the decision to go back to school to become a physician's assistant.

Someone else was happy to see Detra—Devan Bowers. He and Detra were honeys, childhood sweethearts. She was the only girl he ever cared for. But for some reason, they seemed to always drift apart just as they were becoming close. He seemed awkward at dating, always uncomfortable. Detra was a beauty but never fed into it; she avoided all excessive comments and attention. She confided in Tressa that she was ready for a meaningful relationship, and since she decided to retire from her steward's job, it may be possible. Tressa believed Detra traveled to get away from Devan; he didn't seem to be able to commit, and she was too frustrated to hang around.

One month later, Detra got the chance to meet

Marcus, and she was impressed. He met Tressa and Detra at their favorite restaurant. Running a half hour late, he made his excuses and introduced himself to Detra and kissed Tressa. Seating himself, he said, "Traffic was brutal, I'm sorry to be late. So, I finally get to meet Detra. You are a legend; I've heard all about your notorious friendship." "Notorious?" "Yes, I heard about the school cutting, the exchange of tests, the ..." "Wait ..." Detra interrupted what she was about to say, "Just wait a minute, none of that is true. Did you tell him that Tressa?" Waving Detra's question away, Tressa said, "No, don't listen to him he's making it all up; I think he's fishing." "Probably is. Let's tell him some real juice; let's tell him about ..." Frantically shaking her head, Tressa said, "No Detra! He knows all he needs to know ... for now!" Marcus looked at Tressa and winked. "Secrets, Tressa?" "Maybe."

After months of praying, Tressa was in a better place. Simone gathered up the nerve and invited Tressa to meet with the family. It had been months since Tressa had talked to them; perhaps it was time. They agreed to meet at Tressa's home after church the following Sunday. Like clockwork, everyone showed up and hugged each other before they began to talk. Jesse already had tears in her eyes; she never thought her family would be going through something like this. It aggrieved her that her children were not speaking, and that there was such a chasm between them. Perhaps today would be the day of healing; it had to be. Jesse prayed and fasted, asking God to bring healing to the family. She did not minimize the pain Tressa was feeling, but she also saw the pain and anguish of Devan and Simone. Tressa said nothing; she let everyone else say their piece.

Standing with his hands in his pockets like a child, Devan began. "Tressa, I'm deeply sorry for hurting you. I thought I was doing the right thing. I didn't want to hurt you. In hindsight, I should have been honest. I made a bad call. I never dreamt this secret would destroy our family and hurt you so much; please forgive me. I miss you, and the family is broken." Breaking off, he shook his head before adding, "I don't know what to do." Devan began to tear up, but Tressa remained stone-faced, which made it uncomfortable for Simone and Jesse to express themselves. Tressa wanted to start next but knew that would be inappropriate.

Simone comforted Devan and began to cry. "Tressa, I realize you are the victim here, but you could at least welcome us into your heart. You are so cold and acting so heartless." "Heartless... heartless?!" Tressa replied, her voice rising. "You want me to be warm and fuzzy. You want me to say I understand and give you a great big hug? No; I'm not going to do that." She began to rant, "The way I see it, I have the right to sit here and listen to your stories and react anyway I want. I want you to feel my pain and embarrassment if that's possible, but it's not. For the three of you, it's been over for years, but I'm still living this horror. Talk to me; explain what happened and why I should forgive you for such an indiscretion." Tressa screamed, "Tell me, Simone! And you, Mom, do you know how I feel? Well, I'll tell you. I feel like you favored one child over the other. You are always holding yourself as a woman of truth, virtue and righteousness, not so. But, you're going to tell me you were trying to protect me. Seeing me with this man that had actually had sexual relations with my sister and marrying me and you said nothing!" "Tressa, I had no idea you would run off and marry that fool ..." "I don't care, Mother! Even if we never married—he had a relationship with my sister, and neither one of you did anything, said nothing! I'm sure Gregg felt he had free reins of the family. Did he do you too Mother?" Jesse's jaw dropped. She was hurt. "Tressa that was uncalled for and cruel." "Yea, how about that; how could I be so cruel?" Tressa began to cry. She had no idea the betrayal was still so painful. "Get out of my house! The three of you, get out." "No Tressa, I'm not leaving. I came here to say my piece, and that's what I'm going to do," said Simone. "I know you are hurt, and it's an awful thing that I did. I don't blame Gregg; I did this, knowing that you were my sister, I should have resisted his advances and told you about it, but I didn't. I enjoyed his company. He was a shoulder to cry on when Craig went away, you have to understand, I was so lonely. Tressa, what you did not know was that Craig was experiencing a nervous breakdown, even before he entered the service. How they overlooked it, I don't know. He wasn't doing drugs and never drank. I asked him to talk to me, but he wouldn't. He said he was a poor provider, and when he came home for good, he would be better prepared to take care of me.

Then he began to act really weird, walking off of base. He went missing for days at a time until finally he was discharged for medical reasons. I didn't know until he died that he had been seeing a doctor because of a massive brain tumor, and the accident was no accident; it was suicide. This I never shared because I was too ashamed, but Gregg was supportive."

Even though Tressa didn't want to, she was

feeling Simone's pain. Simone continued, "Tressa, the irony was, after we had sex, Gregg and me, he professed his undying love for you. He said he was sorry it happened and begged me not to tell you; I felt like a piece of trash. I felt betrayed and abandoned, but I got what I deserved. He went back to you, and a year later he married you. Tressa, I was in a lonely and defeated place at the time. I wanted to tell you, but I couldn't, I couldn't. I confessed to Devan and Mom not knowing that Ms. Vye had told Mom. Devan and Mom said I should tell you, but I was too ashamed, and I swore them to secrecy. Please don't punish them for my sin." Jesse cut in, her hands clasped together, "Tressa, we were all wrong; what we did was unthinkable. We didn't trust you, and we allowed Gregg to spin his web of deceit." Simone grabbed some tissues and handed them to Tressa as their mother continued. "Tressa, I am your mother. I will not let this go; I will not walk away from this situation. I intend to call and come around. You will have to hang up on me or close the door in my face. I'm your mother, and I should have known better, and I didn't give you the benefit of the doubt or protect you from that demon. I do pray you will forgive me, no, forgive us all."

Tressa wiped the tears from her eyes and took a deep breath. "I can't imagine the pain you experienced Simone, and I'm sorry for your loss, and I'm sorry you couldn't share it with me. I'm not sure you cared about my pain; I think you just took it in stride." Simone interrupted, "Tressa, this is not an excuse, but I always thought you were stronger than me; I felt you could bear the pain as stupid as that may sound. I didn't want Gregg; I just wanted to be loved, to be comforted. "Yes,

Simone, I got that, and I believe you. However, there must be something wrong with us that we are so protective for the wrong reasons. For me, forgiveness is not the issue; it's the forgetting. It's the secrets and our history of one being better than the other, the silly insecurities." So what now! Where do we go from here?

Chapter six

Marcus thought of dozens of ways to propose to Tressa; she had waited patiently and was getting a little antsy. He wanted the proposal to be loving, fun, heartfelt, and most of all, memorable; something she would be talking about for a lifetime. He felt they had grown to know each other quite well over the past several years, and he knew she was the one. So, he came up with a brilliant idea—he hoped.

He worked every assignment that paid him top dollar; his plan was to amass enough money to pay cash for Tressa's engagement ring, take an elaborate honeymoon and make a sizeable down payment on their home. He had reached that goal; it was time to put his plan into action. In addition, for the sake of their relationship, he decided to only accept assignments in the States.

The plan was put in motion. On a moonlit Friday night after talking for hours, he asked Tressa to go shopping with him the next day. He said he needed some new shirts and new bedding. This was right up Tressa's alley; she loved to shop. Marcus knew, however, that he had to stay focused.

Early Saturday morning, he picked up Tressa and ate breakfast at the local diner. He sat lingering over his breakfast longer than usual. "What's wrong babe, you don't like your food?" "Yea, it's good," she replied. "I am just so tired; perhaps we should have started later." "We can go home, you said all you needed was shirts and bedding." "Actually, Marcus, we can order them online." Why did Tressa say that? She knew Marcus hated online shopping. "I know, before you say anything, I know that's not your bag." Marcus playfully kicked Tressa under the table. "That my dear man is what's called sweet brutality." "What Tressa? You're not going to do a thing, and anyway, I didn't hurt you girl. Let's go, it's time to get the show on the road." Little did Tressa Bowers know what she was in for. Tressa laid a twenty dollar bill on the table. "Gee, are you paying, dear Tressa." "Of course, I can pay for my man; after all, I'll probably get a new pair of shoes or dress or hat or ..." Marcus looked at Tressa. "Not today, my dear; your honey is broke. I haven't been to the bank, and I have just enough on my card to get my purchases." Tressa's eyes widened. "Is that so? I've never known you to be low on funds; this is something new. I am happy I could afford to pay for our meal. Next time, let me know when you're low on funds, I would be happy to spot you a couple hundred."

As they walked out the diner, Tressa asked Marcus sarcastically, "Do you think you'll need gas money? As I said, I have a couple hundred on me." Marcus smiled. "If you have a couple hundred, you can pay for my purchases, little missy." "And I can too." "Tressa, keep your chump change; one of my shirts cost two hundred dollars. You would be broke at the end of the day fooling with me." Tressa slapped him on the arm. "Enough said, Mr. Dallas; I know when to keep my mouth shut." Tressa was a generous woman. Marcus wasn't used to this type of generosity from a woman, but he loved her for it. "By the way Tressa, don't load up on food today; I would like to take you to dinner tonight, are you game?" "Sure, if you promise not to feed me all day." Taking her hand, he said, "I tell you what, I'll take you past all the stands that hand out food on those toothpicks. After about ten of those samples, you should be full!" "Now that's clever Dallas. Only you would come up with such an ingenious idea." Marcus laughed. "I know, got cha!"

As they pulled out of the parking lot, Marcus turned on the radio; some of Tressa's favorite songs were playing. "Marcus turn that up, that's the Temptations." She began to sing "Will you marry me; I'm gonna love you forever ..." After the song ended, Marcus laughed at Tressa. "My love, you can sure get into a song, you really killed that tune." "Shut up Marcus, you know I can sing. Didn't you hear me hit those high notes?" Marcus gave a short laugh. "I heard you screaming those notes." As they pulled into the mall, he added, "Come on babe, we're here."

Entering the mall, Marcus led Tressa to a local jewelry store. He told her he had to get his watch repaired. She patiently waited for him to transact his business, which took forever. The doorbell to the store rang, and a young couple entered with stars in their eyes—it was sickening. They walked to the bridal rings and asked to see several sets. After looking at about five sets, the girl asked Tressa, "Miss, can I impose upon you?" Tressa responded with a nod, "Sure, how may I help?"

"Which one of these sets do you like—I mean if you had to choose one?" Tressa pointed to the set that had a three carat center stone shaped like a heart. "This is beautiful." Inside, Tressa was feeling jealous; this was her dream ring, a heart-shaped diamond with a red heart in the center of the setting. She had priced these rings when she married Gregg, but it was way over their price point. "Yes," looking down at the ring, she said, "this is the one I like as well. But it's way over our budget." "Miss, can I impose upon you again?"

Tressa interjected, extending her hand, "My name is Tressa." Returning the courtesy, the girl said, "My name is Sylvia. Now that we know each other would you try it on for me? I want to see what it looks like on your hand."

Tressa tried it on, "Wow! This is magnificent, a perfect fit. You're a lucky woman," said Tressa, holding up her hand. "Who wouldn't want this baby!" Just then, Marcus approached the counter. "What are you looking at babe?" Tressa held out her hand to show Marcus. "What a sparkler? How much is that?" Marcus looked at the guy and pointed to the young lady, "Man, if you purchase that, she'll love you forever; no let me take that back; she'll love that ring forever." Tressa smirked, "Marcus have you no romance in your soul?" "Yes, I do," he said smiling, "but it depends on how much love costs, or should I say, how much that ring costs." The young man held out his hand to Marcus. "Hi, my name is Patrick, and this is Sylvia, happy to meet you too. By the way, if it's not too personal, how much is that ring Marcus asked about?"

Patrick turned to the salesman. The salesman took a deep breath and said with his sales pitch. "If you are prepared to purchase this today, we can offer you a twenty-five percent discount." "That's not what I want to know," said Patrick, "How much is the ring?" "Without the discount, it's in the ballpark of $29,000." Marcus almost screamed, "Some ballpark." "We are running a special this week, and this week only!" Tressa, looking at the couple whispered, "Come back next week, and it will be the same week long special." The salesman overheard her and replied, "No, this is definitely this week only. We can offer you 25% off," he said, punching numbers on the calculator, "which would include the seasonal discount, making your total $17,400, including tax. So how about it?" "How about it?" replied Patrick. "No way can we afford that; can you show us something between one and two thousand?" "Of course, but you need to step down to the next counter. That ring you just tried on was our exclusive premier collection." Tressa looked at Marcus, and Marcus looked sideways at Tressa. "Marcus, when and if you ever shop for a ring for me, please don't bring me into a jewelry store and make me go through that. Just surprise me, please!" "Mr. Dallas your repair is ready," a voice called out. Marcus retrieved his watch and escorted Tressa out of the store. "So, which ring did they choose?" asked Marcus. "Actually, neither," said Tressa. "I guess not; after that brother heard the price, he quickly made his getaway." "I did overhear the salesman give them the name of another jewelry store in the middle of the mall that was less expensive." "That so?" "Yes, that's so."

Marcus continued his journey. They visited several men's shops. He liked well tailored clothes, and he did need some new shirts. Once in the store, Tressa picked out four shirts she liked and a suit. "Tressa, I don't need a suit, I have two or three suits I haven't worn." Ignoring him, she said, "Marcus, you don't like this? It's 50% off. I love it, try it on; let's see how it looks." "Tressa," Marcus grumbled, "I don't feel like trying on clothes." Tressa gave him the "man try on this suit" look and reluctantly taking the suit, he went to the dressing room.

Waiting for him to exit the dressing room the same song came on by The Temptations. There's that song again. That's the second time I've heard it today. Just then, Marcus appeared wearing the suit. It was a perfect fit, and he looked dashing in it. Admiring himself in the mirror, he said, "I must say, Tressa, this is nice." He looked at the price tag and sighed, "Maybe, I'll see." He laid the suit on the counter and continued to look for shirts. Tressa thought to herself, they must be doing a tribute to The Temptations. Marcus decided to purchase three shirts and the suit when Tressa handed him a dress bag containing the suit. He was surprised and startled. "For me?!" "Yes for you. A special gift. I'm hoping you wear it on our next special occasion." "Mr. Dallas," the salesman asked, "Will this be a delivery?" "No, Mr. Mitchell, I'll pick it up." Marcus being sincere, whispered, "Tressa, that suit cost three hundred and fifty dollars, that's a lot of money missy; are you sure it's not going to dampen your next shopping spree?" "Don't worry baby, I got this; that's chump change!" Tressa winked at Marcus as they exited the store. "Where to next Mr. Dallas?" "Well, Marcus Daye Dallas, look at you and your woman. If I knew I was going to run into you and her, I would have worn your favorite outfit." The newcomer swung about seductively, hands on hips. "You know, the one you really like, that you bought me!" Marcus froze, it was Tia. "Aren't you going to introduce me?" Marcus sighed. "Tressa, this is Tia, my ex; no, let me rephrase, the ex." Tressa stood looking at Tia and her dog, speechless. Tia was tall, well dressed, and her makeup was flawless; she dripped in luxury. She was carrying a Gucci bag and coordinating shoes and wearing a Cartier watch. Despite her arrogance, she was quite articulate and came off as a first-class snob. She could see the physical attraction. "Tressa is it!" Tia extended her hand to Tressa. Refusing the handshake, Tressa responded with a short, "Hi Tia." "No handshake, afraid to touch me? I heard so much about you Tressa, and may I say Marcus did not lie," she said with a laugh, "I am taller than you, and might I say I'm also better looking!"

Tressa looked at her with a smirk as Tia stood admiring Marcus. "Don't flatter yourself, Tia, not in your wildest dreams could you measure up to Tressa—not in looks, style, personality, or class. This has been eventful and tiring; we have to go," said Marcus. He took Tressa by the waist, and they walked off. Tia stood looking at them walk away. "Next time, maybe we'll talk and carry on an adult conversation," she called out, still with her phony smile. "Oh, has anything eventful happened in your lives lately?" Shaking his head, Marcus called back, "Yes, as a matter of fact, I fell in love." Stunned, Tia started to respond but abruptly turned and walked away. "So, I finally got to meet Tia. She's not bad. Actually, she's quite pretty, a bit on the arrogant side." "I never said she was hard to look at, just hard to be with," Marcus said, heaving a breath. "Tressa, there are many crazy attractive women out there, and she's one of them." Marcus looked at her admiringly and clarified, "That does not include you, Ms. Bowers." "Thanks, Marcus Daye Dallas; I appreciate that!" They visited several more men's shops. Marcus purchased a tie to match his new suit and headed to the gas station to get his car oil changed. "Oil changed?

Marcus, you didn't tell me I would be out running around all day. Can't you get your oil changed next week or something, I am tired." "Tressa, how can you be tired, we've only been to a few stores. You know it doesn't take long to change the oil, now pipe down woman and come on! Oh, and after that I need to go to the market." "To the supermarket?" Tressa chided. "You're going to the market? Why? And to buy what? I know—you're planning a romantic evening for me; you're going to cook a fabulous meal for me." Marcus shook his head. "No, my love, I am going to the market because the cabinets are bare." "I thought we were just going to the mall; I didn't know you were going to hogtie me all day." Tressa, just go with the flow; this is quality time, Tressa thought, quality time, my foot I'm ready to go home! "Just drop me off before you get the oil changed and ..." "No Tressa, you told me you would spend the day with me, and I am holding you to it. I am not dropping you off!" Being persistent, Tressa said, "OK, then drop me off ..." "No, I am not dropping you off anywhere! Just be patient it will only take an hour or less and I'll be finished. What do you have to do that's so important Tressa?" Tressa was outdone. "Marcus you tricked me. You know I would have never consented to this madness if I had known your plans." "That's true, Tressa, that's true." After Marcus had run Tressa around all day, he took her to his house to relax. Later, they would shower and change for dinner. He knew that Tressa was tired, but he had made up his mind to spend the day with her, and the day was not over. The phone rang, and he asked Tressa to answer it and if necessary take a message. "Hello, he's unavailable at the moment, may I help you? Yes, I'll tell him, he will be glad to hear that. Marcus that was Cavaliers, you forgot your receipt and credit card." "Gee," Marcus said, his hand on his brow. "I got to go back. Well, that will push back dinner, but the restaurant is only down the road, I'll call them and let them know we will be a few minutes late." Now Tressa was really getting tired. "By the way, Tressa, you have a change of clothes in my closet if you want to change. And before you ask, you left them when we had the storm." "Oh, yea, now I remember. Yes, I think I'll change. It's a good thing this is a dressy outfit because if it wasn't ... " and before she could complete her sentence, the song came on AGAIN, "I am gonna love you forever, for better or worse ..." "Am I going crazy? Marcus, are you having that song played?" "Me!" Marcus swung around. "How can I have a song played all day girl, it's just coincidence."

Tressa looked at Marcus. "You know, I am remembering when we first met, and you had that buddy of yours escort me to the meeting; now that was high-handed, only a man with connections could do that, so I don't think it's impossible for you." "Hold it, Tressa, I have no connections with radio stations, and I certainly would not have them play a 'will you marry me song,' that's just not me." Rolling her eyes, she thought, don't I know it? Well, a girl can dream.

They relaxed for a few hours. Marcus fixed Tressa a light snack, and they attempted to watch a movie but fell asleep. Hours later, Tressa was awoken by her cell phone. It was Ma Lizzy, and she decided not to answer. Ma Lizzy left a recorded message. "Tressa, this is Ma Lizzy. I was wondering what you and that handsome man of yours were doing this evening. I have a pair of extra tickets to the theater. Call me back by five, thanks!" "I'll call her back later, much later. As a matter of fact, I never received the message."

After resting, they dressed for the second half of their day. Marcus parked and hurried in Cavaliers and returned in less than ten minutes. Soon they were seated at Chantilly's. Dinner was served in record time, and Tressa was happy, she was starved. When the food arrived, Tressa quickly recognized it was not what she ordered. Marcus flagged down the waiter, "Sir, this is not what we ordered." "No," he said, "it is not," looking at his pad. "This must be the order for table nine." He removed the plate and came back with Tressa's order, but it was cold. "This will not do! This food is cold. Marcus, I am hungry," said Tressa. "Let's go, I'll call Lou Chang's for Chinese Carry Out," said Marcus. "That sounds good." Marcus and Tressa excused themselves and left. Tressa looked at Marcus with curious eyes, "That was odd, don't you think? Something is up; I know it! Are you planning a romantic dinner for me at my house, Dallas?" "Sorry to say I'm not." "Actually, this might work out better because I am tired and could use some food and relaxation." "Tired? We just woke up from a three-hour nap, how can you be tired?" Marcus shrugged, "I don't know, but I am."

Once in the car, Tressa leaned back to relax. "This has been an interesting day, Marcus. I can't believe you brought flowers for your den, and lobster for dinner tomorrow; like you know how to cook lobster." "I don't," Marcus said, "I was going to get you to do it." "Me!" Tressa looked horrified. "Are you for real? I can't kill those poor little creatures!" "You eat those poor little creatures." "Yes, I do. I also eat chicken, but I don't watch them being ... well, you know." "Yes, slaughtered!"

"OK, let's end this conversation." "Oh no, not again, when is this going to stop?" This time Tressa decided, "I'm calling the station, there must be a reason they keep playing that same song; it's creepy and beguiling at the same time." Marcus frowned. "Tressa, it's just a song, what's wrong with you? Is it the words that's creeping you out?" "Yes, I guess. OK, maybe I am taking this too far. But you know what's really creepy about this, it's the events of the whole day." Marcus shook his head. "You poor thing, a song; what's gonna happen when I do propose to you." Tressa rolled her eyes. "I'm still waiting for that day." She clinched his arm. "At least I know you're thinking about it," she replied. "Tressa, I am always thinking about it."

Looking at Tressa with sympathetic eyes, he said, "I just don't have the funds right now. I want to buy you a big, pretty house, and I want you to have the wedding of your dreams, but right now, money is tight." On the way to Tressa's, Marcus made a call to his answering service. He said a couple of yes's and no's then hung up. "Is everything alright?" Tressa asked. "Yes, I have to call and hopefully meet with a client to Marcus took Tressa's hand and held it. "Tressa, I love you with all my heart, and when that day comes, I promise you all the bells and whistles. You will want for nothing, I promise you that." Tressa slid over, and they rode the rest of the way in silence.

Marcus walked Tressa into her house, and she abruptly stopped. "This is strange, why are all the lights off?" Just then that song started to play "I am gonna love you forever, love you for better or worse..." "No, not again." "Yes, Tressa again." Marcus opened the dining room door, and there was a loud shout "Surprise!"

Tressa was scared out of her wits! "What's going on? It's not my birthday, what's up!" "Just wait a minute," said Jesse walking up to her. Tressa was stunned, all of her family and friends were there, and then Marcus entered carrying a velvet pillow and on it was a beautiful diamond.

He sat Tressa down in a chair he had transformed into a chair for royalty. It was covered in purple velvet and had gold piping in the seams. Tressa sat down and looked Marcus in the eyes as he knelt in front of her. "Tressa, I have planned this moment for the past year. I wondered how I could make this moment memorable. I pray that you will cherish this occasion." He took the ring off the velvet pillow and slid it on her finger. "Tressa Bowers, will you marry me?

Tressa was blown away. Tears began to roll down her cheeks, "Yes, Marcus Daye Dallas, I will marry you. My God, Marcus, this is the ring that was in the store today and ... and that's the suit I purchased for you. You're wearing my suit; I mean it's your suit!"

Tressa didn't know what she was saying. Then there was loud applause. She said yes! Devan ran to his sister feeling elated. "Oh Devan, everybody knew," and then the biggest surprise of all, in walked her best friend, Detra. Tressa jumped up and ran to greet her. "Detra, I am so happy." They hugged and cried and cried and hugged.

Then Tressa looked around, "Where is Simone?" Everyone looked away from Tressa trying not to make eye contact. Jesse walked up behind Tressa to whisper something in her ear. "Do tell," said Tressa. Well, that's not going to spoil my night.

There was a crowd of people. Jesse had

prepared food for at least forty people, but the word must have gotten out as there was well over sixty people there. The music was on, and the fun began. Everyone wanted to personally congratulate the couple, especially Les and Avery Dallas, her future in-laws. Tressa couldn't believe her finger; the ring was a perfect fit, and the diamond was huge. Marcus had outdone himself. Tressa couldn't wait for all the people to leave. She wanted to be with Marcus and tell him how much she loved him and how much she appreciated the beautiful ring and engagement party. Then she thought, I actually got engaged and had an engagement party at the same time, cool!

Tressa was feeling bad that her one and only sister wasn't there. She had decided to phone her when the doorbell rang. Marcus answered the door, it was Simone. He motioned for her to go into the study and Tressa was quickly ushered out of the room into the family room. "What's going on now?" "OK, Tressa, when we count three, open your eyes." She took a deep breath and opened her eyes. Standing before her was a group of men dressed in 70s style clothes, each wearing a huge bush. When the music came on, the group introduced themselves as the "Tempos" a group that sang only Temptations songs. "One, two, three hit it! I got sunshine...on a cloudy day..."

Tressa held her heart. When they finished their first song, they paused and congratulated Tressa and Marcus on their engagement and continued with all of Tressa's favorite songs. Then, from out of Tressa's study, appeared her sister Simone. She was dressed in a wig and outfit resembling Etta James and began singing one of Tressa's all-time favorites. "At Last." Tressa was moved beyond words. The guests got more than what they came for. Les and Avery each gave a beautiful speech and toast to the engaged couple. Avery Dallas was so proud he was in tears. This was the engagement of the century, and one Tressa would never forget.

The party went on for hours; the food and wine flowed. It was almost 2 a.m. before all the guests left. "What a night this has been," said Tressa. "I am so tired; I want to just lay down." "You do that Tressa," said Devan, "We will clean this mess. You have to get some sleep so you can get to church today; remember you're leading the young adult choir." "I haven't forgotten Devan, but I was hoping for a moment to get someone else to ..." "That's not feasible young lady, now off to bed." "No, hold it a moment, Miss Bowers," said Marcus, "you come with me." Marcus grabbed Tressa by the hand and led her to the small sitting room. "Are you happy Tressa?" "Babe, never in my wildest dream would I ever have imagined a day like this. It exceeded my every dream, and I promise you, I will never forget it." She thumped him hard on the shoulder, "You set me up! Blushing, all day in your own way, you were proposing to me!" "Yes, I was; all day I was setting you up for the big 'question' and you said yes!" With a look of love, joy, and pleasure, they hugged and kissed passionately. "Wow! I can look forward to this for the rest of my life." "Yes, you can if you're a good boy." Marcus held up his hand. "I promise to be good. Now, you really need to get to bed, but I must ask you one question ..." "What's that?" He hitched up close to Tressa and whispered in her ear, "Can I spend the night?" "No boy! What's wrong with you, you have got to be kiddin'." Marcus was rolling with laughter, "Yes, I am pretty lady, yes, I am." Jesse and Detra knocked on the door, "May we enter?" "Yes, come in." Marcus kissed Tressa again and said he would call her later in the day; perhaps they would go out to dinner. When he left, he could hear Tressa, Detra and Simone in the room screaming with joy. "Women, they are really crazy."

The next day, Tressa was in for another surprise. Following the engagement festivities, Rev. Rayford invited Marcus, Les and Avery to the Second Baptist Church. He informed them that he was going to announce the couple's engagement at church the next day, and he wanted them present. A man of his word, just before giving the benediction, Rev Goode asked the congregation for their attention. "Brothers and sisters," grabbing both sides of the pulpit he leaned back and forth and said "I need your full attention. I had the pleasure of attending a most auspicious occasion yesterday. It is my pleasure to announce that Tressa Bowers and Marcus Dallas are engaged. Will the engaged couple please come forth?" Tressa came down from the choir stand as Marcus slowly walked up the aisle. They grabbed hands and stood before the congregation. There was loud applause and then everyone stood. "You're a lucky man, Mr. Dallas," said the pastor. Quieting the congregation, he added, "Now, in keeping with the tradition of the church, we will say a prayer for the couple." Everyone bowed their heads as Rev. Rayford prayed.

After the service, Les and Avery invited the family out to dinner, and guess who invited herself? Yes, Ma Lizzy. Tressa knew this was going to be interesting. Ma Lizzy did not disappoint. Once alone, she told Tressa she was hurt she had not been invited to the engagement party. She said she considered herself a member of the family and demanded she be told why she was not invited. "Ma Lizzy," Tressa said, desperately defending herself, "I knew nothing about the engagement and or party, so how could I have invited you?" Jesse overheard the conversation. "Ma Lizzy, I must apologize; it was my fault, and it indeed was an oversight." Ma Lizzy was irate. "I do not accept your apology. I was embarrassed by the entire congregation, finding out the way I did. Don't you realize who I am?!" Jesse was floored, and before she could stop herself, she responded, "No, I obviously I don't know! Who exactly are you?!" "How dare you question me, you ..." Marcus immediately stepped in to try and diffuse the situation, after all, this was his area of expertise. "Ma Lizzy, you must know that this was an oversight," he said, facing her and caressing her shoulders. "You're one of the family, and I promise you this will not happen again. You mean the world to us! Please accept our apology."

Ma Lizzy was touched. There was a little twinkle in her eye. "For you Marcus, I know you're sincere. I do accept your apology," she said, glancing at Jesse as she nestled up to Marcus. "You could tell me anything. Your sweet smile and tender touch just drive me crazy." Everyone laughed but Tressa and Detra. They saw something sinister in her eyes. But it was not over. Avery posed the question to Ma Lizzy. "Ma Lizzy, who exactly are you? What I mean dear lady is; what is your role in the church and in Tressa's life?"

Now she really was angry. How dare this man question her? She responded loudly, "I'm the mother of the church, Mr. Dallas. I am second in command of the church body here at Second Baptist Church. The pastor and all the others confide in me and keep me informed about all the goings on. They seek my advice, and my dear man, they come to me for special prayer and revelations. Ask Tressa, she's often sought me out for direction. Now, Avery Dallas, have I answered your question?" With a sharp tongue, he replied, "I suppose you did, dear lady, I suppose you did." With a stern look after dinner, Devan asked Tressa if he could talk to her alone, as there was something he needed to discuss with her. "Yes, of course. This is not about whether or not you're going to be in the wedding is it?" Devan didn't smile, "No Tressa it's not." He was serious. "I'll meet you at your house, actually no! Can you come to my house? I need your undivided attention." "Let me check with Marcus to see if he has anything planned." "No Tressa!" Devan said firmly. "If you have plans, cancel them, we need to talk." "Devan, you're scaring me," Tressa said nervously. "I don't mean to," he said, gently holding her hands, "but it's serious." "OK, I'll be there around 4 p.m." "That's fine, Sis." "See you later."

Tressa did not discuss the meeting with Marcus. She felt guilty, but she didn't want him to worry. Whatever the problem, she would share it with him later, but there would be no secrets. Then she thought, what if it's another celebration? No, they wouldn't do that two days in a row, and it's not like Devan to be so serious. Please Lord, not another awful family secret; I don't think I can take it.

With butterflies in her stomach, Tressa promptly arrived at Devan's by four. Besides Marcus, Devan was one of the slickest dressers she knew, but not today. He had on a pair of worn jeans and an old

T-shirt that looked like a scrub rag. "Man look at you, was I not worth a decent outfit?" "Yes Tressa, indeed you're worth it, I just came in from washing my car." "That explains things." "Do you want me to change?" "Would you? I think I could take you more seriously." Devan excused himself and went to change. Tressa went to the kitchen to get a beverage when she saw an envelope lying on the counter with her name on it. It read: "TRESSA BOWERS –CONFIDENTIAL."

She picked up the envelope and stared at it. She could hear Devan yell, "Whatever you do, do not open that envelope!" Tressa placed the envelope on the counter and returned to the living room. When Devan appeared, he was half smiling. "Boy do I know you, Sis; I knew you would wander over to that envelope." Tressa was leaning against the kitchen counter when he took her hand and led her to the sofa. Motioning for her to take a deep breath, he said, "Now I want you to sit back and relax. What I am about to share with you is serious, but not earth shattering."

He began by telling her about the week before. He and several officers responded to the office where Tressa worked. Tressa's tenure at Lewis and Benton was almost over, and she spent less time in the office and more at home. "We responded to a call from your supervisor, Mr. Goode, who found an envelope tucked in the secretary's desk." "Who, Sheila?" "Yes, Sheila."

Devan picked up the envelope and removed a stack of papers, which included scraps of notes and some pictures. Tressa was a little unsettled. "Wait, Devan, before I touch this should you have this information? Is this Sheila's property?" "No, it's not. Sheila was fired and left the envelope in her desk along with some other corporate information she had no business having. Mr. Goode gave this to me to share with you. Shall we move on?" Shuffling from side to side, she said, "Yes, of course." "Tressa, some of the notes contain comments about Marcus, which are damaging to his character. What I mean by that is if any of it is true, he has not been honest with you. That being said, it could also mean that the information could have been blown out of proportion and not worth mentioning." Devan handed Tressa the envelope and stepped out to give her time to concentrate and thoroughly read the material. He said he would be back in about an hour.

Tressa slowly read each page and scrap of paper. She studied every picture. The paperwork contained a police report for Tia Montgomery filed by Marcus Daye Dallas just weeks after they had started seeing each other. There was pictures of them holding hands and hugging outside of Cavalier's restaurant with him wearing a recently purchased black cap that she had given him. In addition, there was a photo of them in his condo relaxing on his sofa with his arms around her, and they looked as if they were enjoying themselves. Tressa felt her blood pressure rising. On the scraps of paper were notes, cryptic notes with an email address: dallas.guys@3generations.com. What is this? It certainly wasn't Marcus's email address. As she turned the piece of paper over, there were two words written in bold "WATCH OUT." "Hum," said Tressa, "this is mighty suspicious." The one thing she had decided was to have faith in Marcus. So what if he had seen her a few times since they had started dating, she had met Gregg on occasions in one of his moments of desperation. There were about ten photos; one included Sheila. That was puzzling; Tressa had no idea she knew Tia.

Tressa stuffed the pictures and papers back in the envelope and laid the package on the table. She leaned her head back and prayed. "Lord, what is this all about? Should I be worried? Has Marcus deceived me?" The Holy Spirit said, "Trust in Him, trust in Him." Tressa felt a peace come over her and thanked God. She heard the door open and saw Devan enter with Marcus. She glanced at them both with wondering eyes. "Devan you didn't tell me you were going to get Marcus?"

Devan shook his head. "I wasn't; I saw him on his way to your house and stopped him. I told him what I had discovered and asked him to come with me." Marcus without hesitation walked over to the cocktail table and picked up the envelope. "Is this the envelope that contains the incriminating information about me and Tia?" "Yes," said Tressa and Devan in unison. He opened the envelope, walked to the dining room and sat at the large table. He spread all the papers and photos out and arranged them according to their dates. His objective was to create a timeline. After reviewing the information, he conceded that there were some he could account for and others he could not.

Marcus, Devan and Tressa sat around the dining room table. Marcus reminded Tressa about the incident the weekend of their first date and how Tia tried to run him down and that he filed a report on her for charging items on his credit card. The name on the credit card was M. D. Dallas. She knew his password, and when they asked for verification, she was able to supply it. Marcus knew he didn't spend $2,000 for a purse, but he knew who did. It wasn't the first time Tia had used his credit cards and name for personal gain. She had a habit of introducing herself as Mrs. Dallas, so much so, people believed her. This time he had had enough. He pressed charges. Of course, she said she thought he wouldn't mind, and as usual her daddy paid for the purse and had the charges squashed.

But what caught Marcus's eye was the scrap of paper that had "WATCH OUT" on it. This was the message he had received on his email when he and Tressa first started seeing one another. This was remarkable because not even his sophisticated electronic friends at the Pentagon could trace the email address. He scrolled through the rest of the information and found an address to a company called "Rapid Tec." This had to be the company they used to send those emails. "Marcus, I need answers. For instance, the picture with your arms around Tia wearing the cap I had just purchased for you. Please explain that one to me." Marcus had to digress for a moment. He held up the photo of him and Tia in front of their favorite restaurant wearing the sports jacket and cap that Tressa had purchased for him. I'm sorry I can't give you one. I would never take Tia to our favorite restaurant, and I wear that jacket all the time. You probably don't believe me; I don't know how she doctored that photo, but I was never there with her, I swear.

All the time, Devan was silent. He sat observing the interaction between Marcus and Tressa. He saw the sincerity of them both, each trusting the other, seeing their faith being tested. As far as he was concerned, if it was a test, they passed. Devan believed Marcus, and so did Tressa.

"Marcus, I don't understand this either, but

I trust and believe in you; we will get to the bottom of this, I will not and cannot let this go." Devan was puzzled; he wondered if Tressa had read all of the notes because the one he felt was most disturbing Tressa had not reacted to. "Tressa, you showed no concern regarding the note about your engagement and wedding. You don't think that was serious?" "What note? I didn't see anything like that."

Devan walked over and emptied the envelope again. He turned every piece of paper over, "Where is that ..." instinctively he looked in the dining room, and on the floor was a piece of paper folded in half. He walked over and picked it up. "Yes, this is it." He handed it to Tressa. She read it out loud. It read: Dear Tressa: I wish you both anguish and pain. I pray to the God I serve that happiness does not find you. I hope misery becomes your best friend. It is my desire that every child you bring into this world brings you sorrow. Others may be happy for you, Tressa Bowers, but I am not. You stole something very precious from me, and I will do my best to get it back, even if I have to die trying. To give you a hint: I was at your engagement party, and I hugged you. But when I did, I cursed you. To prove I was there, look under your sofa, I placed a piece of greasy chicken under the cushion. I hope I stained your satin sofa (ha! ha!). You will never guess who I am, you're not that intelligent. Keep wondering, stupid. Signed, a dangerous enemy." Tressa turned red. "I guess she means business." Marcus shook his head in dismay. He took the letter from Tressa and placed it in the folder. "Perhaps we can trace the handwriting." He leaned over to Tressa and caressed her head against his shoulder. "Babe, I am so sorry. I seem to have brought you so much pain. I don't know how to fix this." "Marcus, this was intended to hurt us; we have got to be strong," Tressa said in a humorous but serious manner. "I need to go home and see if there really is a greasy chicken bone under my beautiful sofa." Devan hugged his sister. He actually felt bad that he had brought this to her attention. But in the end, he knew it was the right thing to do. "Devan, thank you bro, I love you and for your information, you did the right thing. I know you, and right now you're kicking yourself for bringing this information to us, but we needed to know." She hugged Devan as she and Marcus left. Tressa wished this was the end of things, but she knew she had to confess to Marcus that she had seen Gregg since they had been dating before this came out. When they reached Tressa's house, she asked Marcus to come in for a little while, but Marcus was beat. He was tired of talking; he just wanted to go home and rest. "Tressa, no more, not tonight; I don't think I could take anyone talking."

She stood motionless but gathered up the nerve to ask him to come in, impressing upon him the need to finish the conversation. She offered him a cup of coffee and headed for the sofa in her sitting room, and there it was, the greasy bone and a note that said, "This is just the beginning hussy." She did not show the note to Marcus; enough was enough.

As they sat drinking coffee, Tressa opened up to Marcus. She told him about the few times she had seen Gregg since they had been dating. She explained the reason and tried to assure him that there was nothing going on; she just felt sorry for him. Marcus put down the cup and headed towards the door, "Tressa, I know all about it! Gregg got a lot of pleasure telling me about the times he had persuaded you to meet him. I did not take it personally; I was dealing with a nut! I also understand that when a person has been in your life for as long as they have, and you have shared a meaningful relationship with them, you oftentimes become victims to the past. It's alright. I was wondering when you were going to tell me, but I also prolonged telling you about Tia. For the record, I trust you with all my heart. So, as he leaned down to kiss her, he whispered, "Let's not sweat the small stuff, I love you, Tressa Bowers. That $18,000 ring you have on should testify to that or at least to the fact that I am now broke." He winked at her and left. "My God, My God, what a day! I don't ever want a day like this again. Please protect us Lord from this craziness, strengthen us because the enemy is busy. What a man, he had to be heaven sent." Tressa lay down on the sofa and fell asleep.

Chapter seven

Over the next year, Marcus and Tressa made plans for the wedding and the purchase of their home. Marcus's career opportunities exceeded his wildest dreams. He was promoted Chief Executive of the entire east coast and European division for diplomatic training located in Washington, DC. His decision to take the promotion in addition to financing the honeymoon and purchasing a home would also enable him to live his dream of going into business for himself, and for that he needed big bucks.

To be a success, he would need influential contracts and the loyalty of former clients. He knew Tressa could comfortably take care of herself; however, he wanted to be able to provide for her and his future family. Marcus had amassed well over seven hundred thousand dollars. The money was a result of careful investing, savings and gifts.

Little did Marcus know how much of an asset Tressa was; she was no pauper. In partnership with Devan, they sold real estate right out of high school. They purchased properties with endowment money left by their father. Devan convinced Tressa that managing properties, going to college and trying to build a career was tiring and time consuming; he wanted out, and Tressa agreed. They sold all their properties and walked away with well over a million each. They both saw their financial standing as a sense of security, something to fall back on. The Bowers were upper middle class with all the trappings, from the luxury cars, vacations, clothes, and homes and yet, were not snubs.

Jesse often reminded them they could lose everything in a twinkling of an eye. Her crusade was "not to think too highly of things or themselves," think more of Christ, and that's the way they lived. The Bowers were very generous, not only with their money but with their time as well. They volunteered at the local homeless shelter. Tressa taught GED classes, Devan, Simone and Jesses taught acrobatics and cooking classes at the local junior college.

Of course, there were some that despised them no matter how humble, generous or well meaning.

The search was on; Tressa, Jesse, and Simone visited every bridal shop in Maryland but could not find that one special dress. Marcus wanted her to wear something straight, something showing her curves but no cleavage, and she wasn't sure what she wanted; she knew she would know it when she saw it. So, the ladies decided to travel to New York in search of the perfect gown, but before they could book train reservations, Detra called Tressa and asked her to hurry to the "Elite Salon" located in Cumberland, Maryland. She said she thought she found the perfect gown. Tressa was hoping it wasn't true; she knew her mother wanted to be the one to say "she found the gown." Jesse had impeccable taste, and Tressa relied on it.

Tressa also had a lot of faith in Detra's taste, so she hurried over to the salon without her mother and sister. Detra gave her directions to the salon and told her to make sure she was there by 3 p.m. "They only give customers a 15 minutes grace period, and then they move onto the next scheduled customer."

"Gee whiz, what kind of place is this?" It was tucked away inside an old building on the second floor. When Tressa entered the salon, it took her breath away; it was beautiful. Before she could take it all in, she was approached by a sophisticated woman wearing an old tailored suit with the collar turned up, rhinestone glasses and a hairstyle from the fifties. That being said, the suit was fabulous; it was well maintained, as well as her fifties hairstyle. This lady had style, class, and a whimsical personality. As Tressa approached the front desk, the saleslady walked up to her. "My goodness is this the bride to be? Honey, you're a vision, a true beauty," she said, twirling Tressa around. "Yes, yes, yes, the gown will be beautiful on you. My name is Sophia; I am the manager of this illustrious salon. My staff and I will try our best to make this the most delightful and unforgettable experience of your life."

Tressa didn't have time to respond. The saleslady ushered her to the back of the salon where Detra was waiting. Detra gave Tressa a hug. "Girl, I am so happy you're here, that woman is about to drive me crazy." Tressa nodded. "Yes, I see; she's mighty pushy, or one might say a real go-getter." They laughed. "Detra how did you find this place? It's not in any of the bridal directories." "Ah, my dear friend, technically this is not a bridal salon. As I was told, it specializes in custom made couture gowns and dresses made only for the elite." Detra leaned over to Tressa and whispered in her ear, "Those with really big pockets." "I see, and you're sure my pockets are deep enough for this place?" Looking around, she said, "This place looks like something out of a French salon for the rich and famous." "Technically Tressa, that's exactly what it is.

It has been hidden away from us peasants for years."
"You mean centuries."

Another saleslady approached Detra and
Tressa and introduced herself as Maddie. She was far
more sophisticated than Sophia. She was wearing a
well-tailored black pants suit that was encrusted with
rhinestones on the pockets and on the collar; and
five-inch black heels that had an enormous black
patent leather bow on the sides, which was also
encrusted with rhinestones. Her hair was long with
what looked like diamond hairpins holding up each side
of her hair. She was soft spoken and particular. Extending
her hand, she said, "Ladies I will be assisting you today.
Before I show you dresses, I would like for you to relax,
and have some wine and/or cheese and crackers. I will
pull several gowns in addition to the one we have on
hold; please relax." "Lar-de-da, miss thing, what have
you gotten me into," said Tressa. Detra and Tressa
declined the wine but ate some of the appetizers and
drank some distilled water. "Detra, you never did tell
me how you found out about this place, now tell me,"
said Tressa. "Actually Tressa, it's not a pretty story. I
happened to mention that I was going to be in my best
friend's wedding and how excited I was, and that's
when one of my patients told me she had ordered a
gown for her daughter. She wanted to surprise her; it
was her dream wedding dress. However, two months
before the wedding, her fiancé cancelled the wedding.
It's not that he didn't love her; he was badly injured in
Afghanistan, and despite her daughter's pleas and
reassurance that she loved him, he couldn't commit.
Her daughter never knew she had ordered the gown.
She described the gown, the salon, and the price, and

I called you ..." she cleared her throat, "pardon me, and that's how I found out about the salon." "That is very sad. I'll pray for them, even though I don't know their names. It can still work out." "Tressa, you're always so sympathetic towards others, bless your heart." Tressa was feeling uneasy that her mother wasn't there. She actually felt troubled. She knew she had to make that call. What if she found the gown, and her mother wasn't there? She told Detra her feelings and decided to give her mother a call. Jesse told Tressa she was only twenty minutes away. Jesse called Simone and told her what was up and asked if she could meet them at the salon. Simone told her she would drop everything and be right over.

Maddie reappeared with a rack full of beautiful gowns. Tressa and Detra's jaws dropped when they saw them. "Holly molly, these gowns look like gowns for royalty. I don't think I can afford any of these," said Tressa. "Tressa, act like you can; after all, it's only money, and we both know you have plenty of it." "Yea sure. Maddie, I don't know how this works in this salon, but I would like to know the prices of these gowns." Maddie looked at Tressa with a raised eyebrow. "Why, of course, madam," she said, handing her a book. "Madam, each dress is numbered and presented in this book. It includes the name of the designer, where it was made, the fabric, and the price." Tressa picked up the book and slowly turned the pages. "Thank you, Maddie," I would have to sell my prized car, and cash in my 401K to be able to afford one of these babies." Tressa heard Jesse's voice and stood when she saw her mother, and to her surprise, Simone, and Ciera. "Gee, you're just in time; I was just going to try on the first gown." Tressa hugged her mother and whispered in her ear, "Follow my lead." "OK, I will."

The first gown, number 21, was too plain. Number 33 was over the top, full of lace, a hood and some kind of draping down the back; Tressa knew that wasn't it. Number 4 was right on point, it was a dream gown, but it was pricey. Finally, Maddie showed Tressa the gown, number 22, the one ordered for Detra's client's daughter. With bated breath, the dress was unveiled. Tressa almost fell over. She couldn't believe her eyes. It was so magnificent; she could never have imagined someone creating a gown so beautiful. Detra stood, walked over to the gown and gasped, "My God, this is stunning."

Jesse, Simone, and Ciera stood there looking and imagining just how much the dress cost. It had to be in the thousands, no hundreds of thousands, and it was. Jesse quickly thumbed through the pages to find the gown. Jesse held her chest and blurted out, "It cost what? Tressa we will have to mortgage the farm for this." "Mom don't tell me the price until I have tried it on." Tressa went to the back, and when she returned she could see Jesse well up. "Mom, do you love it?" "Do I love it, it's magnificent, and you will definitely own one on your wedding day. "Baby, this is the gown, it's a perfect fit. It is everything I could have imagined you wearing on your wedding day."

The gown was straight, made of satin, off-white with crystals inlaid throughout. It was off the shoulder and as it reached the bottom, it flowed in layers of plain satin and a layer of satin with Swarovski crystals. The train was also encrusted in crystals, which looked like diamonds. Everyone was breathless. Simone was floored.

"What a gown, I mean, is this an original?" "Yes," replied Maddie, "All of our gowns are originals until they are copied!" She smiled. Finally, the moment Tressa dreaded. "How much, Mom?" Jesse looked at Tressa for what seemed like hours and finally said, "$40,000."

"What! How much?! Lord, let me take this thing off right now." "No, no, no," said Maddie. "It's not $40.000." Tressa breathed a sigh of relief, then Maddie said, "It's actually $70,000." "Well, this dress is coming off, this is ludicrous. I don't have that kind of money for a gown." "Wait hold it, Miss Bowers, I know it sounds like a lot of money. This gown was designed for ..." "Maddie, I know it was designed for Mrs. Deauraux's daughter." "Yes, but did you know that it was designed by a famous Paris fashion designer. And here's where it gets interesting—the gown included all the accessories that a bride needs, everything! That includes the headpiece, shoes, and any alterations. The accessory package alone totalled over $6,000. All you have to do is pick them out." "But still the gown would still cost $63,000." Sophie heard the commotion and came over. "I told you, my dear; I told you and ..." Tressa stopped her. "Yes, she told me, but I cannot afford to pay $63,000!" "No, no, my dear, the gown has been reduced that's why it's still here." She walked away and came back holding a ticket. "Let me see. Yes, that gown is now $30,000." "$30,000, that's more up my alley," said Tressa, "and does that include the package that Maddie was talking about?" "Yes, it does. You can choose from the pictures on the following pages." Everyone was looking at each other in shock and delight. "Mom what do you think?" "That's still a lot of money, Tressa.

I wanted to pay for your gown, but sweetie, that's way out of my price range." "Tressa get the gown, I will help pay for it." "Really Simone?!" Tressa asked, astonished. "Yes, I know you didn't think I would, but you're my kid sister, and I cannot imagine you wearing anything else. Just let me know what my bill is—no, I will write you a check and that will be my share, OK?" Simone took out her checkbook, wrote a check for $10,000 and handed it to Tressa. "Sis." Tressa grabbed Simone and hugged her. "Stop girl, the dress is not paid for yet!" "Oh, yea, I better turn off the waterworks."

Jesse was so proud of them. Given their history, she wasn't sure she would ever see this day. Then Jesse took out her checkbook and handed her a check for $10,000. "Now, my dear, I think you can pay the remainder." "Yes, I think I can." "Well, that's not the final cost, unfortunately. There are taxes and the shipment fees for the accessories, and just in case you need alterations, you will have to pay the shipping and handling." Detra smiled and said looking at Sophia and Maddie, "Well, I guess the taxes are on me. What's my bill? I thank God it's not in the thousands." "Ladies, will you be taking the gown with you today? It is a perfect fit. The accessories will be mailed directly to your home?" "Yes, we will be taking it," said Jesse." They all squealed and hugged; Tressa couldn't believe what just happened. She had purchased a $70,000 gown for $30,000, what a blessing. She felt so blessed. As they all ventured to their individual cars, Tressa asked everyone to keep the purchase of the gown to themselves. Tressa gave Detra an extra hug and thanked her over and over again. "I'm so grateful Detra, God truly used you, and I am so happy." Everyone was happy, hugging and smiling, accept Ciera. She later told Simone she was happy for Tressa; however, she hadn't realized that she and Tressa had patched things up, and she was surprised that she had that kind of money. Simone reminded her that she had worked very hard to patch things up with her sister and as for the money, "Why wouldn't she have ten thousand dollars?" "Ciera, are you really asking me why I spent so much on my sister? I can tell you because she's my sister and I love her!" Ciera turned her head to look out the window while rolling her eyes. Tressa asked Jesse to take her gown home with her; with all the strange things that had been occurring, she felt the gown would be secure at her mother's. Tressa also decided to pay for the gowns of the bridesmaids. She was grateful for Detra's generosity, but she knew she could not afford to spend additional money on a gown.

Sitting in her home office, Tressa began to add the proposed cost for the wedding. Including the venue, gown, caterers, favors, limos, etc. the cost was now in the thousands, but she did not care. She had saved all her adult life and couldn't think of any other thing she would spend so much money on. She and Marcus had talked about purchasing a home, but that would be a joint investment.

As always Tressa thanked God for the beautiful gown and for connecting Detra with the patient, and she thanked him for the generosity of her family. As she was showering, she heard the Holy Spirit whisper Psalm 37:4 to her: "Delight thyself in the Lord: and he shall give thee the desires of your heart." Tressa began to well-up with tears of joy and gratitude. "Oh Lord, you are so kind and faithful, and I am so undeserving."

Everywhere Tressa and Marcus went, people marveled at Tressa's ring and wanted to hear about the proposal. Of course, Marcus and Tressa were obliged to tell the entire story. Finally, Marcus had six weeks off, and Tressa was determined to sit him down so they could make wedding plans. "First the wedding date, Mr. Dallas, what's it going to be?" "Did you bring your date planner?" "Yes, I have it." Marcus pulled out his planner but paused. He took out a sealed envelope and handed it to Tressa. She took the envelope and saw her name on it. Not again, it was deja vu; she had already experienced this. She had started to open it when Marcus snatched it out of her hands. "Oh no you don't, this is personal!" "But it has my name on it, and I want to see what it is!" Marcus gave it to her as if she had caught him with some kind of secret. Tressa hurriedly tore open the envelope and removed the contents. It read: Tressa, I know we have not formally met, but I want to wish you and my son the best. He is very happy, says his father. I pray I am invited to the wedding. As you know, Marcus and I seldom communicate or see each other, but I would love to see my first son get married. If there's anything I can do to be of assistance, feel free to contact me; my information is enclosed. Cordially, Desiree. "Gee, where did you get this?" Tressa asked, full of surprise.

Chapter eight

"My father gave it to me. My mother calls him several times a year. So obviously she called within the last few months. She sent my father a picture of my brothers to give to me and included was this note for me to give to you." "Oh, that answers things." Marcus nodded. "Yes, of course, she's invited; the entire clan can come, can't they?" "Sure, why not?" and turning more serious, he said, "Now, let's get back to the planning." Tressa knew there was friction between Marcus, Desiree and Avery, but she stayed out of it. She figured he would talk about it when he was ready.

The wedding would be held in the fall the following year at the Cathedral of All Saints, which was large and beautiful. They prayed Father Gooding would allow them to use it. The reception would be held at the Belvedere Ballroom, the prettiest and priciest ballroom in the State of Maryland. Marcus didn't ask or care how much it cost; he wanted the best for Tressa.

A week later all was secured. Father Gooding confirmed the use of the church, and the ballroom was available. They hurried and placed their deposits and sighed with relief; the rest was a piece of cake, so to speak. Tressa shared the news with Marcus about her wedding dress and how it all unfolded. He sat numb, and then asked, "How much did this dress cost?" "How much? Is that really necessary for you to know Marcus?" Really, some things should be ..." Marcus was squeezing Tressa's leg, a terrible habit he had. She screamed, "Marcus, stop, that hurt!" "I know it hurt, Tressa, answer my question." Tressa shook her head. "No, I will not! It's none of your business." Marcus gave a sly smile. "You know I'll eventually find out, so why not tell me now?" Tressa snuggled up to Marcus and whispered in his ear, "Silly boy, trust me on this, I am not telling. I can afford it, and it's not costing you a dime. It's my business," she said with a smile and an Italian gesture, caprice! "No problem Miss Thang! But don't come running to me for funds; I have to pay for this fabulous honeymoon and get you a home, caprice that!"

Tressa later regretted telling Marcus about the gown; she knew he was a bit controlling, but she never imagined he would be so inquisitive. Based on this revelation, she decided to only share what she thought was necessary, after all, she was paying for the wedding.

Marcus and Tressa decided to sell their homes to purchase one of their own. Tressa sold her home to Devan, who had always admired it. She made a vow to the Lord that she would never shack. Her mother insisted she move in with her, but Tressa declined, so Devan allowed Tressa to stay in the house until she and Marcus found a home. Marcus and Tressa looked at countless houses, but none of them was right. Again, Tressa saw one of her many prayers answered. Returning from a client's home, she took a wrong turn and found herself in a part of the city that was unfamiliar. The houses were huge and gated, yet it was only about ten blocks from the inner city. Stopping at a light, she saw a house perched on a hill that looked vacant. From the street, she could see that it was Victorian with plenty of character.

She decided to take a peek. The outside was fabulous; it had a long, impressive driveway that led up to a wraparound porch. The front had beautiful stained glass doors and windows, and the front door was massive. She slowly drove around the back of the house and saw a stream that ran through the back. The home appeared abandoned and in desperate need of repairs. She decided to look the house up on the public records as soon as she got home. Taking out a notepad, she wrote down the address.

The next day Tressa made it a personal mission to find out about that house. What she learned was astounding. The house had been abandoned for approximately five years. It was city owned, and to her surprise was up for sale. Tressa arranged to meet Mr. Ingram, the city representative. The next day, she was in seventh heaven.

Upon entering, the first thing she noticed was a beautiful spiral staircase that was situated in the center of the house, which she loved. There was a foyer with the original marble floor that led to the living room. Some of the wood was water damaged, and the house smelled of mildew. Tressa wondered what had caused the damage but pressed on. "Mr. Ingram, how bad is the damage?"

He hesitated, and said, "It's not as bad as it looks Ms. Bowers. The house is beautiful. The previous owners and the city were in conflict over a broken water pipe that burst during one of the city's cold spells. Technically it was the city's responsibility to repair the pipe and make repairs to the owner's property, but they were determined to make the owners insurance pay for the damages. It was a terrible feud and the owners abandoned the property. I am going to let you in on a secret—there's a proposal for a strip mall and a financial district to be built in the next two years. The city desperately needed the revenue, which would be in the millions and are, therefore, looking for a resolution. The other problem, Ms. Bowers, is that the house sits on the line that divides the city and county; though the city claims ownership of the property, the county wants to share in the revenue." "So what you're saying is that it's a zoning problem in addition to the plumbing?" "Yes, Ms. Bowers, that's exactly what I am saying."

Tressa thanked Mr. Ingram for the heads up and continued to tour the house. When she walked in the kitchen, she could not believe her eyes. It was gigantic. It was completely remodelled. It had updated appliances and a window seat. It could use some work, but so far, so good. Upstairs were five bedrooms; two were small, two medium and the master, which was approximately 20 X 60, not including the master bath and a balcony. Each bedroom had a balcony and bath. At the far end of the hall was a large room that was used as a family room. It had a small refrigerator, stove, washer, and dryer. What a house! Tressa knew she had not seen the entire house, but she decided to leave and return the next day with Devan. "Thanks, Mr. Ingram. Is it all right if I return tomorrow? I need a fresh pair of eyes." "Of course, call me on my cell, and I'll meet you here, let's say about 10 a.m." "That sounds good, but I'll have to call you back to confirm."

They shook hands and left. Tressa did not tell Mr. Ingram she was a real estate attorney, just in case he was hesitant about revealing any information.

That night, Tressa couldn't sleep thinking about the house. Devan had agreed to meet her at the appointed time the next day. She prayed Devan wouldn't give her a hard time. He was the type that had little or no patience for haggling, and she was sure he would not see her vision. Marcus was not in town. Devan had carpentry skills; she was sure he would be able to point out problem areas that she would miss, or if she were getting in over her head.

When Devan drove up, his first words were, "Tressa are you kidding, this is a wreck!" Before seeing the inside of the house, he suggested Tressa purchase the house and grounds and demolish it. The land was massive, and they could build their dream home. "Devan, give it a chance; wait until you see the inside, you'll love it I am sure." "OK, Tressa, but I see a money pit." Once inside, Devan was impressed. It was indeed a beautiful and charming house. However, he was concerned about the cost to rehab it. The water damage was evident. The floors were puckering, and he was fearful of mildew.

Tressa took her time and walked through the first floor. There were several rooms she had not seen on her first visit. In addition to the living room, dining room and huge kitchen, there were three other rooms. One off of the kitchen that could be used as a family room; one room could be a private office and the other a sitting room. The house had five fireplaces; two wood burning and three were gas. They proceeded down to the basement. It needed a lot of work. Mildew was apparent, and the smell was unpleasant. Mr. Ingram pointed out the areas where the pipes had burst and showed them the water damage.

To Devan's amazement and surprise, Mr. Ingram explained the proposal being offered by the city for the sale of the house. He said the city was ready to sell the property. The city council had agreed to offer a one time only deal to fix the pipes and to repair any landscaping that was damaged because of the flooding. "Mr. Ingram, what is the house selling for?" "To date Mr. Bowers, the house has been appraised for $475,000, but the city is offering it for $250,000.The city could not afford to update it for resale, and it was too valuable a property to destroy. Now I guess you're wondering why no one has snatched up this property. I'll tell you; it's a cash sale." Tressa took a deep breath and responded "It's a what?" "I kid you not Ms. Bowers; it's a cash sale; that's the only way the city can afford to make the necessary repairs." "Are you sure, Mr. Ingram? That's an awful lot of money and ..."

Mr. Ingram held up his hand to quiet Tressa. He decided to call the office to confirm the price. "Hey Marty, yea, Ingram here. I am at the house on Crescent Falls; yes, the abandoned house. Can you give me any current information you have on that property? Yes, I have a young lady here that's interested...you're kidding me; sure, sure I'll let her know. What's the phone number there? OK, yes I'll tell her. Well, young lady, I have some good news and some bad news, which do you want first?" Tressa turned to look at Devan; turning back to Mr. Ingram, she said, "Give me the bad news first." "Well, despite the value of the home, the bad news is the house is slated to be torn down in 10 days if it's not sold. The city is tired of worrying about it. It is a cash sale; however, the good news is if there is a buyer, the city will accept $200,000 for the property because they have acquired a grant for some of the repairs, and they guarantee the repairs for ten years. In addition, they will pay all closing costs as long as the buyer(s) agree to purchase the home 'as is'."

Tressa was stunned and amazed. She knew she could afford the house; the only problem was it would put a dent in her wedding plans. She did not feel comfortable cashing in a mutual fund, but she would if necessary. "Well, if I want the property, what do I do?" "Take this number and call as soon as possible. Marty just told me they have received several offers; I'm thinking it's because of the grant information that the city concealed as long as they could, which is now out of the bag." Tressa put two and two together and figured the land developers put up the $50,000 difference. Tressa thought, What's for me, is for me. I'm not going to worry about that. Devan wasn't getting it; for a piece of property this size he couldn't imagine a real estate company not snatching it up, but he kept his mouth shut.

Tressa called the office and received a voice mail. She left a message and decided to be at the real estate office first thing the next day. "Tressa are you sure you want this house? It's going to need a lot of work. I realize the price is remarkable, but it will eat up all of your savings." "No it won't Devan; remember I have a partner, we will share the cost. Anyways, I just sold my home, and that can pay for the house." Devan frowned. "Tressa, I thought that money was for the wedding; never mind, you're going to do what you want." "I really want it, and I am praying Marcus will agree." Devan seemed unconvinced. "Good luck with that, Sis! I don't see Marcus jumping for joy when he sees this house." "We shall see; we shall see."

Tressa tried feverishly to reach Marcus, where could he be? He didn't answer his phone or respond to her text messages. She called his father, and he apologized. "Tressa, I'm so glad you called; Marcus lost his phone, and he said he tried reaching you, but his phone kept going dead. He's in the process of getting another phone, and he will contact you as soon as possible." Just then her phone rang. "Thanks, Dad, this is Marcus now." "Hey love, did my dad contact you? I thought I lost my phone, but I picked up one of the clients' phones, and he picked up mine by mistake, so I'm good."

Marcus listened as Tressa described the house and all the improvements it would need; she gently told him about the conditions in order to purchase the house. Marcus could hear the longing in her voice. "Tressa has anyone else inquired about the property?" "Yes, I was told they have several offers on the table, and we only have a few days to make the purchase. Marcus, I really love this house, it needs some work but ..." Marcus stopped her. "Babe, can you fax me some pictures of the house?" "Check your phone I already sent a few." Marcus looked through his phone and paused. "Are you looking at them?" "Yes, I am." Marcus was thoughtful. "Can I call you back in about an hour? I need to really look at these pictures." "Sure, take your time, I'll wait for your call." Tressa was a little disappointed. Marcus didn't immediately see her vision. She hung up the phone and took a deep breath and prayed this prayer: "Lord, it's in your hands; please guide and direct us. Amen."

When Marcus hung up, he called Devan to get

his opinion of the house. Devan told him he thought the house was a money pit but did admit it had potential. He advised Marcus to get at least two inspections. Marcus walked the floors, and after careful thought he called Tressa. "Hi honey, I've been waiting for your call." "I am sure you have. Tressa, I don't think the house is worth it. I called Devan, and he said the house was a money pit, and looking at the pictures, I must agree." Tressa listened, then began to make her case. "Marcus, I am willing to forgo a big wedding and a fancy reception if you think it's a matter of money." "Tressa, I don't think the house is worth the trouble; it's not the money, and we wouldn't have to forgo our wedding—there are other houses!" Tressa said nothing for quite a while, and then without apology she said, "Marcus, I am going to purchase that house whether you like it or not. I love it, and I think it's worth the price, good night!"

Marcus was stunned but not surprised; when Tressa wanted something, she went headlong into it. He decided he needed to take some leave and head home; this decision was too important for Tressa to make alone.

The next day, Marcus arrived on Tressa's doorstep; he took his key and opened the door. "Tressa, Tressa Bowers, are you home?"

Tressa couldn't believe her ears, was that Marcus? She rose up in the bed, and before she knew it, Marcus had fallen on top of her and given her a long kiss and a warm embrace. "When did you get home? I wasn't expecting you! Let me look at you—wow, my man." "And I'm happy to see you too!" Marcus told Tressa he had to return in five days. His assistant was holding down the fort. He said he felt it necessary to come home to help in the decision-making of the house or their future home. "Marcus, I already told you I plan to purchase the house, if not for us, then as an investment property." Marcus sighed. "I know, I know, but, you seem to be so enthusiastic about it, I ..." "Marcus come, we're going to see the house right now!" She called Mr. Ingram, but he was busy; however, he told her the key to the house was in the key box, and he gave the combination. Tressa thanked him and promised she would secure the house when they left.

Marcus could not believe his eyes when he saw the house. He didn't immediately respond. He was reminded of an occurrence that happened to him several weeks ago. He was bewildered when he heard the spirit speaks these words, "Meet her halfway." He heard this three times, once in Seattle at the conference, once on the plane coming home, and in the car coming to view the house. He silently prayed. He didn't want to say the wrong thing, and he wasn't sure this was what the Lord was talking about. "So this is it!" Marcus was impressed with the entrance to the property. The long bricked driveway was quite impressive. "Let's see the inside of the house first, OK!" Tressa managed to get the keys, and when she opened the door, she squealed. Marcus quickly jumped in front of her. "What in the world was that?" Tressa thought she saw a shadow in the living area. Marcus walked slowly, peeking in the living room and dining room, but saw nothing. "Girl, you almost scared me to death." "Sorry, I was sure I saw something." They held hands as they walked through the house. He nodded and groaned and Tressa led him. Finally, Marcus said, "Tressa, I like it; as a matter of fact, I love it." "You do! But you haven't seen the upstairs or the basement or the grounds!" "I know, but it's something about it that I love. However, I must admit, it's going to need a lot of holy water," he said with a smile. They toured the upstairs and the basement and then went outside. He could imagine the family in the pool and having company stay in the guest house. Yes, he loved it. Tressa was shocked; she just knew he would give her a hard time. Walking to the car, he paused, raising his hands as if he envisioned a huge steel sign across the front entrance, "Welcome to the Dallas Estate." "Really Marcus, I don't see that." "What do you see?" "I see 'Dallas Estate'." "Oh, you want to leave out the 'welcome'." "Yes, I do, let's leave out the 'welcome' folks just might take us seriously." "You know pretty lady, you just might be right!" "OK, Tressa, how do we get this property?"

Tressa again explained the conditions and the deadline. Marcus agreed to go with Tressa to the city's real estate office the next day. As she was locking up, she heard a noise. "I know I heard something rumbling in the house Marcus. Do you think we should call the police?" Tressa asked anxiously. "Maybe we should if you really think you hear something." "No, don't call the police." Suddenly, out jumped a scruffy-looking man wearing an old navy blue suit, his hair was matted to his head, and he looked and smelled like he had not bathed in years. Marcus was in kick butt mode. "Who are you?" The man sneered. "Now the question is who you all are. This is my house! I've been taking care of it for near thirty years! I attended to every family." Lowering his head, he added, "They don't stay long on account of the pipes, but that only means they are not devoted like I am." Displaying his diplomatic prowess, Marcus extended his hand to the man. "Sir, I'm Marcus Dallas, and this is my fiancé Tressa Bowers; we are interested in purchasing this property, and if we do we will be devoted." "That's what they all say," the scruffy man scowled. "But sooner or later they leave, as you will also." "What is your name if I may ask?" "You may ask; it's Thomas Crenshaw the third, and I am the caretaker. I know it's a bit overgrown now, but that's because they won't allow me to do my job. I have to sneak around like I don't belong. I am going to take you at your word Mr. Dallas," he said, looking at Marcus with a sly grin. You know things happen to people that cross me." Tressa looked at Marcus as if to say let's go! "It was nice meeting you, Mr. Crenshaw, but we must lock up." "Lock up young man, I don't want to get you in any trouble." Marcus had a thought. "By the way, Mr. Crenshaw, how did you get ..." "Mr. Crenshaw ... Tressa, where did he go?" "Come on Marcus, let's lock up and get out of here!"

Marcus found the situation humorous. "Tressa, you're running away from a house you desperately want. What's it going be? Are we going to put in a contract on this house or not?" "Of course, I want the house. That little display of fright doesn't change anything." Marcus was fine with that. He loved the house but shared Devan's optimism. He saw the potential and concluded the property needed a private inspection in addition to the city inspectors. That included the heating system, plumbing, furnace, roof, the pool, etc. He wasn't sure Tressa considered all these things, and he needed clarification regarding the terms of the purchase. Tressa looked befuddled. "Marcus, I already shared that information with you." Marcus frowned. "When, I don't remember that?" "Hon, you said you read the contract. Attached are updated copies of all recent repairs and inspections including those issues you just discussed?"

Marcus was annoyed; he didn't like Tressa talking to him as if he were clueless. "Let me see it again. I don't recall reading that." He snatched the document from Tressa and searched for the documents as she stood staring at him, frowning. "Yes, I see. It's all here, I apologize." Tressa took the contract from him and said, "Your apology has been accepted." She was miffed, and he knew it. Marcus and Tressa had just had their first disagreement. On the way home, Marcus again apologized. "Tressa, I'm sorry for being so abrupt." "I accepted your apology, Marcus, I just don't know why you were so ..." Marcus stopped her. "So much a donkey's behind, I was embarrassed." Tressa wasn't one to hold a grudge, and she said, "It's been settled my love, let's forget it, OK?!" "Ok."

Three days later, they were homeowners. The Dallas men converged upon what was now the "Dallas Estate." Les and Avery were beside themselves with pride. They slowly toured the house pointing out imperfections and things they especially liked. Avery loved the impressive entry hall and large kitchen, and Les fell in love with the guest house. Looking in every room, every nook and cranny, Les said, "This guest house needs a little work but is it beautiful! This is indeed a dream home." "Yes Dad, this is a humdinger of a house. I can see many parties and family dinners here." Marcus joined them. "OK, gentlemen, what's the verdict?" Les hung his head as if disappointed. "Son, I don't know about this." Then he raised his head "This is fantastic, great job." "You like it; you really like it! I have your approval?" Les looked at Avery. "Yes, you have our approval!" Marcus needed his father and grandfather's approval. Now, everything was good, he was ready to get married.

Avery and Les often visited the property overseeing the progress. They were there so often the workers looked for them and often jokingly asked if they were doing a good job. Tressa knew Devan was anxious to occupy the house and give it his personal touch; that being said, she decided to move into the house. Marcus had several offers on his condo, but it had not sold. Though Les and Avery were licensed contractors, Marcus preferred to use outside contractors. He felt it would cause less strain on the family unit. They needed the grounds landscaped, the hardwood floors refinished; windows needed to be washed, the pool cleaned, etc. As far as Tressa and Marcus were concerned, they had one major issue; whose bedroom furniture would be put in the master bedroom? They each loved their own sets. Marcus's furniture was too masculine for Tressa, and Tressa's too feminine for Marcus. "I have the perfect solution. As a wedding present, how about I buy you guys a set you can both agree on?" said Les. Tressa hesitated because she wasn't sure she wanted Les to spend that much money, but, Marcus dove right in. "Great idea, Pops; we'll take you up on that offer!" "We will? I am not sure ..." the look on Marcus's face changed Tressa's mind. "Ah, yes, we will, thanks, Pops." Tressa moved in, wandering from room to room trying to decide where their furniture would be placed. She had to decide for both of them. She knew Marcus would have different ideas about decorating the living and dining rooms. To her surprise, he left it up to her.

"Carte blanch," he said, "do whatever you like, you have impeccable taste." Tressa was shocked and slowly turned a house into a home. She later learned that Avery had given Marcus a pre-marital lecture about what to relinquish to the wife, and one of those things was decorating. "Son, leave her to it, after you're settled, you can go back and rearrange a piece here and there, and she'll probably never notice." Tressa appreciated the advice and ran with it. First things first, the house had to be fumigated and painted.

Marcus's condo finally sold, and he moved in with Avery. The wedding was only months away; he figured he could be comfortable and useful there until the wedding. He was at the house every day after work helping Tressa get it ready. They discovered they liked seeing empty places come to life. Combined with each other's furnishing, every room was tastefully decorated. Tressa's favorite was the sitting room across the hall from the living room. She had no idea Marcus had his eye on the same room as his study. "This looks good Tressa, why is your sofa in here?" "Why?" "Yes, I thought this was going to be my study!" Batting her eyes, she said, "Darling, you never said a word; if you had, I may have considered letting you have it. As of now, it's my mine." "Well, we'll see missy. Let's settle it with the toss of a coin." Tressa thought about it for a moment, "OK, but I'll provide the coin." Marcus couldn't help but laugh; Tressa was onto his two-headed coin. "You win Tressa, the room is yours, but .." he said, his hands clasped in begging mode, "I really wanted it!" "You'll get over it in time. Help me move this box in the hallway, I need to vacuum." She looked for an outlet but couldn't find one. Marcus pulled out the sofa and stumbled. His head hit the wall and a door popped open. "What in the world, Tressa look!" "I see; gee, a secret door. Move the sofa out a little further, so we can explore!" "Explore, I don't ..." "Marcus don't be a wimp, get the flashlights! Come on, we might find a fortune in gold or something."

Marcus located two flashlights and they slowly crept down the stairs. They could feel a breeze, and as they slowly walked through the room, their eyes adjusting to the environment, they could see old dusty furniture. There was a crib, a disconnected stove, a bed, and in the far corner was a large dilapidated pool table. "Tressa this place is spotless, a bit dingy, but spotless." Marcus walked over to where the front of the house would be. He saw an old cloth and pulled on it. Under the cloth was a window that had fake stained glass on it. He forced it open. Where was this? He didn't notice it on the outside of the house. "A window, is it more than one?" Marcus flashed the light around the room. There was another window that had been boarded up and painted over. "I can see the guest house from here." "The guest house? I've lost my bearings; let's see, we're directly over the living room aren't we?" Marcus shook his head. "I don't know, let's continue looking." "There's another door over there; Marcus go open it." He pulled and pulled, but the door wouldn't open. He told Tressa he would be right back. He went upstairs and found a crowbar but when he returned Tressa had opened the door. "Oh no, you didn't, how did you open that?"

"There's a skeleton key in the lock." "So, what did you find?" "Nothing. It leads down a long and wide hall, and I was not going without you." Marcus walked in front of Tressa, both flashlights lighting their path. They discovered two additional rooms and a bathroom, which was neat and clean. At the end of the hall was a door; Marcus forced open the door that led outside. "This is interesting. I don't recall seeing this on the blueprints, do you, Tressa?" Tressa shook her head. "No, I don't recall." "You aren't frightened are you?" Marcus asked. "No, you're with me, I am not frightened, but I don't like it down here!" "Let's see if there's a light switch." Marcus located a light switch, but there was no bulb. "There's the problem; no light bulb." He took one from the bathroom, and this time when he turned on the lights he jumped and screamed, "Good God, where did you come from?"

Avery couldn't contain himself, "Son, you asked me to come over. I came into the house and saw the door open. I called out, but no one answered. I saw the open door and came down here. What is this room?" Marcus shook his head. "I'm not sure, it look like old servants quarters or something." "Marcus, let's go back upstairs please; this is creepy." "You go up, babe. I want to show Dad what we discovered." Tressa couldn't wait to get back upstairs. "See Ya!" "What do you think Dad?" "I don't know, I feel like Tressa, this is a creepy place." "What's this?" Avery found a big black book lying in a crib and a long round black container. "Let's take it upstairs and see what we've found." Marcus and Avery were pumped. This was a real mystery, an adventure. In the container were family photos, love letters and other memorabilia. "These must belong to the previous owners." "I guess, Dad, but which previous owners? There were so many...." "Well, I am tired; it's been a busy day. Let's go through this on Saturday. We

can come over on Saturday and continue our discovery."
"Yea, Dad, that's a good idea." Before leaving, Marcus
asked Tressa if she felt safe. Tressa said she was fine,
but her body language said no; she was putting on an
act. She was frightened, and Marcus knew it. Marcus
called Detra who agreed to spend the night with her.
Avery and Marcus walked around the perimeter of the
house checking for any doors and windows that could
provide access to the house. The security system would
be installed the next day, which would provide a sense
of safety.

On Saturday, both families converged at the
Dallas Estate to bless the house and help Tressa finish
unpacking and arranging furniture. Tressa prepared a
lavish brunch, but no one seemed interested in the
spread. Tressa, Jesse, Marcus, Avery and Les were
captivated by the old pictures in the album. There was
writing on the cover of the album that was worn. Jesse
carefully wiped off the dust to discover the name,
"Tilton's" in what was gold. Most of the pictures were
dated, which made it easier for them to recognize each
generation.

They discovered the family owned a string of
gas stations in Maryland and Delaware. Three generations
of Tiltons lived in the house at the same time. The pictures
reflected a happy family. There were pictures of
Thanksgiving, Christmas and birthdays celebrations.
Avery pointed out the fashions and joked with Les.
"Dad, do you still have any of your clothes from that
period?" "Of course, I have a few pieces. As a matter
of fact, the shirt I have on is one." After much laughter,
he said, "Let's see what else is in the container, we may
find something sinister. Avery shook the container and

a folder fell out. "These are blueprints; I wonder if they are blueprints of the house?" Tressa ran and got her copy of the blueprints they received at closing. They laid both sets together. "What are we looking for?" Devan asked. "They don't know," remarked Simone, shaking her head, "this is like seeing the Three Stooges, Abbott and Costello and the Marx Brothers looking for a needle in a haystack." "Simone if you're not going to be helpful, go to another room." Simone shook her head. "Not me, I am staying right here. What if someone comes out of one of those secret doors?" Initially, the blueprints looked alike, but upon close observation they found discrepancies. "How could this happen?" said Tressa, "the layout is different." "We must keep in mind the house has been remodeled over the years, and there would be major changes in the layout of the house. "But what happened to all those secret passages?" "That's what I want to find out," said Les. "We're getting to that, Dad; just hold on." "Look there's a door that was right here in the dining room." Les walked over to the wall and started tapping on it, it was hollow. "I think I found something!"

They all started banging on the wall. Devan pushed against it, but nothing happened. Tressa said, "Where is this going. I don't want my house tore up, and, don't you dare tear open my wall! Perhaps we need to let sleeping dogs lie."

It was like the guys were now determined to find something, anything, and decided to go in the basement and explore. If there were secret entrances or passageways, they would find them. They roamed and roamed until finally Devan made a discovery. "Here, come here!" Avery ran so fast that he fell. "Good

God, boy!" said Les, helping Avery to his feet. "What's the matter with you?! Do you think we found gold or something?" Devan showed them some stairs leading where to they did not know. The staircase was covered with cobwebs. They found a stick, and removed them as they proceeded up the stairs. At the top of the stairs was a brick wall. Devan used the stick to bang on the wall. Jesse heard the banging, grabbed a pot and began to bang. Devan yelled, "Keep banging until I come up." Tressa and Simone joined Jesse. The banging sounded as if it was coming from the side door leading out to the yard. Then again it could have been coming from the hallway, which was it?

Avery and Less encouraged Devan to continue knocking while they joined the girls. "This is it; we found it." The entire first floor and perhaps the entire house have secret passages that's going to take time to discover," said Les. In addition to the secret panel in the sitting room, they found a panel in the hall closet that revealed where the steps were. "This is amazing; Tressa there's no end to the secret passages. We are so lucky!" "Marcus, are you crazy? This isn't creepy to you? Quite frankly, I don't want to know where they are. I fear I'm going to come home and find my home dismantled." Deep down she knew this was just the beginning. She hoped that the planning of the activities surrounding the wedding would taper their investigation and her newfound fears. "Now can we do what we're here for, remember?" said Tressa. Les, being the senior member of the family was therefore given the privilege of blessing the home and the food. Everyone gathered around and held hands.

Les prayed fervently. It was powerful and

heartfelt. Afterwards, they sat down to eat. Looking around the table, Marcus's heart was full of pride. He not only had two loving parents, but he was now blessed with a caring extended family that was supportive and kind. He had not realized it until today, but he had come to love Devan as his brother. He grew to depend and lean on him, and he never disappointed. They made a toast. "To the Dallas and Bowers, God bless and keep us, Amen."

Chapter nine

The wedding was the event of the year. Everyone wanted to be invited, and those who were bragged about it. Four weeks prior to the wedding, the girls threw Tressa a lavish bridal shower. Over one hundred and fifty family, friends and colleagues were in attendance.

The shower was held at the Palace Room in the Ramsey Hotel, beautifully decorated in cream and lavender, the colors of the wedding. Jesse was impressed; the women were dressed to the nines and on their best behavior, so far. Tressa was wonderfully surprised; the ballroom was beautiful. The moment she saw the room, she welled up in tears. "Mom, this is beautiful, I'm touched." "Nothing but the best for you Tressa; nothing but the best."

Tressa tearfully gazed around the room. There were large pictures of her and Marcus suspended from the ceiling, bouquets of balloons. Tressa especially loved the giant framed picture of the night they were engaged, with Marcus on one knee proposing. On the top of her cake was a replica of her engagement ring. The women were quite colorful.

The games and jokes made a hooker blush. So much so, Jesse had to ask them to cut it out. Her gifts ranged from raunchy to elegant, and surprisingly, Tressa loved them all. She held up one of the more revealing gowns and playfully gave it to Jesse. "Here Mom, you might need this," and winked. Jesse shocked

Tressa with her response. "I could have used this a few weeks ago," and winked back. The girls put on a play depicting Tressa's life up until her engagement; it was hilarious. The players included her immediate family, her high school teachers, some old neighborhood friends, and church members. They really went down memory lane.

Mrs. Fern, her fifth-grade teacher, stole the show. She recalled the time she caught Tressa and Sonny Vale passing notes. She said she dismissed the first few notes but soon tired of their foolishness. She asked them both to come to the front of the class and read the notes aloud. Sonny and Tressa slowly strolled to the front of the class. Sonny was dumbfounded and useless while Tressa took the bull by the horns. Taking a deep breath, Tressa said, "Mrs. Fern before I read these notes, would you allow me to ask you a few questions?" Mrs. Fern decided to play along. Tressa placed a chair at the front of the room and asked Mrs. Fern to take a seat. Tressa began by asking some pertinent questions, and Mrs. Fern began to act out the scene imitating Tressa's voice. "Now, Mrs. Fern, are you sure you saw a note? And, are you sure it was intended for Sonny Vale? I pretended I was being questioned by Perry Mason and finally relented by saying, 'I confess Ms. Bowers, I'm not sure, I can only say what I thought I saw,' and pretended to cry. The class applauded, and I collected the notes and sent Tressa and Sonny to the principal's office, who in turn sent for their parents. They were both punished and had to write a letter of apology to me and the class." Tressa had forgotten all about that. She hugged Mrs. Fern and took the opportunity to thank her for putting up with her and all her shenanigans.

Before the evening got away from them, Simone grabbed Tressa and took her aside. She handed her a small gift bag. "Here, Sis. I wanted to give you something from my heart." Tressa unwrapped the gift and smiled. Tears began to roll down her face. "This is so sweet Simone. Look at us, we were so happy." It was a collage of four pictures of Tressa and Simone when they were teenagers. "Simone, these were our happiness times." "I know, and I pray we can find our way back to that happy place." "We're doing a great job kiddo." "Tressa, please forgive me for all the cruel and unkind things I've done to you," Simone said, embracing her. "I love you so much. I lost myself, but I am in a better place now." "I know you are," Tressa replied. "I can see it and feel it. Let's keep praying for one another. And, Simone, I do forgive you and I love you." "May I interrupt this tender moment?" It was Ciera, with an armload of gifts. "Where do these go?" Simone and Tressa ignored Ciera and gave each other another strong and warm hug. "Stay sweet Sis." "Oh, so you and Miss Queen of the universe are tight again, I never thought I'd see this day." "Ciera," Simone said sternly, "What's your problem? Aren't you pleased that Tressa and I are growing closer? If you're not, I am. I've been praying and praying for my sister's forgiveness. Do you realize how much I hurt her?" "No, it's not that SIMONE! You're the one that has carried on this hateful vendetta against her all these years, and I suppose I'm surprised to see you so ...whatever." "Let me get you straight Ciera. I know you have, for some reason, enjoyed the Bower sister feud. You have relished in our discord, but no more. I will not let you talk about my sister!

Or discredit her in any way. And, if you cannot be happy for her, I suggest you leave, NOW!"

Ciera was shocked and thought, how dare she talk to me that way! She seems to forget I have the ammunition to tear them apart. Or might I say, I have the power to hurt them both; mess with me! All her dirty deeds I ... well, forget it; she'll need me again.

The party was a hit, a beautiful celebration, which went off without a hitch. Tressa thought Ma Lizzy would show off, but for some reason she was quiet; you could say she was unusually quiet. She barely mingled but seemed to enjoy herself. There was one mystery. Simone accidentally knocked a bottle of hand soap off the counter in the ladies bathroom. When she went to pick it up, she saw some of the shower programs in a small trash can torn up. She reached in and picked up several of the torn programs. She was surprised to see the face of Marcus ripped out, and it looked as if someone with the mind of a child had scratched through Tressa's face. Who could have done such a thing? Simone decided to share this with Jesse, who was furious.

They began to realize that someone at the party was Tressa's enemy. Simone told Jesse she had just had it out with Ciera, but though annoyed with her, she didn't think she was that petty, Jesse agreed. While Tressa was enjoying her celebration, the guys were throwing Marcus a basketball themed bachelor party. It was one of a kind. At least forty guys showed. The invitation suggested gifts from local hardware stores. Julian, Marcus's best friend from his college days, arranged an assortment of games. Surprisingly, he discouraged basketball; Julian said he wanted the guys fresh at the end of the day. After the games, they stuffed themselves and drank. The music was pumping, and the guys rocked the latest line dances. Les performed some older dances that wowed the crowd.

When Marcus opened his gifts, he was pleasantly surprised. They were just what the doctor ordered. Some of the guys chipped in and brought an outdoor grill that could do everything but turn the burners on and off; Avery, Les and Mr. Dan, Avery's best friend, gave him a riding mower. Other gifts included an electric saw, a plunger, a drill, and hammer. "Thanks, guys, I love these gifts. On behalf of Tressa and me they are appreciated." When he opened the last gift, Marcus heard a lot of commotion and loud voices. "My Lord it's Tressa and her posse. Hi babe, come to crash my party?" "We sure did. I wanted to make sure there were no strippers here," she said with a wink. "You just missed them; they just pulled off." "I know that's a lie, we would have seen those hootchie mommas," she said smiling, her hands on her hips.

Two weeks before the wedding, Tressa called Father Brown to confirm the date for the rehearsal. "Hi Father, this is Tressa Bowers; I'm calling to confirm the date for my wedding rehearsal." She gave him the date they had selected. "Wait sugar; let me get the scheduling book. Now, you said you've already penciled that date in because I am not showing it on the books." "Father Brown, check again, please! We sat in your office and marked the date on your calendar, June 21st, 6 p.m." Father Brown, scratching his head, did recall meeting with Tressa. "Hon let me call you back."

When he returned the call, he told her for some reason the date had been erased and another activity scheduled in that time slot. "Now are you sure you did not call the office to change the date?" "I'm quite sure, Father. Would you ask Alesha if she changed it? If she did, she had no right." Tressa was getting angry. "Tressa calm down. I'll find out what's going on and will get back to you."

Tressa called Marcus and informed him about the mix-up. "Babe, that's an easy fix. We can have the rehearsal at your church. It's not a problem!" "It is a problem Marcus," Tressa protested. "The caterer is coming for the rehearsal dinner, and I've already sent out rehearsal reminders listing the cathedral as the address." There was silence. "Tressa, you're getting ahead of yourself. Father Brown hasn't called you back; hold on, it'll be fine." "OK, Marcus, I'll have faith and try to chill!" "Please do." "You can hang up now Marcus; I need to go lie down." The phone rang, Tressa assumed it was Father Brown until she saw the ID number. "Hello." "Hello, may I speak to Tressa Bowers." "Yes, this is she." "Ms. Bower, this is Kenny Bentley from The Belvedere Ballroom. This call is in reference to your booking on June 21st." "Yes, it's my wedding reception!" "That's correct, Ms. Bowers. I want to confirm the assigned ballroom and the number of people that will be in attendance. I would like to review your contract information; its standard for us to call and review the contracted information as the event draws near." Tressa sat up in the bed. "Please wait while I retrieve my copy of the contract." "Yes, I'll hold," Mr. Bentley said.

Tressa did not feel good about this. However, he did say it was standard procedure. She found the contract and returned to the phone. "Mr. Bentley, per my contract we will be located in the Chrystal Room, and there will be two hundred and fifty in attendance." "Ms. Bowers, someone made a huge mistake. The Chrystal Room is a small room that will only accommodate up to two hundred people comfortably, and your number is two hundred and fifty." "Mr. Bentley, what exactly are you saying, and why would you call me after my wedding invitations have been mailed? I was told by the sales representative, let me see, Ms. Sawyer, that the room was perfect for my needs. My fiancé and I checked out the space, and it appeared to be large enough for the guest, band, and dance floor. Are you sure we're talking about the same room?" Mr. Bentley laughed, "Yes, I am. I've been working here for fifteen years." "Mr. Bentley, I'll call you back." Tressa hung up, poured herself a cup of tea and sat on the deck. She whispered a quiet prayer and concluded that she had not received devastating news; nothing was catastrophic. Details had to be ironed out, and everything would be fine. She had to keep the faith.

Tressa heard a car pulling up in the driveway. Oh no, she wouldn't; Lord, this is not a good time. This is what I get for leaving the gate open. "Hi, Ma Lizzy what a surprise; I wasn't expecting company. And, as a matter of fact, I'm not in the best mood." "Dear girl, I was on my way to see Sister Blue, Jackie's mother, you know the ..." "Yes, I know who she is Ma Lizzy," Tressa said with a sigh. "Well, I noticed where I was and wanted to see this lovely house that everyone is talking about." Wiping a hand across her brow, Tressa said, "Honestly, Ma Lizzy, this is not a good time. Tomorrow would be better."

Paying no heed, Ma Lizzy walked pass Tressa, entered the living room and picked up a picture of the

Dallas men that was on the mantle. "My word what gorgeous men. Tressa, you're a lucky woman to be in their company; to be surrounded by such worldly, fashionable, spirited good-looking men, especially, this one." Tressa didn't see which one she was ogling over, but she was smitten. Boy, here we go again. Tressa stood in front of Ma Lizzy and started snapping her fingers. "Ma Lizzy, may I help you?" Coming to her senses, Ma Lizzy answered, "No dear, I came here to help you." "Help me, why?" Ma Lizzy began to pull out bags of what looked like weeds and twigs out of her purse. "I am going to purify and place a spirit of calm throughout your home."

Just before she could start her purification, Marcus walked into the house. She stopped, held her chest and almost dropped the bag. "Oh my, this is my lucky day." She hurried over to Marcus, grabbed him around the waist and tried to kiss him on the lips. Marcus pushed her away. "Lady, what's wrong with you, are you right in the head?" Tressa was astounded. "Ma Lizzy, I think you better leave. It was nice of you to come by and do your thing, but I assure you my home, my fiancé, and I are fine." "I will remember this visit for months to come. Too bad the other Dallas men aren't here. I am ready to give them a run ..." Marcus ushered Ma Lizzy out the door. "You take care now and have a nice evening. Tressa, where did that kook come from? That woman gives me the creeps. She always brings a spirit of gloom and doom. I am sure her purification ritual would have brought on negative energy instead of good." As they sat talking, it dawned on Marcus he did not hear her drive off. He peeked out the window and saw her car door open and Ma Lizzy walking around the house shaking sticks and sprinkling something. "Tressa, she's out there with her witchery, what shall we do?" As they were leaving to confront Ma Lizzy, the phone rang, it might be Father Brown or Mr. Bentley. Tressa ran to get the phone, and Marcus proceeded to chase Ma Lizzy off the property. "Hello, yes, this is Ms. Bowers." "Ms. Bowers, this is Nicole Sawyer at the Belvedere. I called to apologize for the call you recently received from Mr. Bentley. I don't know why he called; he had no right. Everything is as agreed." Tressa breathed a sigh of relief. "Thanks for calling, Ms. Sawyer. Needless to say, Marcus and I were concerned about the mix-up and especially at this late date." "Yes, but there is one thing, Ms. Bowers; ordinarily, we do not accept packages from our clients for storage at such an early date. We will make an exception this time but ..." "Ms. Sawyer, I don't recall having any items sent to the Belvedere. We will be down to retrieve it as soon as possible." "That's not necessary, Ms. Bowers but feel free to come." Minutes later, Tressa heard a loud crash and Marcus screaming. Tressa ran to see what had happened and found Marcus lying on the ground under a trash can. "What in the world happened?" "A pack of dogs came running from out of nowhere; I couldn't get out of the way quick enough and fell in the trash cans." Tressa helped him off the ground and helped to clean up the mess. "How did you get rid of Ma Lizzy?" "When I opened the door and proceeded down the stairs, she hurriedly got into her car and took off like a bat out of hell."

Turning on the floodlights and walking around the property, they found small packages of Ma Lizzy's potions and tossed them in the trash. Tressa ran and got the anointing oil, and they walked around the property blessing their home, prayerfully removing any mojo she had cast on the property. "Lord, Marcus, what next? We can certainly say this marriage is getting off to an adventurous start." "Yes, and I need to go home and take a bath. I smell my yesterday's salami." "Well, before you leave, I need to update you on the latest news."

Father Brown called Tressa several days later. He told her Alesha said she had received a call from someone claiming they were Tressa Bowers, who said she would like to cancel the rehearsal date because she had secured a smaller venue. Alesha asked her if she was sure she wanted to cancel and tried to encourage her to keep the time slot because rescheduling would be difficult, but Ms. Bowers insisted. "Father Brown, I never called. Does Alesha have a copy of the date and time the call was made?" "Yes, it was recorded on May 2nd at 2:30 p.m." "I see, so how do we stand? I never found another venue." "No, don't worry, we did schedule another couple in that time slot; however we were able to give them an earlier hour and a few perks, and they accepted, so you're good." "My God, thanks so much, a weight has been lifted off our shoulders." Tressa wondered who had called and done this awful thing. One thing she knew for sure, "The devil was in their details." To keep the family from worrying, she chose to keep the matter between herself and Marcus and asked him to do the same.

The next week, Avery called Marcus with some unsettling news; his mother and brothers had decided to attend the wedding. He knew this would not be welcome news for Marcus, although he had relented and agreed to invite them, at this point Marcus seemed indifferent.

The week of the wedding, Avery was jittery and moody. Marcus and Les attributed it to the upcoming nuptials. They decided to spend an evening with him. Perhaps a home cooked meal and a movie would relax him and give him the opportunity to talk about what was weighing him down. Avery welcomed them. He paced and rambled about one thing or another. "Son, what in the world is the matter with you? I have never seen you like this. You act like a man on the edge." Avery invited his dad and Marcus to the kitchen where he had prepared a small feast. "This is enough food for an army. Avery, why did you fix this food? I told you we were going to do this. It would take us a week to eat all this." "I know Dad, I needed to do something, I feel frustrated." "Dad is it about the wedding? You don't have to worry it's all been taken care of, I promise."

Avery sat still, buried his face in his hands and let out a loud squeal and heart-wrenching cry. He pushed the plate away and threw the glass of wine on the floor. "Go away, I love you both, but I don't want any company. Please leave me alone," he said banging his fist against the table. He pushed himself away and went to the sitting room. "What the hell is the matter, Son? This is not like you; you're usually so composed and sure-footed." "Yes, Dad, I know. Good ole composed Avery, always doing the right thing."

Avery was sobbing so hard; Les thought he was going to pass out. Marcus was stunned and afraid. This was out of character for his dad. He remembered the times when he was a youth he would well up, and Avery would wipe his eyes and hug him, reassuring him that everything would be all right. Perhaps, he needed to step in and comfort and reassure his dad.

Before he could make a move, Les sat beside Avery and cradled his son. "Whatever the problem, Son, we can work it out. You need to talk to us; I promise we won't judge; we'll just listen." Marcus sat across from his dad and gently took his hands from his face. He sat looking in the face of his idol, his beloved father. He never knew a man so strong and loving. What could be the problem! Surprisingly, Avery held onto Marcus's hands, squeezing them as hard as he could. Bear with me while I get myself together." Avery sat up straight and wiped his eyes.

Les brought him a glass of wine. "Here sip on this, it might relax you!" Avery drank the entire glass of wine and closed his eyes. He leaned forward and whispered to Marcus; with tears flowing, he said, "Son, your father is a fraud and a liar. I have misrepresented myself for years, ever since your mother and I separated. No, ever since your mother left us. Marcus, I have tried to live my life as a Christian man. My dad, your grandfather raised me to respect God and my manhood, and I tried my best, but I failed." "How have you failed dad? I don't understand!"

Avery slumped down in a position of defeat. He took a deep breath, and to Marcus and Les's surprise, he said, "You never knew it, but I hate your mother. There, I said it, I hate her. I hate that I've put on a false face and lied. I didn't want her to come to the wedding because I would have to face the slut; she betrayed us. She tossed us aside." "Dad, all of this wasn't necessary. Why didn't you voice your feelings to her instead of putting up such a front? I wouldn't have held it against you." "Why because of God, my beliefs; I had to forgive, and; what kind of father would I be if I defamed your mother?"

Les walked out of the room and sat in the living room. He heard Avery go on and on about his feelings, and how he felt betrayed. Finally, he couldn't take it anymore; he marched into the sitting room with his arms folded and yelled "Avery, quiet! That's not the complete truth, and you know it. If you're going to unload yourself, tell the truth, the complete truth!" "What truth, Dad? I'm trying to be honest instead of truthful." "Son, it's about, one—infidelity; she cheated on you; two, rejection; she chose another man and two boys over you and Marcus; three, indifference; she acted like she didn't care; four, fear; you were a coward, you never confronted her because deep down you wanted her back, you loved her; five, anger; you could not forgive yourself for feeling like a coward and; six, you're bitter because you never let yourself love anyone else, until now!" You could hear a pin drop; Les had said it all. Let the cat out of the box. Avery was still; he sat staring at the floor. He composed himself and stood. "Dad, you have always been honest with me, straightforward and encouraging. Why now? Why didn't you give me what for a long time ago?" "You knew all these things, Avery. You wanted to be the martyr, and; you wanted Desiree to feel like she could come back. And; most importantly, you could not admit that you loved her deeply. You could not image she would leave you for another man. So, for years, you felt rejected and unworthy of any woman's love, always afraid you would be left. You strung Bonnie along all these years, not because she's not a loving and faithful companion but because, for the sake of your son, you wanted to be free just in case his mother changed her mind and came back; she never did. "Desiree had the nerve to marry another man and have two other children. She loved them and shunned Marcus except for birthday cards and Christmas gifts, which he rejected. And, you used God as a reason to hide your true feelings and give Marcus the impression that his father was fair and forgiving. Now Son isn't that the truth?" "Yes, that's the truth. But you left out one more crucial thing. Marcus, I deceived you. I hid behind your rejection of your mother. By that, I mean, I wanted you to dislike her, to reject her. I was too much of a coward to do it. I ask for your forgiveness, and I pray you don't think little of me."

Marcus was silent; he didn't know what to say. Forgiving his father was easy, but dealing with the reality of the situation was hard; He sat in silence. "Marcus, before you respond to your father, Avery you need to hear the rest of the story. What I never told you." Marcus braced for this revelation, now what. "I didn't want to lose you, Son. I knew Desiree was homesick and wanted to return to Italy. I feared you would return with her and take my grandson. Our maid, Molly, caught her several times on the phone talking to her beau and told me. You were so happy; I kept it to myself. Well, I caught them together dining in an out of the way cozy café. I confronted her; she begged me not to tell you, and I didn't on one condition—that if she decided to leave you she would not file for custody of Marcus. I knew if she really loved her child, no one could convince her not to fight for her child; she readily agreed. I didn't believe her. I was shocked when she decided to leave and not take Marcus. I felt bad but couldn't tell you about my proposition. I have been carrying this since the day she left. Now, I pray you can forgive me." "Dad before we let this go, I need to know what brought this on? What brought you to this point of confession?" "Marcus, I found myself belonging to two awesome families, the Bowers and Dallas clan. We're always so happy together, it's new and refreshing, and I love it. Most of all ... I envy your relationship with Tressa, and I've longed for one just like it. I realized I would never be happy as long as I lived a lie, this dreadful secret. When Tressa told us about the lady with the blue hair and her telling Tressa not to keep secrets, I couldn't help but feel that message was for me. I kept hearing it over and over again, don't keep secrets. But was it a secret? Yes, because I knew how I felt and purposely kept these feeling pinned up. It was time to be set free, and I knew I ... I had to confess in order to be free."

Marcus took charge; he knelt by the sofa, and Les and Avery joined him. Each man prayed, asking for forgiveness. When they finished praying, Marcus told Avery he forgave him. He admitted he didn't understand it all, but he knew that his father loved him and as quiet as it was kept, he knew his father was in pain. They had spent years protecting each other, running away from disappointments, hurt, and pain. Today was the day they would be set free. "Dad, from this day on we're free; no more looking back, no blaming each other. Let's start healing. And as for my mother, I think it's time I forgave her. I don't have to have a relationship with her, but I must forgive her." "I too must forgive her. So she left, I've lived a wonderful life despite harboring resentments. I want to be happy. "OK, we are all in agreement by the grace of God; from this day on, we will put the past behind and live each day with promise and strength that the good Lord has given us."

The hearts of the Dallas men were set free. They were on the road to joy and peace. Now they could get on with their lives. Except, one thing. "Pop, did I understand you to say Dad was in love? Are you Dad? And who is it? No, don't tell me, it can't be, not Jesse!" "No more secrets, no remissions, yes, I love Jessica Bowers. I don't know if she knows; I've never said anything to her. I hesitated because of you Marcus. I ..." "Dad, go for it," Marcus urged. "An hour ago, I probably would have rebuffed the idea, but I want you to be happy. Just pray about it." "But what about Ms. Bonnie?" "Ms. Bonnie and I called it quits months ago." "Was it because of Jesse?" "Not really, maybe, I don't know. We were on our way out long before Jesse came along. Dad was right, I hung on for the sake of hanging on, and in my own way, I cared about her. When I saw Jesse that night at the show, I swear Son, she won my heart." "Well, that's that, good luck with that."

Chapter ten

"Tressa tossed and turned, trying to sleep. When she finally drifted off, she dreamt she was walking down the staircase in her beautiful gown. The house and lawn were beautifully decorated; every seat was taken. She held Devan's arm to take the first step, and suddenly water rushed into the house flooding the first floor and slowly creeping up the stairs. Guests tried to run but were overtaken by the floodwaters. The water was now midway up the stairs. Devan disappeared, she was standing there all alone. She turned to run, but the waters were too strong. She tried her best to swim but found herself being pulled under. Finally, she swam to the top and yelled, "Jesus, help me!" She sat up in the bed, "Lord, what is going on? We're so close to the wedding. Please protect us from the evil forces that are trying to destroy our happiness, please, Lord!"

This was it, the rehearsal and rehearsal dinner, and then the big day. The entire family was in a joyous mood. Les and Avery were in charge of the menu for the dinner, and the ladies took charge of the decorations. The rehearsal was scheduled for 6 p.m. sharp, and Les wasn't taking any chances; he called everyone to make sure they were at the church and on time. Just before he could complete all his calls, his best friend called to check in on him. "Hey, man good hearing from you." "Back at cha, how's everybody?" "Ford, you should see this place, it's magnificent. Are you and the kids going to make it for the wedding? I won't take no for an

answer." "What do you think, I got a pink suit and ..."
Man stop lying; if you show up here wearing a pink suit,
I'll kill ya!"

Ford and Les communicated at least three
times a week. Keeping each other updated on current
affairs, their families and careers. Ford and Les served
in the air force together and retired at the same time.
Over the last thirty years, they kept in touch by phone
and visited each other as often as possible. Ford and
Marjorie had two sons, who were grown and pains. Les
hated hearing about the two ingrates. Ford had two
sons who graduated from West Point in good standing
and went on to become successful in the corporate
world. However, they were always borrowing or moving
in or making babies. Ford was man enough for them,
he believed in tough love. His sons eventually got the
point their father was not a pushover, and they stopped
begging and depending on him. Les was happy to hear
that Ford and Marjorie would be leaving early enough
to spend a couple of days before the wedding. Les said
his goodbyes and continued to make his calls.

Everyone responded accept Simone. Les
wasn't concerned; he knew the load Simone was
carrying; however, he wanted to be sure they were on
the same page. He called Marcus and asked for an
update. Marcus, in turn, tried to call Tressa, and she said
no one had seen nor heard from her but felt sure she
was all right. By 4p.m., still no one had heard from
Simone, and they were becoming concerned. Devan
decided to check on her. Then his phone rang, it was
Simone's number. "Finally, Simone, Simone where are
you? We've been calling and calling." Then there was
silence, "Simone, answer me!" Devan rushed over

to Simone's, calling the family on his way. Tressa and Jesse rushed to the door knocking and calling her name. Devan unlocked the door and to their horror found Simone's house a wreck. Devan called for backup and ushered Tressa and Jesse out of the condo as he searched for Simone. He heard a groan and found Simone lying on the floor by her bed. Her head was bloody, and her hands were tied behind her back. Devan told Tressa and Jesse what he had found. "Is my baby alive? Devan, answer me!" "Yes, Mom she has a pulse, she's alive. It looks like she has been lying here for quite some time." "She couldn't have been Devan, I talked to Simone around 12, and she was fine."

Simone was transported to Faithful General Hospital. After close examination, it was discovered Simone had a large gash that could have been caused by falling or foul play. When she finally came around, she filled the family in on what happened. All she remembered was bringing in her dry cleaning and being struck on the head. Someone was waiting for her in her condo. She did not see their face but was sure it was not a man. Then she remembered one thing; whoever it was had on an awful smelling cologne. She did not recognize it from anyone she had known.

The doctor assured the family Simone would have a whopper of a headache and knot on her head, but, she would recover with no complications. Devan decided to stay with Simone, and the rest of the family would attend the rehearsal. Les objected, he said he was sure he could walk down the aisle without a rehearsal; therefore, he would stay with Simone, and Devan should go. Simone, now drowsy, asked Tressa if she could speak to her. When everyone left, Tressa sat on the side of the bed as Simone held her hand. "Tressa, I love you very much. I am sorry for the things I've done to you in the past, but you know that I've tried hard to change, and I have. I wouldn't do anything like this for attention or to dampen your joy, please believe me! I want you to be happy. Marcus is a wonderful man, and he loves you to the moon and back. I think this is my punishment from God for the things I've done, and I humbly accept it, knowing you have forgiven me. And, Tressa, I think someone wants to stop the wedding or at least cause you sorrow. I don't believe this attack was about hurting you in a roundabout way. Don't give them the victory. You go to your rehearsal and have a great time." Tressa hastened to reassure her sister. "Simone, the thought of your sabotaging my plans never crossed my mind, and we will find out who did this to you. Now you rest big sister, and Simone, I love you too." Simone drifted off to sleep.

Before the festivities began, Tressa requested everyone hold hands and say a prayer for Simone. The rehearsal and dinner were joyful and perfect. There were toasts and congratulations offered to the future Marcus and Tressa Dallas. The Dallas men put on a show of shows. Tressa never knew they had so much talent; they sang and danced like pros. Avery led a love song "Some Enchanted Evening" that he sang to Jessica. She was speechless and beguiled. "Oh my, you surprised me Avery; I felt like a schoolgirl." "Really?" Avery smiled. "That's good; however, I want you to feel like, "my girl." Jessica didn't know what to say. Everyone was gazing at the two of them, waiting for Jesse to respond. "We'll talk about it later!" "You promise?" "Yes, I promise!" "After we're finished here ..." "No, maybe tomorrow. I need to think about what I'm going to say and how I am going to say it." Avery smiled, "You know Jessica, some things don't require much thought; think long, you think wrong." Jesse gave Avery a peck on the cheek and winked. "Don't worry, Dallas, I got this."

When Simone was released from the hospital, she and Devan went over the incident detail by detail but came up with nothing but that odd fragrance. Simone said it smelled like jasmine or cheap perfume. She thought she smelled the aroma when a group of church members visited her but wasn't sure. Simone did recall Detra was on duty and her visiting from time to time; perhaps she saw someone or could recall someone wearing the fragrance.

When Ciera heard Simone was hurt, she hurried to the hospital, frantic. "Hey, buddy, I heard you were hurt. I am so sorry. Is there anything I can do?" Simone rarely saw Ciera in tears. She gently knelt beside the edge of her bed and nestled up to her. "Simone, I don't know what I'd do if anything happened to you. I know I am a jerk, but I love you, buddy." "I know you do Ciera, I know you do. Do me one favor and ask around; see if you can find out who did this to me?" "I promise, I'll get right on it, you can call me Mrs. Holmes."

The wedding day finally arrived. The men were dressed in tailored suits. Avery objected to the fellows wearing rented clothing and purchased evening suits for all the guys. Julian and Maximillian (Marcus's best friends) were flabbergasted; they had no idea they would be so dapper but knowing the Dallas men they should have known better. "Dad, what am I going to have to sell to repay you for this suit? I don't have any money; you might have to wait for my next few paychecks!" Avery embraced Marcus. "My boy, your father always has an ace in the hole. I had money socked away for an occasion such as this. Money is no object!" "Why didn't you tell me that sooner big spender; I would have rented the extra extended limo?" "Yes, I know you would; I am not crazy, Son," he said smiling. The coordinator made the announcement. "OK gentlemen, you're on!" They stood tall and readied themselves for the grand entry. The church was beautiful. The coordinator did an outstanding job decorating. It looked like a sea of roses and candles. Devan told Tressa how beautiful she looked and how proud and happy he was for her. "Sis, I've never seen a bride as beautiful as you or seen a man as happy as Marcus. I wish you both years of happiness and many babies." "Thanks, Brother; coming from you, that means a lot.

You would mention babies on my wedding day. Tressa gave Devan a bear hug and kiss.

At the sound of four trumpet blasts, Jessica was escorted down the aisle, and from out of nowhere appeared a woman wearing a beautiful lilac gown, worming her way past the ushers and bridal party, and proceeding to walk down the aisle. It was Desiree; it couldn't be. Les and Avery immediately recognized her and without skipping a beat rushed forward, each one grabbed her by an arm and escorted her out of the church without anyone noticing and informed security not to allow her back in the church. Desiree performed; she screamed and yelled, fighting the security guards. 'I have a right to be at my son's wedding. Take your hands off of me."

"Miss, if you don't calm down, we will call the police and have you locked up for public disturbance." That's the last thing she wanted. She jerked away from the guards, found her rented car and sat motionless. Her sons would wonder what happened to her and come looking for her, she was sure of it.

Meanwhile, the wedding processional continued. After Jesse was Taylor, the junior bridesmaid, and the bridesmaids and groomsmen, walking side by side. There was a short pause and the trumpets blew again. Les and Avery slowly began to walk down the aisle. When they reached the front of the church, Marcus walked the aisle, very sure and proud. He was suave and sophisticated. Heads turned when the Dallas men walked the aisle, some of the women applauded and whistled. It went on so long the pastor made a gesture for the guests to quieten down.

Then two girls walked down the aisle ringing bells and announced, "The bride is coming." Two young men rolled out the runner. The center of the runner was satin and the edges were velvet. The guests slowly rose to their feet. When the doors opened, there was Tressa in all her glory and Devan dressed like a prince; he was gorgeous. All that could be heard were oohs and aahs. Marcus held his chest; he could barely contain himself. Julian whispered to Marcus, "She's stunning." Marcus knew Tressa was going to be beautiful, but this was beyond words. She was glamorous and radiant. She looked like she had been dressed by royalty. There were two girls carrying her train; it had so many crystals, it lit up the church. The guests were whispering, pointing and holding their chests in surprise and awe. When they reached the alter, Jesse, Simone and Devan held

Tressa's hand. When the pastor asked "Who give thee?" Jesse, Simone and Devan said, "Marcus, we are entrusting Tressa to your care. We expect you as a member of our family to be caring, honest, loving, and patient. You have proclaimed yourself to be a Christian man that is deeply devoted to the Lord. We pray that your spiritual beliefs be an intricate part of your marriage. All three placed Tressa's hand in Marcus's hand and took their seats.

When they were pronounced man and wife, Marcus gently kissed Tressa and held up both their hands as a sign of triumph. They jumped the broom and walked down the aisle on a runner that was now illuminated in big, bold writing and read, Mr. and Mrs. Marcus Dallas. To their surprise, Les substituted the limo for a coach and driver dressed in period clothes to take Marcus and Tressa to the reception. Bystanders and guests were taking pictures as they were slowly driven to the reception.

Les and Avery made the decision to tell Marcus that his mother and brothers were at the wedding and that his mother had attempted to walk down the aisle to represent him as the mother of the groom. Marcus was livid, outraged. He told Tressa what Desiree had done and informed her that he, his father and grandfather were on the way back to the church to make sure she and her sons were gone. Based on her behavior, they weren't sure she would not act up at the reception. Tressa was heartbroken; why would she pull this at their wedding? Detra assured Tressa that everything would be alright. She led her to the bridal suite and gave her a cup of tea; hopefully, to calm her nerves.

When Avery and Les reached the parking lot, Desiree and her sons were just pulling off the lot. Desiree noticed Avery and backed up so she could confront him. She exited the car so fast she stumbled. "You rotten dog, how dare you stop me from seeing my son! I came all this way to show my son love and support on his special day." She was yelling and shaking her fists at Avery as if he were a child. Avery couldn't take any more. From out of a deep and ugly place, he responded, "You no good piece of trash, you should be happy he allowed you to come in the first place." Storming up to her face, he uttered, "This was my fault, I encouraged him to invite you and his brothers, but I did it before I had come to my senses. "Let me tell you something, you have no right to be here. You were never a mother to my son! It took me years to figure out why I've been so compliant, so understanding; until I finally realized a few weeks ago." "Shut up, you spineless man; you encouraged me because you wanted me back. You wanted to hear me say I love you to you and the boy, but I didn't!" Holding her chest, she said, "I mean I didn't love you, I loved Marcus." "You're lying Desiree; if you loved him, all you had to do was claim him. Act like you wanted him, insist on joint custody. No, instead you sent token gifts and senseless cards with empty words and sentiments that he saw right through. He tore up every card and trashed every gift. Still I tried to encourage him to accept you, to include you in his life. Let me tell you something, you selfish, heartless b****; I agree I wanted you to come back."

Desiree lifted her head in agreement and pride. At the sight of her piety, he responded, "Oh no not for the reasons you're thinking. I wanted you to come back so I could torment you, make your life miserable and perhaps even humiliate you." "That's not why you were angry; it was because I chose Daniel over you. I wanted to go back home to my beloved Italy, and you knew that, but you wouldn't let me go. So I found someone that would go with me and be a real man to me." "A real man, Desiree, what you wanted was a fool, a puppet; someone to follow you around and give in to your every command. You stopped caring for me when you realized I wasn't going to be your lapdog. I was not going to demean myself for your so-called love. You quickly changed once we came to America. As for Daniel, he's the one that's spineless and pitiful. You could have found someone that wasn't such an Olga; he's so damned unattractive, one day he'll just be ugly anyway." "Why Desiree, why did you want to come here so badly? Marcus can't stand you, and I couldn't care less about you. Was it for his brothers? No, it was so you could go home and brag, not feel ashamed. I get it now, Desiree. Your family and friends don't know you left Marcus; you probably told them I wouldn't let you have Marcus and you put up a good front all these years by showing them you cared by sending gifts and cards. You made sure your folks saw you shopping and mailing gifts. Am I right? Of course, I am. And, I bet Daniel doesn't know the truth, the poor fool. Now, I am through; I've had my say. Goodbye and go to hell from my son and me."

Avery had no idea Marcus was standing behind him listening to every word. He was proud of his father. Marcus spoke, "Finally, the truth. Desiree, don't you ever call or come see me again. As for my brothers," Marcus approached Ethan and Franco. "I don't know what hold she has over the two of you but, if you don't cut the apron strings, she will suck you both down a dark and ugly path. You're welcome to call and visit but know I do not feel close to you. Perhaps in time things will change. I do consider you my brothers, and I pray in time we can become closer."

This was a big step for Marcus; he surprised himself. Ethan and Franco held out their hands, and when Marcus extended his hand they pulled in close and embraced him despite the look of disgust on Desiree's face. "Marcus, I am ashamed of my mother's actions today. We had no idea she was going to pull this stunt. Yet, we should have known she was going to do something to include herself. Avery was right; the family back home doesn't know your history, not even my father. He knows part truths, and he adores my mother. We will be leaving tomorrow morning and promise to keep in touch. Please don't hate us, Marcus, we too are pawns in my mother's evil plans." When they got in the car and drove away, Les, Avery and Marcus stood side by side watching the car as it drove off. "Well, Dad and Pop, let's go and enjoy my wedding day. I desperately need to find my wife."

The guests hurried to the reception. When they arrived, instead of the usual social hour before the bride and groom arrived, they were escorted to a room with theatre seats. The seats reclined and were covered in velvet. There were small portions of popcorn, hotdogs, boxes of candy and soda awaiting each guest. Once seated, Devan demanded their attention. "Ladies and gentlemen, we would like to present 'The Love Story: Tressa and Marcus Dallas.'" A big screen came down, and a film began. It was photos of Marcus and Tressa from their first date, vacation pictures, their new home, the engagement and bridal shower and rehearsal and behind the scenes of their preparation of their wedding. It was touching, enjoyable and moving!

When the film ended and the screen was lifted, there stood Marcus and Tressa. It looked as if they walked through the screen. The guests went wild. They had never seen anything like it. Another door opened, and there was the grand ballroom; it was magical. Soft lilac roses and crystals were centered on each table. The tablecloths were organza and satin lilac. They had video cameras throughout the ballroom that took candid pictures of each guest to be placed in beautiful picture frames. The pictures would be presented to guests prior to their leaving. The guests took their seats and were served warm cloths to wipe their hands after eating the tasty sweets. "Patsy, this is really classy; I wonder who they copied this from." "You better lower your voice; you don't want to be overheard criticizing Ms. Bowers or shall we say the new Mrs. Dallas!" They looked around, hoping they were not overheard.

Dinner was served. The menu was tailored to the palette of the guests. Marcus invited people from all around the globe. The menu included soul, Italian, Greek, Asian and Latino foods. Marcus and Tressa left the ordering of the food, with their final approval, to the venue chef, who did a fantastic job. There were three dessert stations, which included cookies, candy, ice cream and a fruit bar. Everything was over the top. Marcus and Tressa requested soft jazz music to play as the guests dined.

The photographer took unforgettable pictures. Marcus had given him a list of shots he desired. "Sir,

I've taken all the pictures you requested; I think we can now move inside to the reception." Marcus was annoyed. "Mr. Young, I don't just want the pictures; I want photos of the scenery and the entire bridal party; you know candid shots. Can you do that?" "Yes, yes, I can." He wants candid; I'll give him candid! Devan came rushing out the door. "Marcus brace yourself; we have another fire to put out." "What now? Lord, I can't take anymore. Is Tressa all right?" "Yes, Marcus, it's not Tressa though she could use your support about now. I was told to back off and let you handle this fiasco." Avery and Les were exhausted, what next. This is starting to seem like a brawl instead of a reception. When they opened the door, they froze.

Marcus couldn't believe his eyes. "Is this fool for real? Jesse and Vye hurried over to Marcus and asked him to be patient; they felt they could contain the situation. Gregory had entered the reception uninvited; he shuffled up on the dance floor and took the mike from the MC. He was seated on a stool singing a medley of sad love songs dedicated to Tressa. He was on his third song when Marcus arrived. No one could believe he was wearing the same type tuxedo as the ushers, allowing him to fit in. Tressa positioned herself by her husband and tried to usher him to the nearest exit, but Marcus wouldn't leave. "Marcus, please do this for me. I want to avoid a scene, and I don't want to give our guests a show." Marcus shrugged away from Tressa. "Not this time." This was their wedding day; first his mother and now Gregory Montgomery. Marcus was not going to allow Gregory Montgomery to sabotage their reception.

When Gregg finished his rendition of "Use to

be by Girl," his mother tried to convince him to leave the floor, but he shook her off. Marcus stomped on the dance floor, put his arm around his shoulder and thanked him for serenading the guests, all the while Gregg was struggling to break free. Devan attempted to assist Marcus by grabbing Gregg's arm, but Marcus gave him a cold stare, and Devan backed off. Marcus took the mike and thanked Gregg for entertaining the guests and literally dragged him off the dance floor down the aisle and out of the building while all the time Gregg resisted. Avery, in the meantime, asked the DJ to play some loud upbeat music. The DJ was well aware of what was happening and started a line dance. The guests readily responded; soon, they were all dancing to the latest line dance with their minds on keeping in step. Mr. Young, the photographer took every shot; all close ups of Marcus and Gregg, frame by frame.

They had almost reached the exit door when Gregg broke away from Marcus and yelled "You bastard, I'm going to get you, wait and see. I wasn't doing anything wrong. As a matter of fact, I'm sure Tressa was enjoying herself; she looked as if she was lost in time, remembering our wedding day. You forgot about that, didn't you, Marcus Dallas? You're not her first husband. I am the one who swept her off her feet not you; you glorified Romeo.

The groomsmen and Devan eventually joined Marcus. "What the devil is going on out here?" said Julian. "Marcus, do you need some assistance?" Before Marcus could respond, they lifted Gregory off his feet to throw him out of the building. Gregg fought them, and in his anger yelled, "You better watch out, Marcus Dallas, you better "watch out!"

Marcus realized those were the words sent to him in the email. He yanked Gregg away from the ushers and pushed him to the ground. "It was you, you sorry excuse for a man! You sent those emails warning me to stay away from Tressa. However, buddy boy, as you see they didn't intimidate me, we're married!" Getting to his feet, Gregg asked, "What emails? I didn't send you any emails; you take yourself too seriously. I don't know your email address, and if I did, I'm man enough to threaten you personally. I've been thrown out of better places you creep." "I know that's a lie," Marcus retorted, "you've never been to a better place."

When Marcus turned to enter the reception, half the guests were in the hall watching the altercation. Standing in front was Ma Lizzy and Ciera. Ciera was in tears; why was she crying? Perhaps she was being sentimental. The idea of someone causing such a disturbance was disheartening.

Les directed everyone back to the reception and Avery and Devan took Marcus to the men's lounge. Tressa joined Marcus and asked everyone to leave them for a while so they could relax. They tried to make sense of the day. They decided that it was God's will. He permitted every detail to take place, and they got through it. They stretched out on the sofa and held each other. "Marcus, do you realize we haven't eaten or danced our first dance? Let's get back out there and reclaim our reception, show everyone we are happy and undefeated." And they did. The rest of the night was perfect. As a matter of fact, it seemed as if a couple of new relationships were brewing.

Jonas Point Dexter and Maximillian seemed to have found their lady loves. Point Dexter was immediately smitten with Ma Lizzy; they were inseparable; they danced the night away. Who would have thought! What a pair! The guys were flabbergasted at Point Dexter's outfit. He was dressed in a brown polyester suit with a striped cotton shirt. His bow tie was black and brown plaid, and he was wearing cologne that smelled like a mixture of alcohol and roach spray; it was awful. Ma Lizzy was dressed in a long flowing green gown with a huge bow on the shoulder; a ridiculous silver hat with long feathers pointing off the top of it, and a pair of silver shoes that were at least four inches high. She and Point Dexter were having a good ole time. They cleared the floor. They jitterbugged, did the twist and then Point Dexter tried to do the moonwalk and fell. He jumped up and continued to dance, never skipping a beat. Les loved it. "This man is crazy, where did he come from?"

Marcus introduced Point Dexter to the family as the man that agreed to be a witness in the case against Tia. "Jonas Point Dexter is my name, and we won't talk about that awful day, let's concentrate on this wonderful occasion and my hopefully new gal." Marcus smiled. "What in the world is he wearing Marcus? He looks like a throwback from ..." "Dad, let's not go there. He's doing his thing, however strange." Maximillian shadowed Ciera all evening; wherever she went, he was there. Fine or not, she was already leery of him. She cornered Simone and asked, "How well do you know this man? He's been following me all evening; I get the feeling he could be a stalker." "I don't know him that well Ciera, you need to talk to Marcus; he's one of his best buddies." "Yea, I will."

Chapter eleven

Marcus and Tressa enjoyed all the wedding traditions. Avery caught the garter, and Jesse caught the bouquet. Avery took this as a sign; he thought this must be fate. Wesley didn't think so, but unlike Bonnie, he was a gentleman about the whole thing. Bonnie, on the other hand, made her position clear later when she and Jesse found themselves alone in the ladies' room. Bonnie was sitting on the sofa relaxing with her shoes off, admiring herself in a mirror when Jesse walked in. "Good evening, Jessica; I must say, you look very pretty." "Thanks, Bonnie, and you look lovely as well."

Bonnie closed the mirror and strode over to the sink to wash her hands. Just as Jesse was exiting the ladies room, Bonnie stepped in front of her. "Not so fast, Jessica; I am taking this opportunity to remind you that Avery is taken and has been for the last twenty-plus years, and I have no intention of freeing him." Jesse, feeling very sure of herself, responded, "Well, Bonnie, maybe it's time for a change."

Bonnie scowled. "Really, why do you feel he needs a change? Avery asked me to attend the wedding with HIM, that's why I am here, and for the record, Marcus is like a son to me. Do you really believe he's going to give me up for you? Get a grip woman. You don't strike me as a naive woman; do you think you're the first woman he's run after since we've been together?

And I am still here—the woman he always turns to." "Ms. Bonnie, a lot has happened today, and I am tired. But, I would like to take this opportunity to proclaim my intentions. Dear lady, I intend to take your man from you. So if you want him, you better pull out all the stops, because, for let's say, Valentine's Day, I expect to be the one he's sending the traditional two dozen roses to." Bonnie laughed. "Jessica, let me give you a sweet warning—like I said, many a woman has tried. I think you're in for a rude awakening, my dear. And, by the way, since we don't keep secrets, I'll inform him about this unpleasant chance encounter. He'll laugh and assure me that I'm the one he wants. As a matter of fact, his exact words will be, 'Really babe, how did she come to that conclusion'? "I'll say, 'I have no idea; perhaps it's because of the new Dallas/Bower merger; or the fact that she's made herself available and throwing herself at you ...'" Jesse interrupted, "Or maybe if I can be so bold, it will be because you have worn out your welcome. I don't recall throwing myself at Avery; I recall him feverishly pursuing me. My dear, you've done a terrific job, but your contract is not up for renewal." "We'll see Ms. Jesse; we'll see. I promise you I won't give him up without a fight; trust me on that!" Jesse saw the look on Bonnie's face; she was hurt and now silent. Tears began to stream down her cheeks. She walked to the door, opened it, and turned around and said, "You know Jessica, you might be right; you just might be right." Jesse felt horrible, why did she say those things to her?

She wanted to run after her and apologize, but her pride wouldn't let her. After all, Bonnie had known Avery for years, and he did bring her to the wedding, and she was part of his family. Jesse shared the incident with Simone. "Simone, what do you think; did I cross the line?" "Mom, obviously, Ms. Bonnie has been through this countless times and is always the victor. But didn't Avery say they had stopped seeing each other long ago? I feel he has the right to see anyone he chooses. But, on the other hand, she does make a point; he does seem to gravitate back to her. I think you need to find out where you stand once and for all." "But Simone, Avery and I have gotten so close in the past year. I've never felt he has been seeing anyone else." "Mom, I don't think you have the right to belittle her." "Simone, that was not my intention, she did approach me first, and I feel she got just as good as she gave." "Well, Mom, why did you ask me if you felt that way?" "I am sorry I did."

Bonnie was a striking woman, well dressed with some class. She could see what Avery saw in her. Jesse was feeling convicted; she felt awful she had made Bonnie cry. What would Avery say when Bonnie told him about their confrontation?" Jesse returned to the reception and saw Bonnie snuggled up against Avery; she smiled and took her seat. "Where have you been, I've been waiting for you?" "I am here now Wesley, let's dance."

Mr. Young did a fantastic job; the photos were awesome, although he took a few that were a little too candid. There was one of Ma Lizzy and Mr. Point Dexter doing the booty call, and boy were they calling. Ma Lizzy was livid. "This is awful; I demand another picture of Point Dexter and me. I can't show this to my church members, especially not the pastor." Mr. Young felt obliged and took a picture of the two of them in the lobby by the water fountain. "Now that's better, this will go on my mantle. Point Dexter was full of himself, did that mean he and Ma Lizzy were a couple?" He hoped so.

True to form, plans changed for the newlyweds. A major thunderstorm was expected, which caused a delay in the honeymoon. But it was a welcomed cancellation. Marcus confessed he was tired and could use some rest. It was ditto for Tressa. They used the time to open gifts, count their loot, rearrange furniture, look at wedding pictures, wrote thank you cards; reminisced about their wedding, and spent quality time alone in their beautiful home. They were grateful the family gave them space. No one visited the entire week. The airline called to reschedule their plans for the following week.

They were already packed and ready to go. Marcus did not tell Tressa their destination, only that she needed to pack for the beach and the mountains. Tressa didn't question it; she was ready to go. On the day of their departure, Les, Avery, Detra, and Devan went with them to the airport. Marcus gave Avery an itinerary and told him to only call in case of an emergency.

Marcus and Tressa had plenty of time to talk about the events of the last two and a half years. They tried to figure out who sent the emails, who left greasy chicken under her sofa pillow, and all of the rest of the crazy events that seemed to mount up. They discussed Ma Lizzie's bizarre personality; the coming together of the family; their future career plans and when they wanted to start a family. Tressa said she wanted at least one year to enjoy being married and the freedom to come and go. She also wanted time to build up her contractual clientele because once they had children she was going to work from home. Marcus agreed, and they laid out plans to make improvements to the property and assist their new combined families as much as possible.

Their honeymoon exceeded Tressa's expectations. The first stop was Fiji. They basked in the sun, swanned and danced the night away, then were off to Europe for fifteen days. Tressa was excited and impressed. He pulled out the red carpets. Each hotel was five-star, and when possible, he booked the honeymoon suite. On several stops, Marcus took Tressa to visit some of his clients. Tressa loved staying in the quaint village on the Isle of Capri in Italy; dining in the Eiffel Tower in Paris, visiting the Rock of Gibraltar in Spain. Every place was something out of a picture book.

On their visit to Greece, Marcus and Tressa were invited to dine with one of Marcus's coworkers, Chantelle Tibbs. She assisted Marcus with all of his Mediterranean conferences. Chantelle was married and had a beautiful four-year-old son, Bobby. She told Marcus she was opening her own consulting firm and asked him if he would consider being her representative in the States. Marcus told her he would give it some consideration and get back to her; he and Tressa had to talk it over. "Why would you need to talk it over with her? Aren't you the king of your own castle, or should I say, do you have a mind of your own? Because that's the impression you've always given me, Dallas." "Yes; however, in the past, I was the king of my own castle, but I didn't have a queen in the castle; now I do, and as for me having a mind of my own, I now share it with my Mrs." Marcus didn't understand Chantelle's abruptness but immediately made the decision without consulting Tressa that he wanted no part in Chantelle's business venture. He vowed to stay away from anything or anyone that could potentially cause any friction in his marriage.

On the plane going home, Marcus told Tressa about the proposition and his response. She patted his hand and said, "Good answer Dallas; I would have said the same thing. Quite frankly, I'm not so sure if she wanted you for your braun or your brains." Marcus smiled; he never thought of Chantelle as a love interest. Devan met them at the airport and took them home; he had to hurry back to work. When they entered the house, they were pleasantly surprised. In the hall was a bouquet of flowers, on the kitchen counter was a variety of their favorite foods, and in the living room was a recent video of the wedding. It was signed, the Family. What a thoughtful welcome home gift. Marcus took the luggage upstairs and heard Tressa screech. Lord, we just got home, what could Tressa be screeching about? "Marcus come down here; hurry, I got something to show you." Marcus almost fell down the stairs. "What is it, I almost killed myself ...Oh, my God!" "Isn't it awesome?" "Yes Tressa, yes it is."

They guessed both Les and Avery took it upon themselves to add an addition to the patio to the outer court of the house. It was Tressa's desire to have a large enclosed patio that extended from the living area to the kitchen. When the patio doors opened, it was an additional 100 feet of indoor/outdoor space. The patio had beautiful red brick; the wall extended up to about eight feet and the rest of the space was covered in indestructible plastic. The plastic would withstand gale winds, heavy snow, and rains. Electrical outlets were installed as well as a heating and cooling system, and indoor-outdoor lighting. Tressa and Marcus were ecstatic. Initially, Marcus had his reservations because of the cost, but as a gift he loved it. "Tressa, I wonder how much this set them back? Where did they get the finances to pay for this?" Tressa shrugged. "I don't know hon, but it's done. Let's just thank them and keep it moving." Marcus called his dad to let him know they were home and to thank him for the gift. "Hi Dad, Yes, we're back. The honeymoon was memorable; we had a wonderful time. No Dad, you won't be a granddad anytime soon. Dad, Tressa and I want to thank you and probably Pop about the patio; it is awesome. You know Tressa is beside herself. She's already planning a celebration just so we can use it." "Son, I don't know what you're talking about. You know I've been out of town, and I don't recall Pop saying anything about a project on your home. Besides, Son, I wouldn't do anything as massive as that without consulting you first." "Dad, are you kidding me? Are you sure?" "Son, I am dead serious; we did not do that work, now I wish we had." "Dad, can I call you back? I need to talk to Tressa?" "Yes, Son, please. Call me back. I would like to know who gave you such an extravagant gift."

Marcus hung up and pondered who could have done this. He was worried because whoever the benefactor was had to have access to their home. "Tressa, I called Dad to thank him and Pop for the patio, and he said it wasn't them, they didn't ..." "I know Marcus, here's a card. I found it on the hall table with the flowers. Guess who paid for the addition, guess? No, read the card."

Dear Tressa and Marcus: This is a token of my love and affection. I needed to do something above and beyond a mere "I'm sorry." I wanted to make you happy, very happy. Once Mom told me you wanted the patio, I made up my mind to have it done. If I overstepped, please forgive me. I pray this token of love will make the both of you happy and give you many years of enjoyment. Your loving sister, Simone Touched wasn't the word; she was grateful and felt a bit beholden. Marcus held Tressa and began to well up himself. "This is one of the grandest gestures anyone has ever shown me, Marcus. Simone has gone out of her way in the last year to prove she has changed. But this is beyond my wildest dreams." "Yours and mine, Tressa. Let's call and thank her ..." "No, Marcus, let's go to her; let's carry her something, perhaps a warm hug, but not now it's late, and we're tired."

The next day, they headed over to Simone's. When she opened the door, they found her in her pajamas at 3 p.m. Surprised, she welcomed them and gave them each a hug. "Hey Sis, welcome back; how is Mrs. Dallas? And, how is my handsome new brother-in-law? Boy, you know you look better and better, especially with that tan!" He actually blushed. Marcus had never been to Simone's home before. It was modestly decorated, but comfortable. On her mantle were pictures of the family at all ages. Marcus had never seen Tressa as a youth; she was adorable. His favorite picture was of all three siblings in their Easter clothes. A man (Marcus guessed it was their father), was standing behind them with his arms around the waist of a young small woman wearing such a large hat you could barely see her face, but he knew it was Jessica Bowers. "Simone, we had to come to personally thank you for the patio. We are touched and grateful. How do we thank you?" "I ... I ..." Tressa couldn't contain herself. "Tressa, you have given and given, and I've just taken. It was time I gave back. You deserve that and more. I've paid for the upkeep for the next five years. The contractors will come out and make sure the structure is safe, and any structural problems will be taken care of."

Ciera actually found the contractor and she paid for the warranty; so be sure and thank her. She wanted to remind me and you that she was family and felt she had not given you guys anything "special." "That was very kind of her and totally unexpected. We will be sure to thank her. For the record, we did bring her something back; perhaps her gift will let her know that we were thinking about her."

Simone took an envelope off the mantle and handed it to Tressa. "This is your guarantee; keep it in a safe place." Marcus took the envelope and hugged Simone. "Are you alright now Sis?" Simone nodded. "Yes, I am fine. I have to regroup." "Tell me, you sneak when did you have this done, and who else was in on this special project? "All of us actually," Simone admitted. "Mom, Devan, and Taylor. Taylor suggested they covered the patio with plastic." She jokingly said, "When you have children, if they are anything like you, they will eventually break all the windows and ..." "OK, you like telling folks I was a tomboy. That I was in and out of trouble until my early teens." "Is that a fact? I didn't know that Mrs. Dallas." "So are my girls going to be tyrants?" "Probably," said Simone. "Anyways, Sis, we brought you a souvenir, we hope you like it." Simone opened a small jewelry box. She gasped, "Oh, Tressa it's lovely." It was a gold pendant that said "Big sister." She held it to her chest, "I'll wear it always." She thanked Marcus and Tressa and caught them up on the events that happened while they were away. Tressa and Marcus stayed longer than they planned. This was the first time in a long time Tressa and Simone laughed and talked about issues other than the painful past. It felt good, they had finally bonded. God had answered their prayers.

Now that Tressa and Simone had become closer, it seemed Ciera had begun to spend less time with her. Simone asked Jesse for advice; after all these years, she didn't want to lose Ciera's friendship. Jesse told her she might want to give her some space. Perhaps she needed to spend more time with some of her other friends. Simone disagreed, "Mom that is not what I want. I miss Ciera, and I don't want her feeling like she's not wanted." "Simone, Ciera should be happy you are mending fences with your sister. You have gone out of your way to keep your friendship alive, what more can you do? Perhaps she wants to be left alone." "Mom, it's deeper than that, and you know it. Ciera and I have leaned on each other for years. She has kept my deepest and darkest secrets, comforted me when my heart was broken; took care of my child when I was too despondent. I've depended on her, and she has always come through. I can't do what you ask." "OK Simone, you do what you want. I've never talked against Ciera, but baby, she is troubled." "Let's call this conversation closed, please." "OK," Jesse reluctantly agreed.

Simone decided to find out what was troubling Ciera. She planned a wonderful day for the two of them. First the spa, then shopping and dining on the cruise ship around the harbor. At first, Ciera resisted but eventually gave in. It was just what the doctor ordered.

Slowly, Ciera began to talk. She told Simone

she was frustrated with her job; felt rejected by her old beau; her family was being their predictable nagging selves, and she felt like she could do nothing right. "Simone, why is everyone around me so happy and I'm so miserable? I feel like I am sinking; like I have no purpose. The people I love have abandoned me, and I can't figure out why. To be honest, I am jealous of you and Simone's new found relationship. When the both of you were at odds, you leaned on me, you depended on me, and I needed that, now ..." she broke off, hanging her head. I know I'm being selfish; I want all of your time because I've been so lonely." She took a deep breath and sighed, "Paul and I were doing so good, and then he stopped calling; then Maximillian and I started seeing each other, but honestly Simone, he's a bore and controlling in a nice gentle sort of way. In addition to that, my supervisor expects me to do everyone's job; I hate to go to work." Simone could feel Ciera's pain. "Ciera, you're like a sister to me. I've tried to reach out to you, but you rejected me, and quite frankly you were downright cruel. I feel at times you went out of your way to hurt me." "I know, I know; I can't apologize enough for my behavior." "Sister girl, from now on, please feel free to lean on me. But this must be a two-way street, Ciera," Simone warned. "I am sorry, Simone. Are we good now?" Simone nodded. "Yes, we're good."

The summer was coming to an end. The Bower and Dallas families converged at the "Dallas Estate." The patio was the main focus of family activities. Les and Avery couldn't believe their eyes when they saw it. "Boy this is something; I know this cost a fortune." "Yea, a small fortune," said Devan. "Simone is not hurting for money; believe me when I say she's not broke. Guys, let's not concentrate on the money, let's concentrate on those steaks and ribs." They were like kids in a candy store racing to see who would control the massive grill. "By the way, Marcus, a Mr. Crenshaw stopped by to see you. He said he came by to get his pay; he left this envelope." "His pay for what?" "Marcus, have you noticed the grounds? They're immaculate. He cut all five acres, planted bushes, trimmed hedges, and everything else the grounds needed." "No, Dad, I didn't pay it any attention." He opened the envelope. "Gee, he works cheap. I can't believe he did all that work for just three hundred dollars. Professionals would have charged twice that amount, this is a bargain." "Son, if he deserves more, give him more; don't shortchange him. He's an elderly man trying to make a living, and you can afford it!"

When Mr. Crenshaw received his pay; he was flabbergasted. He called Marcus to express his appreciation. "Mr. Dallas, I've never received this much for a job. You must be really pleased with my work. I was wondering, Mr. Dallas, am I going to be receiving this amount in the future or is this a one-time thing?" "Mr. Crenshaw, we'll work that out. My wife and I felt you earned more than the invoiced amount because of the extensive amount of work that was needed." "So, does that mean I can no longer occupy the basement quarters. You know I've been living there for the past twenty years." Marcus was stunned, "You've been living in the basement, Mr. Crenshaw?" "Of course. Didn't you see my bed and notice the place was nice and clean? I only stay there when I'm in town; when I have jobs outside the city, I stay at my other home." "Mr. Crenshaw, quite frankly, we were not aware you were living in the basement. Tressa and I will have to get back to ..." "But, does that mean you're throwing me out?" "Like I said, I must talk this over with my wife. Gee, do mysterious unfold." Tressa's answer was no. "I don't want him or anyone else living in our home." Marcus nodded. "Tressa, I concur. I'll call him in the morning."

Life for Marcus and Tressa was heavenly. They experienced all the normal ups and downs of married life. Tressa found herself lonely when Marcus was out of town. Fortunately, Tressa's job kept her busy, and her family kept her company. Her tenure with Lewis and Benton had ended prior to the wedding. However, her skills were so valued, they asked her to renew her contract for another three years. She agreed based on certain stipulations. The firm agreed to allow her to take on outside clients; to work from home at least two days a week; to have all holidays off; be considerate of her time when she decided to have a family and increase her salary by 15%.

Tressa was paying a high cost for the fringe benefits she had negotiated. She and Marcus were constantly scheduling and rescheduling plans. When they were home, they shut out the world. The money was good, and they had made a commitment to each other to spend at least seven to ten days a month with each other until their current assignments were complete. Tressa found herself away from home almost as much as Marcus. On an assignment in the Midwest for the firm, she became sick on the plane. She had been feeling poorly for some time. She had just gotten over the flu and thought she had recovered. Detra (now a physician's assistant) suggested she not take the trip; however, this case was a big deal. She would finally meet Daniel Langley, the Regional Director for Real Estate Licensing, who had assisted her in the past with some challenging issues.

Because Tressa was determined to go, Detra decided to accompany her; good thing she did. When the plane landed, Tressa was rushed to the local hospital. Detra called Marcus and informed him what had happened. She tried to assure Marcus that he did not have to travel to Wyoming. That she would keep him informed, and if they decided to keep her, she would contact him as soon as possible. Detra called Mr. Langley and Mr. Goode from the home office to let them know Tressa had been rushed to the hospital.

Meanwhile, Tressa was being put through the grind. Hours later, Tressa was informed that she had a bad cold, not the flu and that she was also pregnant, yes pregnant! "You have got to be kidding me; that can't be true, we've been careful. This was not on my radar." Detra stood looking at Tressa as if she didn't know how things worked. "Lord, I can't be pregnant! Wait until Marcus hears this; we had decided to wait for at least a year." Detra sat down beside Tressa and laid her head on her shoulder. "Sis, this is the day the Lord has made, let us rejoice and be glad in it." "You're right, Detra. Let us rejoice and be glad in it, and let's go home."

Tressa was quiet all the way home. For the first time, Detra could not read her. Was she happy, sad, disappointed or just in shock? "Tressa, I am happy, as a matter of fact, I am ecstatic." "Yea Detra you would be; you're the happiest person on the planet. I am in shock, and I am scared."

Detra frowned. "Scared of what? Women have been doing this for centuries, and if they can do it, so can you." Detra stayed with Tressa until Marcus came home. She gave him a thumbs up hug and a kiss, laughed and left. "What's wrong with Detra? She doesn't usually give me a hug and kiss me; I must be getting to her!" Tressa didn't find him funny. She sat stoic with a blank look. "Babe, what's wrong, what did the doctor say? You're not going to need an operation or something. Tressa your face is pale; there's no blood in your face." "Marcus, I'm pregnant!" Marcus seemed to have frozen as if in deep shock. "What?! Pregnant?" Then realization dawned. Ya-hoo! Oh boy! We're going to have a baby. Thank you, Jesus!" Marcus held Tressa so tight she had to break loose. "When is the baby due? Are you feeling alright babe?"

Marcus tried to encourage Tressa to lie down, but she couldn't. "Marcus Daye Dallas, we were going to wait; we were going to take a trip to Fiji on our first anniversary, remember!" "Fiji, Tressa are you crazy? We can't go to Fiji; we're going to have a baby!" Marcus was beside himself. He rushed to the phone and called Avery. "Dad, guess what!" Before he could answer, Marcus said, "You're going to be a grandfather. No, Dad, she just told me. I have to ask her—again. "Tressa, when is the baby due?" "In about seven months." "Dad, did you hear that; in about seven months." "Wait, Marcus, I have to call your grandfather; we need to put him on speaker phone." Minutes later, Les Dallas was on the phone. "Hi Pop, Dad is on the other line. You're on speaker phone." "OK, what's happening, is everything alright?" "Pop, you're going to be a great-grandfather!" "Me? praise the lord! When is the baby due?" "Tressa said in about seven months." "Now boys, we're going to have to get started preparing the room." Tressa went to bed as the

Dallas men went on and on for hours. After Marcus had hung up, it dawned on him to call the Bowers. "Hello?" "Hello, Devan this is Marcus." "I know who it is; what in the world do you want?" Devan asked, glancing at the clock, at MIDNIGHT?" "Wake up, I have good news, exciting news! Hold on, I am going to get Simone and Jesse on speaker phone. It's best I share the news with all of you at one time."

Once Marcus had the hook-up, he made sure he had everyone's attention. "OK, boys and girls, I found out today that I am going to be a father, and you're ..." He didn't get to finish as they all said in unison, "We're going to be an uncle, an aunt and a grandmother!" They laughed, and Marcus was surprised. "Did Tressa call you all?" "No, Detra called on behalf of Tressa." "Why didn't Tressa tell me?" "I figured you were preoccupied with the guys, and it was only fair she tell her folks." Marcus nodded. "OK, I'll take that. goodnight, Uncle, Aunt, and Grandma!"

Early the next morning, Avery and Les called their best pals. Les had to call Paul. "Hey, Paul, it's me. Les, call me back as soon as you get this message, I have important news." Avery called Chester his investigative buddy who lived in Boston. He too left a message. Paul was the first to call back. "Les, is everything all right? Are the boys well?" "Yes, Paul it's good news. I should have said they were fine; I didn't mean to worry you." Taking a deep breath, Les said, "Paul, I am going to be a great grandfather! My heart is overwhelmed. She's about two months pregnant; we'll find out for sure soon. They have to find a pediatrician and make an appointment as soon as possible." "I am excited for you man. Listen, we'll have to get together and build one of our hand carved pieces for the little one. I am willing to come down and stay until it's finished, what do you say?" "Sure, sure; let's wait until she's a little further along. I want to include the boys, you understand?" "Of course, I understand, just let me know."

Les asked Paul to give his wife and children his love and said he looked forward to seeing them. "Whew, that was harder than I thought." Les thought the world of Paul, but he could be a little overbearing. They had the same type of personalities and always felt distance helped make them best friends. Days later, Chester called and congratulated Avery on the blessed event. Avery was beside himself with joy. "Your first grandchild, I am happy for you. When is the blessed event?" "Tressa said in about seven months. Dad called Paul, and they plan to build a piece for the baby. I have to be there to referee; you know those two; they're so competitive." "Yes, I remember Avery. I feel sorry for you, that piece probably won't be completed until the baby is due." "You're right. I hadn't thought about that," and they both laughed. "I'll be calling Avery, keep in touch!"

As the men prepared to meet to build a dresser for the baby, the women were planning the baby shower. It seemed as though this was Jessica's first grandchild. It had been so long since they had held a newborn. The guys got to work on the dresser when Tressa was in her fifth month. That's when they found out Tressa was having twins. They had to re-adjust their dimensions and purchase extra cherry wood. Cost was not a problem, however; nothing was too good for Les and Avery's new baby. Little did they know the plans would change again one month later!

Tressa and Marcus decided to ask everyone to dinner to share their more recent news. Everyone showed, thinking it was a regular invitation to dinner. Tressa had a spread; they all gathered, holding hands to bless the food. Marcus took the lead. "Heavenly Father, we come giving you thanks for an awesome family and the opportunity to break bread together. We also want to give thanks for the blessed little ones you're entrusting to Tressa and me." Marcus cleared his voice and said, "We thank you for the three children, the two boys and one girl that will bring love and joy to this loving family." There was silence and confusion. Avery was the first to catch on. "Marcus, did you say three babies? Did I hear right?" Marcus glanced around the room, scanning the expressions on everyone's face. Devan's eyes immediately locked onto Tressa's stomach. "Tressa, this isn't a joke is it? Are you having triplets?" Tressa had envelopes with copies of the sonograms inside; she handed everyone their personal copy. After their reactions, Tressa wasn't sure this was such a good idea. Les did a Fred Sanford, and fell backward holding his chest. Avery's face became ashen; the blood had drained from his face. Simone took a seat, staring at the sonogram while Devan paced back and forth. "This can't be true; what are we supposed to do with that small dresser we've worked on for the past three months? I've got to call Paul; changes must be made ASAP!" Les exited the room to call Paul as Avery took a deep breath and with a big leap lunged at Jesse. It scared her, and she moved back leaving Avery lying on the floor between the dining room and kitchen. "Good God, Dad, are you alright?" "No, Marcus I am not; help me up. Why did you move woman? I could have split my head wide open!" "You scared me," Jesse said apologetically. "I didn't know you wanted to hug me, because if I did, I wouldn't have moved." "Well, can I, hug you? After all, we're going to be grandparents – together!" Jesse walked into Avery's open arms and returned his embrace.

Devan was dumbfounded; he didn't know what to do, but it was clear he was ready to explode when the doorbell rang. In walked Detra heading for the food when she saw the picture Devan was holding. "Get out of here! Is this for real? Devan is this real? Is Tressa having ...?"

Marcus and Tressa stood glancing at everyone, cherishing their reactions to the news. Les made his way back into the dining room with his cell phone and headed towards Marcus. Handing Marcus the phone, he said, "Here grandson, tell Paul the news; he doesn't believe me. He thinks I am joking." "Uncle Paul, it's true we're having triplets, two boys, and one girl. No, he wasn't joking." "Yes, I know how Granddad is, but he's not joking this time. OK, I'll tell him. Pop, Uncle Paul said he will call you back; he had to tell Ms. Odessa the news, and he said he has to take off more time so we can construct another dresser, this one for a girl." Les was in tears. He excused himself and sat out on the patio. "Please everyone, I know you're surprised, so were we. But I've cooked all this food; let's settle down and have a good meal while we absorb our good news." Avery knew why Les walked away; he was praying. Thanking God for the three little blessings and asking for good health for Tressa.

The shower was held one month before the birth of the triplets. Many changes had taken place.

Devan and Detra were engaged; Simone had accepted her call to the ministry, and Avery and Jessica's relationship had become public. He had declared himself to Jessica, but he must have forgotten to undeclare himself to Bonnie. Jesse didn't know how she found out about the shower; she wasn't invited because she wasn't considered a friend, and she certainly wasn't family. Yet, she did attend. She walked in with a huge box tied with blue and yellow ribbons. One of the attendants took the box, and Bonnie sat in a seat in the front of the room. She participated in all the games, sat at the table with the family, and when the attendant picked up her box, she jumped up, grabbed the box and proceeded to open it herself. "This one is from Avery and me." She asked for assistance, together she and the attendant removed the wrappings and did a Vanna White hand wave. It was a stroller for three. The guests applauded. "What a thoughtful gift; I know it took a lot of searching to find it." "No, Ma Lizzy, actually it didn't; these things are common online. It did cost Avery and me a mint, but it was our pleasure." "Indeed," said Jesse. It was as if Bonnie had declared herself a member of the family. Jesse was pissed. When the shower was over, Jesse and Detra were loading the gifts into their cars. There were so many gifts, they had to call for assistance; about a half hour later, Devan and Avery arrived. "My goodness what a haul; this is enough stuff for ten babies." "Yes, Avery, and it was nice of you and Bonita to give your daughter-in-law that awesome three-baby stroller. The guests thought it was really something." "Say what? What stroller?" "Bonnie announced that you and she were the givers of the stroller." Avery stroked his chin. "Yea, perhaps she was being polite or something; I don't know. I am going to have to talk to her." "You can talk to me now Avery, what do you want to talk about?" Avery didn't see Bonnie standing by the car; she had been listening inconspicuously. "Bonnie, this is neither the time nor place for a heart-to-heart. Let's take this someplace else." "No Avery Dallas, let's discuss this right here and now! I am tired of being jerked around by you. Tell Ms. Thing here if you're her man or mine because I am confused."

She waltzed up close to him and leaned against his chest. "Were you or were you not with me last week? Did you or didn't you take me to a formal affair and spend the night with me? Tell her dammit! She needs to know where she stands!"

Avery stood dumbfounded; what was he going to do? Since Bonnie demanded that he set the record straight right then and there, he decided to do just that, and it was not going to be pretty. He had one thing on his side, the truth.

Looking Jesse in the eyes, he took a deep breath. "Jesse, I did not tell you about going out with Bonnie last week. I purchased tickets to the annual school ball months ago; I was on the planning committee and felt obligated to show. Despite what she's implying at the time, I purchased the tickets, —Bonnie and I had not seen each other in months. She called and asked me to pick her up because her car was in the shop. I knew that was true because one of our friends had been transporting her to and from work. I saw no harm in giving her a lift. As for spending the night, what she neglected to tell you was when we pulled up to the house, it appeared that the front door was open. And upon our investigation, we discovered that someone had indeed broken in, they had broken in the back window and the house was ransacked. I called the police and decided to spend the night because she was so scared. She also did not say that I slept in the back spare bedroom and left early the next morning.

We found out the next day that her son was the culprit; he was looking for drug money. But, I swear nothing happened, it was innocent. I have not been seeing Bonnie behind your back. I told you I cared for you, and Bonnie and I were over, and I meant it! Jesse, I should have told you, but I swear nothing happened, and it was innocent." "You dirty rotten two-faced coward; how could you humiliate me like this? We have been together over twenty years. I am your common-law wife, and I was your babysitter, confident, cook, shopper, and now fool! When did you stop loving me, Avery? When did you say it was over, you deceitful dog!" "Bonnie, please stop this; you're trying to make it seem as if we had a torrid love affair. It's been over for years. Marcus is a grown man. You haven't babysat him in fifteen years. I've dated other people, and so have you. So now that I've found someone special, you're angry?" "OK, Avery!" she screamed. "You wanna play that game; you stand there and convince Jessica that we've only been buddies. 'Have we made love in the last six months?! Have you taken me to dinner?! I need you to tell the truth you bastard!" "Yes Bonnie; we had sex, and it was about a year ago, and yes, I've taken you to lunch." "Sex, is that what it was? Oh, my God is that what it meant to you?" She struck him with her fist, and he jerked away, grabbing his face. "Avery, are you alright?" she said mimicking Jesse. "Avery are you alright?" "Yes, he's fine. I've struck him before, and he liked it. You'll find out he's a real tiger."

Jesse could tell Avery was angry. The blood drained from his face, and he began to breathe hard; his chest was pumping up and down, and he now had his fists balled tight. Jesse grabbed him by the arm to pull him away when Bonnie pushed Jesse hard up against him, and they both stumbled. That was enough for Jesse, she got up and grabbed Bonnie around the neck and started choking her. Bonnie was struggling to pull Jesse's hands away from her neck when someone grabbed Jesse from behind. "Stop this; Mom stop. What's going on?"

Devan pulled the women apart as Avery was regaining his composure. "Take your hands off me. I can take care of myself. And aren't you a member of our finest?" "Well, Officer, I want this woman arrested; she tried to kill me. You had to pull her off of me and don't deny it!" "I didn't see a thing! I was taking gifts to my car when I heard a commotion. I came over to find Mr. Dallas struggling to stand and a bruised face. I asked Mr. Dallas what happened, and he said you hit him and pushed this lady to the ground. Now that's my story, and I am sticking to it, Bonita." "So you win again—I better not ever see you alone, Jessica Bowers; I'll kick your behind. We'll see who the better woman is!"

As they walked back to the car, Jesse called to Bonnie. "Bonnie, wait, here's something for ya!" She dragged the stroller from the car and kicked a hole in the box. "Get your money back and buy yourself a personality!" "What in the world happened?" Devan asked bewildered. "I'll explain later, Devan; I've had enough for one night." Avery was embarrassed.

Nothing like this had ever happened to him. He was a man of class; he now feared Jesse would dump him. He had to get through to her; he couldn't lose her. Later that week, Bonnie called Marcus to plead her case. She cried and confided in him, telling him intimate details between her and Avery; promises he made and did not intend to keep. Little did Avery know that Bonita Dandridge was thinking about suing Avery for breach of promise. "Ms. Julie, what is that going to get you? You have admitted that the two of you had moved on, don't you think that would come out in a public hearing? And, that you have been with someone else." "So you're turning on me too. I should have known, you ingrate!" She called Marcus a foul name and slammed down the phone.

That's it; Ms. Julie was history. Marcus decided to support Jesse and Avery's relationship by being a go-between. He had seen things slowly evolve between Jesse and his dad and knew what he felt for her was real. In the end, they didn't need his assistance. Jesse and Avery had a good foundation. Avery and Jesse agreed to limit communication and meetings with their ex's as much as possible; consequently, their relationship grew stronger and stronger.

Chapter twelve

Tressa was about to blow; eight months pregnant and tired. Unlike many other women, she found it hard to admit she was not enjoying being pregnant, or rather she had her good and bad days. The kicking was unbearable; her feet had swollen two sizes; her appetite was humongous, and she had gained an enormous amount of weight. Yet, Marcus thought, she was the prettiest pregnant woman he ever saw.

Marcus wanted those babies, and he did whatever was humanly possible to make Tressa comfortable and happy. Tressa was on to him. She jokingly told him she knew he would swim the English Channel if it meant his being a father. "Ain't no shame to my game Tressa; I want three healthy children but know Mrs. Dallas, I want you more." Tressa was touched. Perhaps he was just trying to be a good husband. "Babe, we're coming down to the wire, one more month. We've had months of bliss; soon there will be three screaming babies in the house." "Yes, and a house full of folks day and night!" "Don't knock it, sweetie, we'll need all the help we can get." Marcus had a thought. "By the way, Tressa, Pop will be moving into the guest house for a while. Mr. Crenshaw moved out and left the place neat and clean, but it's in need of a paint job. Pop has hired a paint company, but he wants to know if you will approve the color choices. I told him to paint it off-white and be done with it, but he said he wanted to get your approval." "Paint Marcus; really. I don't care what color he paints it; I'm not going to be staying there." "Tressa, you say that now, but ..." "Marcus Daye Dallas, I couldn't care less. Now, please get me my snacks and don't forget the snickerdoodles." Marcus shrugged. "OK, Tressa, whatever you say." By now, they could write a book. Tressa had so many mood swings and cravings; they couldn't keep up. The babies' room was perfect. Each baby had a beautifully crafted crib and dresser. Marcus often sat in the rocker staring at the cribs knowing that soon he would be holding his children. "Lord, thanks for our babies and help Tressa through the pregnancy, and please, continue to give me patience!"

Sunday was Women and Men's day at Second Baptist Church. The family tried to encourage Tressa not to attend, but she was determined. Marcus preferred that Tressa stay home for numerous reasons. First, he feared she didn't have a dress large enough to wear; second, her feet would eventually hurt, and third, she would most likely fall asleep.

Still, she was determined. She tried on dress after dress, but nothing fit. Discouraged, she convinced Marcus to purchase her a suitable outfit. "Tressa, please don't ask me to do this; you're just going to be angry with me when I come home with something you don't like or can't wear." Tressa said nothing; she looked at him and leaned from side to side, which meant, "Now Marcus!" He got the point. Since the women were not available, he called Devan, Avery and Les for support.

At the appointed time, the guys converged at the nearest mall looking for a maternity shop. "Dad, this is a store for large women, let's try this one." "Marcus, are you kidding?" said Devan. "Son, why did you drag me down here; I thought we were going to purchase a maternity outfit. These are clothes for plus size women." "She is plus size, and Avery, this is not about you, it's about Tressa; don't you want her to look good tomorrow?" Yes, Dad, I do, but this is too much." "Avery, I am your father, and Tressa is your daughter; now we're going to find her an outfit, and not just any outfit, one that will showcase her and that big belly." They searched the mall and finally found an outfit befitting a queen. "Pop, do you see how much this cost?" "Are you crazy—for one outfit?" Les calculated. "Let's see; if we each chip in 75 dollars, we can pay for this baby and go home." "I don't have 75 dollars, said Devan ..." "... and I don't have any cash," said Avery." Les was disgusted. "Between the four of us, we don't have 300 dollars. What did you all come for? Marcus, it's your wife, and Avery, your daughter-in-law!" "Lord, this is like a circus; I'll pay for the dress, and I want my money back." "OK, Pop, thanks. I'll fix you up as soon as we eat that dinner that you're going to purchase."

The guys went to the nearest 'all you can eat' buffet. Despite the annoyance, Les was proud to pay for Tressa's dress and take the guys to dinner; he felt needed and appreciated. They laughed and joked about how Marcus was going to react when it was time for the birth of the babies. This was Marcus's posse; he couldn't have asked for a better class of men to be in his life. Marcus's phone started beeping; it was a text message, but he couldn't make out the name. "Who in the world is this?" "It's not Tressa is it?" "No, Devan, it's from Nathan, but no last name. It says to call Nathan immediately; it's urgent." "Let me see the number, Son, maybe it's for me; I know a Nathan." "Dad, why would

he be calling you on my phone?" "Well, call him back."
The guys were all leaning across the table in anticipation.
Marcus dialed the number, but he could barely hear the
person on the other end. "Hello, this is Marcus. Who am
I speaking with?" "It's Nathan; you know, Tia's father."
"Yes, Hi Nathan, what can I do for you?" "I can't talk
right now, but be aware, be aware!" Marcus rubbed his
brow. "It was Mr. Brooks, Tia's father. What could he
want?" "It probably has something to do with Tia and
one of her crazy antics, let's eat." Marcus didn't let on,
but he was concerned. Nathan never called him unless
it was serious. But for the sake of the guys, he pretended
he had put it out of his mind.

That evening while the Dallas men were busy
putting the finishing touches on the dresser, Marcus
received another call from Nathan. "Nathan, sorry I
couldn't return your call. How can I help you?" "Marcus,
I must see you, it's important; no, it's imperative. You
need to know ..." "Nathan, Mr. Brooks, Nathan ... are you
there? What do I need to know?" He hung up or
something, the line went dead. Avery and Les stopped
what they were doing, "Is everything alright Son, who
was that?" Marcus rubbed his brow. "It was Mr. Kingsley,
Tia's father. I was talking to him and nothing, he stopped
talking." Marcus called him back; someone picked up
and said hello and then hung up, it sounded like Tia.
"What is going on, this is unusual; Dad what should I
do?" "Leave it alone, Marcus; if Tia is involved, it's got
to be bad." "I think something is wrong; I'll call Tia's
mother." He called her and the phone continuously
rang, and the answering machine never came on. "This
is strange, but, what can I do?" Marcus took Avery's advice
and tabled the matter. He decided to call the next

day; perhaps it was just a coincidence. Just before leaving for church, Avery received a text message from Nathan; it read, "Avery, I know this is a bit mysterious, but I need to see you before church today, about 10:30 if possible. Meet me on Hackabee and Maine located a few blocks from Second Baptist Church." Nathan Brooks "Oh no, he's not going to involve me in another one of his family's sick dramas." Avery, called Les and Marcus and informed them about the email and request. They immediately responded back. "Dad, I have to take Tressa straight to church. You will have to handle this. Please keep me abreast of any troubling circumstances. Marcus" "Avery, I'll meet you at the location by 10:00. Call Devan and have him meet with us as well. Les Dallas" "Nathan, I'll be there by 10:30, Avery."

Avery, Les, and Devan arrived at the appointed location by 10:15. At exactly 10:30, Nathan pulled up at the lot. Avery could see several other people in the car with him. "Hum, what is this "Shootout at the O.K. Corral?" "Yea, and on a Sunday; maybe we should have said our prayers first!" said Devan. "It's not too late, let's pray." Les said a prayer, and they exited the car to meet Nathan. "Good morning Nathan; you know my father and son-in-law." They shook hands. "You didn't need to bring reinforcements, Avery; I didn't come for a shootout." "I see you have your posse!" "Posse, you've got to be kidding, those old men couldn't fight their way out of a paper bag. They are church members I pick up every Sunday to take to services." For some reason, Devan didn't believe Nathan but backed off. "With all due respect, I need to talk to Avery privately; time is of the essence." Les and Devan sat in the car and waited for

Avery. Within minutes, they heard loud shouting and saw Avery heading towards the car. "Let's go, we need to get to the church. This is something that fool could have told me on the phone; I think he likes trouble." "What's wrong Avery?" "Dad, we're only a few blocks from the church; I'll tell you when we get there."

The car squeaked, turning the corner like a bat out of hell. Within minutes, Avery had parked the car and ran in the church, but it was too late. Rev. Rayford had asked all visitors to stand, and if they would like to walk the aisle to give a welcome address. There she was dressed in black just as Nathan said. It was Tia, ready to give her stunning news to the entire congregation. As Tia's mother watched, panic-stricken, Avery thought fast and beckoned Devan to follow him. They hurried down the aisle; Devan stepped in front of Tia, turned her around and gently pushed her back down the aisle and out the door as Avery followed. Rev. Rayford uttered a sigh of relief and moved the service along.

Nathan hurried by Tia's side to comfort her. Victoria interceded; knowing what the secret was, she did her best to persuade Tia to tell Marcus and his family privately. "Tia, what you attempted to do was very cruel and how your father could support such foolishness is beyond me. Is there any shame in either of you? Tia, I thought we raised a strong, independent, confident woman, but I see you're a vindictive, mean-spirited adolescent, and I'm ashamed of you. And Nathan, what are you going to do when the world learns Tia's secret? Though it's nothing new under the sun, you've always presented our family as upright and moral. Wait until they find out we have dirty laundry; what do you think they will think of the great Judge

Brooks?"

Tia sat in her parents' car smoldering; how dare they interrupt her plan? It was imperative she set the record straight, now! Maybe this was not the right time and place; she didn't care; the hell with the Dallas family, what about her?

Marcus and Tressa and the Bowers decided to take Tressa home; they had no idea what Tia had up her sleeve, Tressa was eight months pregnant, and the health of her and the babies was their main concern. Tia saw them as they pulled off. This was her chance; with her parents still in church; she decided to follow the Dallas's home and let them have it. Out of his rear-view mirror, Marcus noticed Tia following them. He pulled over to the side of the road just blocks from their home. "Marcus, why did you pull over, what's wrong?" "Tressa, we have a situation that has just caught up with us! Please stay in the car." In the meantime, the Bower clan pulled up behind Marcus to find out what was wrong. Before Marcus could explain, Tia exited her car and casually leaned against the door, knowing Marcus would come to her. This was what she wanted, his undivided attention. Devan joined Marcus and Jesse, and Simone got in the car with Tressa. "Simone, should we call Avery and Pop?" "No, not now, let's see what happens."

As Marcus approached, Tia smugly made eye contact. "I thought you'd pull over; you're wondering what all the hell is about. Let me tell ya! I want that hussy of a wife of yours to know ..." she paused, "... Oh no, this is for everyone to hear! I want the entire family, the collaboration to hear my news. I want you all to gasp and pine and be blown away, especially the old man!" "Tia, this is the only audience you'll get. Say what you have to say or we're leaving." Unfortunately, Jesse decided to call Avery, who called Les, and they were on their way. "OK, everyone gather around, I have something to say. Jesse and Simone played along, but Tressa refused to join them. When Tia saw Avery and Pop pull up, she took a deep breath, waved them over and smiled. "Now that the gang's all here, watch yourselves; get off the road because if a car don't kill you, what I have to say will. I am not going to beat around the bush any longer. Marcus Daye Dallas, I want you to know that the three little Dallas's will not be your first born children. Your firstborn was Marcus Daye Dallas, Jr., born July 3rd, nine years ago. He is buried at the Chimes Cemetery in Pasadena, Maryland. She threw a handful of photos at him. "Look, see for yourself, evidence." Marcus stumbled backwards, the blood drained from his face. "Look at the great Marcus, he's pale; I didn't know you could lose color, I am proud of myself." Marcus sneered. "Tia, you're simply a poor looser. This stunt of yours is useless. I am not coming back to you, and whatever you've done, will not destroy us." "I don't want you back, Marcus. I want you to hurt! And, I don't care how close you and tubby are, I got the last laugh. I carried Marcus, Jr. for nine months. It's not my fault he died; I was a good mother!"

Everyone could see Tia was becoming unraveled. She screamed and yelled and cried. Despite her arrogance, they all felt sorry for her. Les and Avery patiently huddled around Marcus as Devan picked up the pictures. "See I wasn't lying. Look, see my gigantic stomach, and turn the picture over, notice the date! Laughing wildly, she said, "They are time-stamped by the camera ... they are not fakes, boys and girls! Oh, and take a look at the picture of me and your son in the delivery room. Tia began to scream. He was born while you were away, helping the poor in some godforsaken country!"

From out of nowhere, the church van appeared in which Tia's parents and Rev. Rayford emerged. "Tia, what's going on; what stunt are you pulling now?" "Rev. Rayford, this is none of your business, please back off." "Tia, that's no way to speak to the Reverend, you apologize to him, right now!" Rev. Rayford interceded, "Please Mrs. Brooks, she's right it's none of my business. I simply transported you here because Tia took your car." He approached Marcus and the family and told them to feel free to call him if they needed anything, and drove off. "Gee, that was your usual nasty self Tia, the pastor was only trying to ..." "I know what he was doing Mom; I do not want him to know my business, and I don't think the Dallas and Bowers do either!" "That was for me to decide Tia," Marcus said. "Unlike you, right now, I could use some spiritual guidance." "Yes, Mr. Holy-err-than-thou, born again, sanctified, Marcus." "Thanks, Tia, I'm happy you noticed, and it's all because of the good Lord and my wife. Now, let's get back to these pictures and my alleged child." "Alleged? That was your baby; Dad tell him! Show him the documents!"

Nathan was standing there holding numerous envelopes. "Marcus, first I need to let you know that Tia's mother and I knew nothing about this until a few weeks ago. She initially told us the baby belonged to her roommate, and we believed her. Then, a few days later she confessed it was her child. We were shocked and hurt, please believe me." He slowly retrieved one of the folders from the envelope and handed it to Marcus. He and Tressa opened it. They looked at several pictures and examined the documents. They couldn't believe their eyes; was this real, did he have a son? Nathan decided to give Marcus all the envelopes and suggested he not open them on the side of the road. "Yes, that's best, Mr. Brooks." Victoria put her arm around Tia and suggested they leave. Nathan again asked for the families' forgiveness as they prepared to leave. Both families proceeded to the "Dallas Estate." It was like a funeral procession. The family was saddened by the news but knew they had to support Marcus and Tressa. The first document was a birth certificate. Baby boy: Marcus Daye Dallas, Jr., born July 3, 2005, 7:30 a.m. at Richford University Hospital, Va. 7 pounds, 6 ounces. Mother: Tia Brooks, Father: Marcus Daye Dallas. Buried: Fieldcrest Cemetery, Va. Les took the certificate and read it over and over again, scrutinizing each detail.

The second document was the results of a DNA test. This document named Marcus Daye Dallas as the father of the baby, and the last document was a certificate of death: This certifies the death of Marcus Daye Dallas, Jr. Died: January 20th, 2006. 3133 Rinehart Road, Virginia. Cause of Death: SIDS. "No, no, no, this can't be true. Dad please, this can't be true! How could she do this? Did I really have a son? Why didn't she tell me? Shaking his head, he said, "Lord, please help me." Tressa cuddled up to Marcus, doing her best to console him. "It'll be alright babe; we have the Lord on our side. Let's put this stuff away for the night." "Son, we'll get to the bottom of this. Right now, you need to rest."

Jesse put Tressa to bed; Simone prepared dinner, and the men sat on the veranda reading and re-reading the documents and looking at the pictures. Marcus lay on the sofa in the family room. When Detra arrived, she gave him a mild sedative, and he eventually drifted off to sleep.

The next day after examining all the documents, Avery knew in his heart it was true. Surprisingly, he couldn't find it in his heart to hate Tia. He pitied her and didn't believe she harmed the baby. But, how did he come to terms with the fact that he never got to meet this firstborn grandson? Les and Devan were angry. Not that the baby passed, but that Marcus and the family had a right to know the child; to welcome him in the family, and to hold him. They had a million questions. Was he baptized? Was he a happy baby? The last packet of documents and photos answered a lot of their questions. There was a progression of pictures depicting the baby's birth and growth. Most of the pictures were of baby Marcus in the delivery room just before he had been cleaned and put in his mother's arms. There were many of Tia holding him, playing with him, and him laughing and smiling. There were a few of him trying to crawl, playing with his feet, eating, bathing and him wearing a cap, the same way Avery put on Marcus. His room was immaculate. On the wall in large letters were his initials. He looked just like Marcus as a baby. He was long and had a head full of black hair. "Well, I hate to admit it, but this is my great-grandson. He looks just like Marcus, and here are the documents to prove he's the father. Tia also included a lock of the baby's hair.

Finally, there was a picture of the baby's headstone. Marcus didn't see that coming; he dropped the pictures and closed his eyes. He had a son, a beautiful boy full of life. What would he have been like or looked like? "My grandson, I pray he's buried someone warm, under a tree to shield him from the elements. I know this has got to be hard on you, Son." "Yea, Dad it is. I pray I can one day forgive that woman because, at this moment, I hate her guts and care even less for her parents." "Marcus, they said they knew nothing about the pregnancy; do you think they're lying?" "I must confess Dad, I have my doubts."

Marcus knew he had to verify all the documents Tia gave him. DNA was a no brainer. He found some old letters she had written, and he supplied saliva and the baby's hair for testing. They also contacted the cemetery to verify the burial of an infant named Marcus Day Dallas, Jr., and contacted the funeral home that Tia claimed received the body. Within a week, all inquiries were in. Marcus asked Tressa to open the envelopes and give him the results. "Babe, according to the test and inquiries, you are the father of Marcus Daye Dallas, Jr. and he is interred in the Fieldcrest Cemetery in VA." Marcus was downcast. "Well, that's that; she wasn't lying. I have to let everyone know."

The following Sunday after church, both families gathered for prayer before heading to Virginia. Marcus rented a limo and driver because he wanted the family to relax and not be distracted. Les was extremely tense. Marcus surmised it was because he feared everyone's reactions, especially his own. Avery and the Bowers were silent; there was no small talk. The radio was turned to a Christian station and every so often, someone could be heard tapping along with the music. When they arrived at the cemetery, they were struck by the beauty of the grounds. The entire driveway was covered in red brick and lined with flowers. Every fifteen to twenty feet were benches; it was so peaceful and serene.

The owner requested the groundskeeper escort the limo to the gravesite. It was just as Avery had hoped.

A tiny grave nestled under a tree with branches hanging over it as if protecting it. The family surrounded Marcus as he took a deep breath and knelt beside the grave. The headstone read: RIP OUR DEAR SON Marcus Daye Dallas, Jr July 3, 2005 – January 20, 2006 Love Always Mom and Dad

Tia Brooks – Marcus Daye Dallas

Suddenly there were wails and loud cries. Marcus fell on the grave crying. "Son, we're sorry, we didn't know, we didn't know!" Stroking the grave, "I wish I could have known you for just those few months. As you can see, you would have been surrounded by people who loved you. Please forgive me, I didn't know." Avery lifted Marcus off the grave. "Come on, Son, get up, you're going to cry yourself sick." Jesse and Simone comforted Les and Avery. Devan sat Marcus on the bench as Tressa retrieved the flowers from the limo. He sat there not wanting to leave his son. "Marcus it's time to leave. You know where he is, you can come see him as often as you please, but for now we must go."

The ride home was livelier. Avery and Jesse sat together holding hands; Marcus laid his head on his father's lap and fell asleep, and Devan rocked Tressa, comforting her while Simone quietly prayed. In a twinkling of an eye, the Dallas family had changed. The Dallas men were no longer awaiting the arrival of their firstborn children, grandchildren and great-grandchildren, but the arrival of three babies that would light up their lives and carry on their bloodline.

Chapter thirteen

Tressa had waited nine months for this blessed event. Now laying on the bed in pain, her only desire was to get it over with. "Marcus," she yelled, "Call Dr. Purnell, it's time!" Not a second later, "Marcus did you call him?" as she tried desperately to get out of the bed. "Answer me, man!" "Yes, Tressa, I called. Dr. Purnell is not at his office; his assistant said he's out of town." "Out of town, that can't be; he knew I was due, where is he? Call him, get him on the phone! Marcus," she yelled at Marcus once more, and everything went silent. Lord, I'm so glad she stopped yelling. Marcus became curious, he tiptoed up the stairs and saw Tressa kneeling beside the bed. Running to her side, he discovered there was no movement. "Tressa! Tressa!" He yelled and shook her; she did not respond. Her body actually went limp. "Oh, my God." He picked her up and headed towards the stairs when the doorbell rang. In a frantic voice, Marcus yelled, "Who is it?" There was no answer. Marcus carefully carried an unconscious Tressa downstairs. "Dear Lord, please help me!" cried Marcus. When he reached the bottom of the stairs, the door flung open; it was Devan. "Devan, man; am I glad to see you." Devan saw Marcus standing there holding Tressa in his arms. "What's wrong with Tressa?" Marcus shook his head. "I don't know. One minute she was calling me, and then silence; she passed out. We have been to the hospital three times in the last two days. Dr. Purnell sent her home; he called it false labor or some such nonsense. Anyways, we're headed to the emergency room. I called Dr. Purnell; he's out of town." "OK, Marcus, let's go! Follow me!" Devan put on his siren as they raced to the hospital. Upon arrival, Marcus scrambled to get Tressa out of the car, but Devan stopped him. "Wait Marcus, let's get some professional assistance." Devan ran to get help. Flagging down the first person he saw, he said, "Hurry my sister is pregnant and has passed out. She's nine months pregnant, but she's a few weeks early." A team of EMTs were just pulling into the hospital. "How early?" the attendant asked. "Well, she wasn't expected to deliver until the end of the month." Running, Marcus, motioned the medics to the car. Two doors burst open, and a medic emerged running with a bed. They carefully removed Tressa and transported her into the hospital; she was still unconscious, and her breathing had become shallow. Marcus called Dr. Purnell again; a voice mail came on with alternate doctors to call in his absence. Marcus did not hesitate to leave a message and call one of the doctors. "Hello, this is Dr. Roberts ..." "Oh, my God, I am so glad you're there. Dr. Roberts, my name is Marcus Dallas, and your name was on Dr. Purnell's voice mail as a contact in his absence. My wife, Tressa Dallas has just been taken to Community Lifeline Hospital. She is nine months pregnant; she passed out at our home. Can you please meet us at the hospital as soon as possible?" "Yes, Mr. Dallas; Dr. Purnell familiarized me with your wife's pregnancy. She's having triplets I believe." "Yes, she is," said Marcus. "I'll be there as soon as I can," replied Dr. Roberts. With a sigh of relief, Marcus thanked Dr. Roberts. Once Tressa was in the hands of the emergency crew, he proceeded to call Tressa's family. First, he called Jesse. "Ma, this is Marcus. No, no the triplets are not here; actually I just brought Tressa to the hospital. We're at Community Lifeline on Chestmount, please get here as soon as possible." As Marcus was about to hang up, Jesse called out, "Marcus relax, I'll call the others, and we'll meet you as soon as ..." Marcus had hung up before Jesse could finish. She immediately called back. "Marcus listen; I'll call the family don't worry." "Mom, I'm so sorry. Thanks, I don't think I can remember everyone's numbers anyway; by the way, Mom, Devan is here, and that's one less person to call. See you soon."

When Dr. Roberts arrived, she asked Marcus to describe in detail what had happened. He answered the best he could; talking with his hands, he described the situation. "We were talking, and she decided to take a nap." We just came from the hospital last night; it was a false alarm. I was sitting listening to music when I heard her cry out; when I ran upstairs, she had passed out by the bed, that's all I know."

Marcus was familiar with the risks of having multiples. Dr. Purnell shared what knowledge he had and referred them to websites about parenting, support groups, complications when having multiples, etc. Tressa and Marcus read everything they could get their hands on, but it did not prepare them for this. As a precaution at 20 weeks, Dr. Purnell performed a sonographic cervical length measurement of gestation to identify if Tressa was at high risk of developing preterm labor. "Were there any signs of bleeding or trauma?" "No, she had both hands and her head lying on the bed." "She wasn't holding her stomach?" "No," said Marcus, "she wasn't." "What type of medication is she on?" "She only took iron tablets to my knowledge; no other medications, none that I know of; I mean no other medications." "OK, Mr. Dallas," Dr. Roberts said, patting his shoulder. "Excuse me, I must attend to your wife. I'll get back to you as soon as I can." "No, Dr. Roberts, I am coming in the room with you; I need to be with my wife." Marcus didn't like Dr. Roberts's bedside manner. She seemed cold and dismissive, and he refused to be dismissed.

When Dr. Roberts examined Tressa, she was surprised that Tressa was indeed ten centimeters along; they did an EKG and took her blood pressure; she was out of it. Marcus, looking helpless at his wife, slowly took her hand and knelt to pray. He prayed so loud and intense that other patients and staff came to the room to kneel as he prayed. Everyone was moved by Marcus's prayer. He thanked God for his three children and his wife's recovery; he also thanked him for the many years of joy he had already promised him and Tressa. It was done. When he finished, Devan entered the room and gave him a hug as he stood. "It will be all right now, God heard my cries." Dr. Roberts wasn't so sure; she remarked that faith was a good thing, but just in case, she wanted to continue her tests. Marcus rolled his eyes at her and said, "You do your thing, Dr. Roberts, as I have done mine." Just as they were about to hook Tressa up to another monitor, she groaned in a weak voice, "Marcus, Marcus are you here babe?" Tressa was dazed but awake. "Yes, Tressa." He leaned over to rub her face and assure her of his presence. "Hi! Are the children alright? Please tell me ..." "Yes, Tressa! You passed out, and they're trying to determine why!" Before Marcus could finish, Tressa said, "I don't know what happened, but I know I'm about to give birth to our children." "How do you know that?" "I know because my water just broke." They both laughed, and Marcus neglected to tell Tressa that Devan was in the room. She heard his voice and beckoned him to come closer. "Hi Sis, it won't be long before you're a mom, and I'm an uncle. Hang in there. Mom and the gang are on the way". "I will." Tressa was exhibiting signs of preeclampsia. Her blood pressure was elevated. "Marcus, I am scared, pray with me." He took her hands, and they prayed their secret prayer. "I believe today is the day; my blood pressure will not be a problem. It is now 9 p.m., the triplets will be here before 11 p.m., that I know and promise. Marcus didn't know what to say, but he believed in Tressa and her relationship with Christ. "Tressa, I believe in you, and I know it'll be alright."

Dr. Roberts was shocked and amazed to discover after they had prayed that Tressa's blood pressure was normal. "I guess the power of prayer has its benefits; this was a first for Dr. Roberts, a true example of a doubting Thomas. Marcus heard the voices of family in the outside waiting room. "Tressa I'll be back." Devan followed him out to meet the family and bring them up to speed. And again, the family joined hands and prayed. "My, oh my, are you all praying again! Tressa should be walking on water by now, she's giving birth, and many have done it before her." Everyone turned to see Dr. Roberts standing with her hands on her hips, looking disgusted. "Mrs. Dallas has dilated ten centimeters, she is in labor." Just then, they heard a scream, "Oh Lord! Please help me!"

Dr. Roberts, Marcus, and Devan rushed into the room just in time to see Tressa in the position to give birth. The nurse was urging Tressa to push, and within minutes a head was protruding. Considering these were multiples, Dr. Roberts called for all medical staffs' assistance. The attending nurse was coaching and trying to calm Tressa, but the first baby came quickly; he shot out of Tressa with little force. Dr. Roberts stepped in front of the nurse so she could receive the firstborn Dallas. He came out wiggling and shaking; he was immediately cleaned and weighed. The nurse said, "A boy, three pounds, and six ounces, born at 9:45 p.m." Marcus cut the cord and followed the nurse to the scale. "My boy, my son, my firstborn." "What's his name," asked Devan?" Tressa and I decided on lots of names but remember, she didn't want to know the sex of the children. Of course, I knew, but ..." "Marcus, focus" said Devan. "I know you're excited, and it's okay." "I better wait until the others are born and clear things with Tressa."

The firstborn had one distinguishing mark, on the bottom of his right foot was a small round black mole. Pointing to the birthmark, Marcus said, "This should help in case of an emergency, don't you think Devan?" "Yea sure, Marcus." "I hope it doesn't wash off or something." Marcus scratched his head, "Wash off, for real Devan."

"Let me see him," said Tressa. "Does he have everything? Who does he look like?" "Tressa, he doesn't look like anyone. He's long, and just looks like a red ball full of hair." Once cleaned, the nurse laid the baby in Marcus's arms. He gushed, he was so proud, he took the baby for Tressa to see. "Wow, he's gorgeous! Just what I imagined." Just then, "Oh yea, I think number two is coming." Marcus gave the baby to Devan, and he gave the baby to the nurse as if it were on fire! "Men, it's not a toy," said the nurse." Devan exited the room to give the family an update. "Ok, as of now it's one boy, three pounds six ounces and the next one is on its way out." Jesse, Simone, Ciera, Avery, Les and several church friends were now in the waiting room, full of joy waiting for the birth of the other two babies.

The hospital staff could have sworn it was a party. There were enough balloons and flowers to fill the entire maternity ward. Devan brought food and beverages for the gang, thinking it was going to take hours. "Well, I better get back in; of course, if you want to go in, Mom!" "No, no, Son; she's so close to you. I'll come in when it's over; the room is already crowded." Dr. Roberts told Tressa it may be a while before the second baby was born. She told her to relax. But how could she? After all, she still had two babies to give birth to. The pain was excruciating. It was now 10:12 p.m. It won't be long, she thought. But time seemed to slow down. Marcus tried to soothe her. He sang to her, read her silly poems and made her guess the next time of arrival of the second child. Looking at the monitor, Dr. Roberts could see the level of contractions, and she told Tressa to get ready to push. Tressa grabbed Marcus's arm so hard he screamed, "AWOL." "I'm sorry." The nurse and Dr. Roberts told Tressa to push.

With one hard push came the head of the second baby, a boy. He was cleaned and weighed and less than fifteen minutes later came the last baby, a little girl. "OK, Mom and Dad, the final tally is three newborns, all present and accounted for. One boy, three pounds, six ounces; one boy, three pounds, one ounce and; one girl, three ounces. Now, all they need are names."

Devan almost fainted. He couldn't believe his eyes. However, the fever caught on. Jesse and Avery rushed the doors. Jesse beat Avery to the babies. They all saw all three babies together before Tressa. She didn't mind; she was exhausted and happy it was over. Her babies had arrived! Cameras were flashing as if the babies were stars, and the family was paparazzi. Tressa knew she had given birth to three special children. Over the years, she had had visions of them. They were just as the Lord had shown her. Tressa heard a loud and intrusive voice in the hall, "Who in the world is that?" "How are the babies? Those babies need to be prayed over immediately! I brought the oil." "Please, Ma Lizzy." Tressa don't need this confusion! "There's a time and a place for everything, and this is not it," said Jesse. "Yawl don't understand," Ma Lizzy replied, "They need to be blessed, and God's covering over them." "Yes, we believe that Ma Lizzy," replied Avery. "But, right now, we need you to calm down and maybe go home." "Not before I see the babies." She abruptly pushed past the family into the room. "Tressa, I need to see the babies, may I see them? Those people out there are trying to make me out to be a kook or something. You know me and what I stand for, don't you?" "Yes, Ma Lizzy, I know. Let her see the babies, but no oil!" Ma Lizzy looked at the babies and began to wail up. "These babies are beautiful. They look just like their father. I can't wait until they're mine."

Tressa wasn't sure what she heard. She asked Ma Lizzy to repeat herself, but she refused. "I meant nothing, honey. I just can't wait to hold and squeeze them. I pray these babies bring you much joy. You are a very lucky child." Tressa was a little set back by the statement "lucky" instead of "blessed" but that was Ma Lizzy.

After everyone had left Tressa's room, Dr. Roberts sat beside Tressa's bed and said in a mellow voice, "Mrs. Dallas, please forgive me. I was rude and unprofessional. I'm not a religious person, but I saw the faith of you and your husband. Never have I met two people with so much faith and who are so in love. You and your husband have a rare and beautiful relationship; I envy it. Keep doing whatever it is you're doing." Tressa smiled and thanked Dr. Roberts. She grabbed her hand and said, "Dr. Roberts, I pray that we touched you in some way. Today we also experienced our faith at work. We trusted God and his promises, and he came through. Perhaps one day you will experience God's salvation. It's the most important thing in our lives." Dr. Roberts looked intently at Tressa and said, "Perhaps." "Now doc, may I see my babies?"

Marcus, Avery, Devan and Les were passing out cigars and sent cell phone photos to family, coworkers, friends and even strangers. Point Dexter showed up with a beautiful wrapped box. His gift was for the parents. Tressa opened the envelope to find gift certificates. There were certificates for local restaurants that offered carryout; there was a gas card, a certificate for a nurse and babysitting service. These gifts were personal and appreciated. When Tressa and Marcus hugged Jonas, he blushed. This man had proven to be an awesome friend.

Five days later, the babies were nestled in their nursery; the room was beautiful. Friends and family made sure the Dallas's wanted for nothing. Tressa had three baby showers, and Marcus's staff surprised him with a shower at work.

The showers provided enough baby stuff to last for more than a year. Tressa knew the triplets would never wear all the gifts so she donated a portion to the church nursery. Marcus surprised Tressa by purchasing a sleep sofa, rocker, TV and a radio for the nursery. She loved it.

Marcus and Tressa were happy to welcome the daily help. Jesse brought her suitcase and planned to stay until she was no longer needed. "Mom, how long is your leave? When are you due back to work?" "Any time I want dear girl, remember I am my own boss." "Yes, I often forget that." Simone and Ciera volunteered their time along with church members, family, friends, and neighbors. They devised a schedule, and for the most part, everyone supported it. The house had at least five to ten people there at a time. It was overrun with people, and Tressa didn't know how to ask them to leave. She was afraid she would need them.

Marcus was always in the nursery. Tressa said he stayed in there to hide from the women and their gossip. Actually, Jesse, Devan, Les and Avery stayed huddled in the nursery, feeding the babies and enjoying each other's company.

Avery enjoyed telling and retelling the monthly accounts of how many children they were expecting. Of course, they expected one, but then two months later there was another child. Avery couldn't help but boast, but Les was worse. He called every old friend, neighbor, and enemy. There would be twins in the family. Devan wasn't surprised, considering twins ran in the family. But, two months later, another baby was discovered.

They thought they would have to take Marcus to the hospital. He couldn't eat or sleep. However, his biggest concern was their future care. "Dad, how am I going to put three children through college, then paying for wedding and cars; I'll have to purchase three cars. And, how are we supposed to take them out? We will need a van for transporting. Dad, do you think I can apply for some type of special aid, you know some assistance?" "Marcus, calm down Son. You have a wife that's wealthy, a father and grandfather that will shower those kids. You worry too much. And, most importantly, remember your children are a gift from God, the ultimate provider. Everything will be fine."

Tressa needed the support but longed for the time when it would be just her, Marcus, and the babies. But, that would be months down the road. For now, she stole as much time alone as possible.

Rev. Rayford would often visit for prayer and fellowship. He confided in Tressa that he had received a call from Tia a few weeks earlier asking him to come get her. She was at a hospital in the psychiatric ward, and she didn't want anyone to know. He said when he arrived, she was sitting in the lobby. She looked as if she had had shock treatment or something; she wasn't all there. "I took her home and started to call her parents, but she refused to talk to them or see them. I didn't know what to do; she needed someone to stay with her. "Stop, Rev. Rayford," Tressa protested, "Why are you telling me this? I don't want to hear anything about Tia." "I think you do, Tressa. The Lord told me he spoke to your heart." Tressa knew that was true. The Lord had been dealing with her about forgiveness. It seemed every time she turned on the TV or radio; it was a sermon about forgiveness and submission, but why Tia? And the Lord said, "Why not?"

Rev. Rayford went on to say that Tia said she had been attending church for the first time in years and had asked God to help her. "She told me that the past had caught up with her, and she couldn't forgive herself for what she had done to Marcus and his family. "Anyway, I called Sister Watkins, and she volunteered to counsel Tia. Now, I don't know how this happened, but instead of Sister Watkins coming, Ma Lizzy went in her place. Tia called the next day and said Ma Lizzy tried to put her in some kind of trance and even believed she put something in her tea. She said she remembered talking a lot, repenting, and pleading for forgiveness. It seemed it went on all night. At some point she heard arguing, two loud voices. One was telling the other to get her hands off of her, meaning Tia, and the other person saying she was in charge and had full authority. Tia said, it was a struggle, and the lady with the blue hair conquered the other lady. She said the lady with the blue hair told Tia to repent, to confess her sins to the Lord Thy God and turn to the Lord, and she quoted scripture: Galatians: 6:7-8 'You Reap what you Sow.' Tia said it frightened her. She knew she had done some cruel things to people, but she somehow never thought about reaping it.

When she finally awoke, Ma Lizzy was sitting by her bed gazing at her. And before she could speak, Ma Lizzy said, 'So what's it going to be?' Sitting up in the bed dazed, she asked "What do you mean what's it going to be, lady are you crazy?! I want you out of my house right now, get out!' Ma Lizzy said she had accomplished her mission and was happy to leave. Tressa was dumbfounded; she knew about the lady with the blue hair, it was her grandmother, and she also knew about Ma Lizzy whom she concluded was CRAZY! "So Tressa this is the hard part, Tia would like to meet with you. Not Marcus, just you. She said she needed to talk." "When does she want to meet with me? Quite frankly, Rev. Rayford I don't trust Tia. Let me get back to you, I need to pray about this." "Ok Tressa, don't take too long."

Tressa shared the conversation with Marcus, expecting him to explode; surprisingly, he encouraged the meeting. He said he felt this was God's way of healing them. So Tressa called Rev. Rayford and agreed to meet with Tia. Tia called the next day and asked Tressa to meet her at the nearby park at 3. Tressa was ready for this long awaited showdown. When Tressa arrived, she sat on a park bench. The sounds of the birds singing and laughter of children playing helped calm her nerves; it relaxed her.

From a distance, she saw a woman limping, walking with a cane. She thought that's not Tia; she looks as if she has aged at least ten years. Yes, it was Tia, what in the world could have happened to her? Extending her hand, Tia said, "Hi Tressa, I am happy to see you." "Hi, Tia, let's have a seat." "Tressa if you don't mind, please give me the privilege of talking before I chicken out of this. I have come to realize that by nature I'm a bully and a coward." Tressa lifted her eyebrow as if saying, you don't say." "I am sorry Tressa, what I meant to say was please hear me out. For openers, it's hard for me to be happy for you and Marcus, but I sincerely want to because I love him. I've been tormented by guilt and shame for what I've done. I not only denied my family the privilege of seeing and holding their grandson, I also denied Marcus and his family the opportunity to help raise him. Marcus should have been told he was a father, but honestly, Tressa, I was too afraid to tell him."

Tia talked the entire time with her head hung down, as a sign of shame. "The pregnancy wasn't planned but welcomed. I was so happy. I viewed this as a gift from God. You see, Marcus had come to dislike me so much. I planned to present his child to him when he was about a year old, and he would realize I was responsible and worth loving, and we would become a happy family. Tressa, I never dreamt he could love another woman like he loved me. I was wrong; he adores you. When our baby died, my world ended and so did any chance of being with the love of my life." Tia was crying, trying to wipe the tears from her eyes. Tressa reached in her purse for a tissue, but Tia objected. "No, I don't want anything from you but forgiveness. I know Marcus hates me, and perhaps I don't deserve forgiveness, but I hope in time they all will. I have come to believe that the loss of my child was punishment from God for all the bad things I've done."

Tia stood and started to walk, limping back and forth as she continued to speak. "Over the last four months, I've been plagued with feelings of guilt and shame. I realized I needed to talk to someone, and I chose Rev. Rayford because I knew he cared about me, really cared. However, I had to admit I wasn't looking for spiritual enlightenment; I just wanted someone to talk too. In time, I began to seek redemption. I had an encounter with Ma Lizzy and a mystery lady. The woman had a beautiful head of blue hair. Her spirit brought me so much peace. She spoke so softly as if she knew me; she was believable. Now, I am seeking an inner peace, trying to find myself. I can't talk to Marcus; he has a way of making me feel worthless and a liar. I couldn't stand his reproving me. I did a horrible thing regardless of the reason. Well, that's what I came here to say. You probably may not believe this, but I admire you. I am a weak woman, too weak for Marcus. He needed me to be strong and steadfast. I realized too late that he needed me to believe in him, trust him and his love for me, but I dropped the ball. Now, I live a lonely, loveless life of regrets."

Tressa thought Tia was doing good up until now. She should have stopped while Tressa was feeling sorry for her. She did believe Tia when she said she was seeking peace, she seemed sincere but, she was skeptical of her reason and timing of this revelation. She decided to be straightforward with her and tell her what was on her mind and see how she responded.

"Tia, you're good, real good. You somehow believe you've laid the foundation for a heartwarming reunion between you and Marcus by creating this bond between you and the baby. You think that the two of you will celebrate the anniversary of the baby's birth and death together and be lifelong fixtures in each other lives. We will remember Marcus Jr., but the birth of our children will hold far more importance. The reason is because Marcus will get to hold and cherish his children. He will read to them, celebrate first birthdays; first day of school and all those events that are celebrated throughout a child's life. I don't mean to be unkind, but wasn't that your objective, to place Marcus,

Jr. at the forefront of Marcus's mind? And then you made sure he had plenty of photos and videos of the baby saying "daddy" that was really touching! Tia let me ask you, was the purpose of the pictures, videos and journals to comfort or torment Marcus? Eventually, Tia, you will get the point; Marcus is a happily married man with three beautiful children. Be assured, I am not a substitute for you, I am the woman he wants." "Well, Tressa Dallas, I guess you told me; I should assume my coming here was in vain. I need you to know that I never consciously thought about the situation as you have so eloquently described to me. But, in hindsight, perhaps I did imagine some of those things happening." Tia took a deep breath, looking Tressa in the eyes and reaching out to hold her hands. Tressa obliged, she said, "I did a horrible thing, and I am sorry. Tell Marcus, I love him and wish him a lifetime of peace and joy. Tressa, I pray I find what I'm looking for, and one day am as happy as both of you are. God Bless." She hugged Tressa and walked away.

Tressa sat in the park reflecting on the meeting. She had looked Tia in the eyes, held her hands and felt her pain. She was being honest; her heart was broken, and she was genuinely sorry. Tressa couldn't fathom the pain and disappointment Tia was feeling. Once and again her grandmother showed up, the lady with the blue hair. She was grateful she comforted Tia and shielded her from Ma Lizzy. Tressa prayed for Tia; she wanted her to find the peace that she was seeking.

Chapter fourteen

"Marcus Daye Dallas, I'm so happy I accompanied you to your conference. I made plenty of contacts." "I'm sure you did. Calvin, the wolf, hung around you the entire three days." "Jealous are we Mr. Dallas?" "Jealous of that fool? He doesn't hold a candle to me. I'm too suave and got too much swag to be intimidated by the wolf." "Wolf or not, I managed to get nine future referrals."

It had begun to rain, first drizzle, and then a downpour. "Babe why is it when we go anywhere there's always a thunderstorm? Perhaps we'll have to find a hotel and spend the night." "Sure Tressa, with three men waiting for us at home with three toddlers. Pop is probably sitting by the window watching for the car." "You're not lying. Pop's patience has begun to wear more lately. He loves those kids, but they're getting the best of him. But, they did volunteer!" "Yeah, that'll teach'em!" They laughed. It was pouring as if the skies had opened. Marcus slowed down. In the rearview mirror, Marcus saw a car coming towards them at a high speed. He couldn't go any faster and pulled over to the side to allow the car to pass.

They saw two passengers, a man and woman. The passengers were Ramone and Lexie Davis. Ramone drove as carefully as possible, but the rain blinded his vision. In the twinkling of an eye, both their worlds would drastically change.

Ramone wished he had called an ambulance

rather than drive Lexie to the hospital. He was halfway there, praying, crying out to God for safety and protection. As he tried to pull to the side of the road, the car swirled out of control. Lexie screamed, "Ramone, Ramone; oh God, please help us," she said grabbing her stomach. "I don't want to lose my baby!" Marcus could see the car spinning out of control. "Jesus, I pray they're OK. Tressa, we need to stop and offer assistance." "Of course, babe, but be careful, watch out for oncoming traffic." Several other cars stopped to assist. He heard a still small voice say, "They need you." Marcus didn't doubt that was the voice of the Lord directing him. Tressa, in the meantime, called the police, an ambulance, and the fire department. He and Tressa quickly ran sliding and soaked to the car. The woman in the car was screaming as several other passersby ran to assist Marcus. They tried to pry open the door, but it was stuck. Realizing his assistance was to no avail, he abandoned his efforts, apologized, and returned to his car. The other drivers heard the ambulance and police and drove off.

The car had drifted off in an embankment. Marcus slid down the hill and with a tug he pulled on the door, and it popped open and out fell Ramone. Lexie was screaming. "Mister please help us!"

Tressa ran around to the other side of the car where the pregnant woman sat. She forced open the door and tried to calm the woman down but knew it was best not to move her. "Miss, please calm down; my husband and I are here to help, and the ambulance is on the way." Ramone was slumped behind the wheel, his head bleeding as he clinched the steering wheel. Marcus checked for vitals, but there were none; he did not have a pulse. He had sustained a huge gash on his head and died instantly. Marcus grabbed a towel from the seat and wrapped it around the man's head. He knew the man was deceased, but he did not want the woman sitting next to him to know.

Drifting in and out, Lexie was calling for her husband "Ramone are you alright? Ms. Please tell me if my husband is OK!" Tressa, looking at Marcus, didn't know what to say, she didn't have to. The police arrived and secured the area, and not far behind were the ambulance and fire departments. Never were two people so happy to see responders. The EMTs immediately ran down the embankment and assessed the situation. Marcus didn't say a word; what if the man wasn't dead? However, his assessment was soon validated when the EMTs looked at each other with eyes of sympathy. With the assistance of the fire department and the EMTs they managed to open the passenger door where the woman was sitting pregnant and wounded; she had passed out. The police arrived moments later and secured the area. Tressa informed them that the woman's name was Lexie, and she was obviously pregnant. She said the woman explained they were on their way to the hospital for the delivery of their child when the accident occurred.

Marcus and Tressa followed the ambulance to the hospital. Drenched they hurried into the emergency room concerned about the progress of the pregnant women. They were told she had delivered a baby boy and was asking to see the couple that assisted them; along with her attorney and her only living relative, her 80-year-old grandmother. The Dallas's were taken aback. They didn't know what to make of this request. Marcus and Tressa asked to speak with Lexie's attending doctor. As they waited, a nurse offered them some blankets, saying "You must be cold." Marcus and Tressa were so affected by the events they didn't realize how chilled they were until the warm blankets were wrapped around them.

The nurse escorted them to Lexie's room. As they neared the room, they saw a group of doctors leaving, one shaking his head. He was overheard to say, "I feel sorry for her grandmother. What a tragedy, she's so young." As they waited, Marcus grabbed Tressa and held her close and whispered, "Babe, I am so grateful right now that we are alive and safe, but I feel so guilty; I can't imagine what Lexie is going through, especially since we don't know if she knows her husband is deceased." Tressa looked up at Marcus and laid her head on his chest. She suggested they find the nearest chapel and pray. "Marcus, why us? I feel we were not here by accident?" "I don't know Tressa' perhaps because we're two compassionate human beings." "Well, that's true, but I think it's more than that, Mr. Dallas."

Marcus phoned the family and informed them of their whereabouts. Jesse agreed to stay with the children until they arrived home. "I can handle the kids, the guys are worn out. Over the loudspeaker, they were being paged; they were asked to come to the fourth-floor nurses' station. When they arrived, Lexie was propped up in the bed; the hospital priest was holding her hand and a gentleman wearing a dark suit was taking notes. What in the world was going on? Minutes later, an elderly woman appeared and ran to Lexie's side.

She threw herself on Lexie and sobbed

uncontrollably. "It's alright, Granny, Ramone and I will be fine." Her grandmother didn't know what to make of that comment, but she steadied herself. Lexie took a deep breath and held her grandmother's hand as she told her Ramone had died, but the baby had lived. She asked her grandmother to remember her and love her grandson always. Her grandmother promised. Then she asked the man, Marcus and Tressa to sit by her.

Lexie explained that her grandmother was up in age and too old to care for an infant. She said she knew it was no mistake that they had arrived on the scene, meaning Marcus and Tressa and that the Lord told her to entrust the care of the baby to them. That being said, she asked Marcus and Tressa to be the legal parents of her child. Marcus and Tressa didn't know what to say. Tressa answered for the both of them, "We would be honored, but why are you giving up your child? I don't understand!" Lexie asked her grandmother if she was in agreement with the request, and she immediately said yes, but why?

Her grandmother knew nothing about them. Then the man wearing the suit introduced himself as Mr. Freed, "I am the attorney for Lexie Davis, and it is my understanding it's her desire to give you her son. If you both agree, I can have the papers drawn up, and your names will appear on the birth certificate. There will be legal documents for the both of you to sign." This was happening too fast for Marcus. He asked to speak to Lexie's doctor, Lexie's grandmother and the attorney in private. "What's going on?" asked Marcus. "Why is she giving up her child?" The doctor looked at Lexie's grandmother and delivered the bad news. "I am sorry, Mrs. Snowden, your granddaughter's injuries are extensive; we were able to save the baby but ..." "Not my Lexie, not my Lexie! What will I do? I have no one else. Why Lord? Why? Just as Mr. Freed had finished conferring with Marcus and Tressa, the doctor summoned them. "Is her grandmother near?" "No, she went to the chapel." "Well, maybe that's best, Lexie just expired."

When Mrs. Snowden appeared, she was taken to a private room where she was given time to mourn the loss of her grandchild. Though Tressa had previously agreed via the attorney, they were asked to give it some more thought. Marcus took it upon himself to talk to Mrs. Snowden again, he had to be certain she was willing to give up the baby, and he had to be certain there were no other family that wanted the baby. Approaching the room, he kindly said, "Mrs. Snowden, I'm so sorry about this; we don't know what to do. We would hate to take the baby and have it challenged in court by other family." Mr. Freed assured them no other family wanted the child. He told them he had just talked to Ramone's only sister and an elderly aunt. They were pleased that the baby would not be put up for adoption or taken to foster care, but they were adamant that they did not want the baby. "In that case," said Marcus in agreement with Tressa, we would love to have the baby. Mrs. Snowden, my wife and I promise to take good care of him." "That's what I wanted to hear. Son, I can't take care of a child, I'm old and tired. This is the best thing. Lexie must have seen something in the two of you; why else would she offer you her child? I promise you I will do all I can to offer love and support to my only grandchild." Between sobs, she asked Marcus and Tressa to allow her visits and promised to love the child as if Tressa had given birth to him. Within hours, Marcus and Tressa were given the privilege of adopting baby Ramone Davis Jr. However, the name on the birth certificate was Ramone Jazzy Dallas.

When Marcus and Tressa arrived home, the family was waiting. They were shocked and amazed. Everyone wanted to hold the new baby. They had to think fast; they needed an extra crib. Les went online and ordered everything they needed, next day service. That night, baby Ramone shared a bed with Budde.

It took weeks before they realized the magnitude of this awesome blessing. Another baby in the family; it all happened so quickly. They were now the parents of four children, all under the age of one. Marcus was beside himself; his dream of adopting had come to pass. This was nothing like he had imagined. He thought he would travel to a foreign land, wait around for days to be handed a baby of foreign nationality. Tressa shared his joy; she instantly grew attached to Ramone. Marcus told the story over and over to anyone that would listen. Devan quickly grew attached to Ramone, and Les's feelings towards Ramone were amazing. He took the baby to be his own, more so than his birth grandchildren. Avery knew why he was attached to Ramone, his father was orphaned, but unlike Ramone, he was never adopted. Avery knew that Ramone would be loved and cared for because Les would see to it.

Out of respect for the Davis's, Marcus and Tressa attended their funeral with the baby. They sat in the back of the funeral home observing the family as they marched in. Marcus and Tressa couldn't imagine why the family wouldn't want the baby. At the conclusion of the service, Mrs. Snowden joined them and embraced Ramone. The family introduced themselves and smiled and patted Ramone, but they did not embrace him. What was wrong with these people? This was a member of their family. They later found out why. The family was afraid the baby had inherited the Davis bipolar disorder. How crazy, like they could catch the disorder. More importantly, they just didn't want the responsibility of raising a child that would be "a problem." "Mrs. Snowden, is there a problem in the family? Are there any family members that are bipolar?" "Let's see bipolar, what is that?" "It's a mental disorder, Mrs. Snowden; does anyone in Lexie or Ramone's family suffer from a mental disorder?" "Oh, you mean are they crazy? No not at all. Ramone's mother, Etta was epileptic; she had seizures. The seizures frightened them, and I guess they mistook seizures for something contagious. So, I must ask, do you still want the baby?" "Of course, we want the baby, nothing has changed." "That's good; I was worried for a minute." "We're leaving, Mrs. Snowden; feel free to visit any time."

When the family learned why Ramone's family didn't want Ramone, they were disgusted but happy for the opportunity to have baby Ramone as a new member of the family. "Son, I love that child so much," said Les. I thank God he was not put in a home or abandoned. I also thank God for your kind heart." "I know Pop, I too am thankful."

Les decided to immediately set up a trust fund for Ramone; he never wanted him to want for anything. He had already invested thousands of his savings in a trust for the triplets and wanted Ramone to have the same privileges and advantages as the triplets. He made a vow to God to never treat Ramone any different than the triplets. He would love him unconditionally.

Marcus had not thought about his grandfather's early years until Ramone's adoption. He asked him if he had ever tried locating his birth parents. Les told him he had once hired a detective to try and locate them, but they came up empty. Avery and Marcus suggested he try again; they reminded Les that this was the age of knowledge. Technology could locate, track, trace all the way back to the Middle Ages; surely, they could trace his genealogy. Surprisingly, Les didn't object.

After all these years, Avery saw a different side of his father. He was always gentle but stern. Now, he displayed a side of himself that was overprotective, gentle and embracing. There was a dearer side of a man that had been in the military, who supervised rowdy men that often saw his herculean personality.

Over the next year, life for the Dallas and Bowers had drastically changed. Devan and Detra became engaged; Avery and Jesse surrendered to their feelings; Simone honored her calling to the ministry; Taylor blossomed into a beautiful and mature young lady; Jonas Point Dexter and Ma Lizzy were a hot couple, and to everyone's surprise, Ciera and Max became the "it couple" and, upon discovering who his parents were, Les was able to finally find peace.

Though strange and unsolved events continued to happen, especially in the house, for the most part, these were happy times. Marcus and Tressa celebrated their first wedding anniversary by vacationing in Fiji as he had promised. They missed the children but welcomed the tranquility.

Jesse had clocked in many hours with the

grandkids. It was her professional opinion that her grandkids were gifted. People often remarked how astute and bright the Dallas children were. They were very observant; curious; learned quickly; had vivid imaginations; excellent reasoning skills, and excellent memories. Marcus hesitated to take them to be tested, but Tressa thought it was necessary. They agreed to wait until they were two. It was determined that all four of them were gifted. Bunne scored higher than the boys. She did everything earlier and better. By eighteen months, she was walking and running and her reading skills far exceeded the boys. Tressa boasted, "Of course, Bunne learned quicker, she after all is the exact replica of her mother. Beauty and brains, what more could you ask for a little Tressa."

The children refused to be separated; they insisted on sharing a room. Marcus and Tressa transformed the upstairs lounge into their bedroom, which housed four twin beds and dressers. They played and embraced each other just as the Bowers did when they were toddlers. Les and Avery built them a table, chairs and a bookcase. They loved to read and act out the characters in the stories.

Les loved being around the kids. He was always available for great-granddad duties. How he managed, no one knew. He found it easy because they learned how to dress and feed themselves at such an early age. They followed him around as if he was a god. As they matured, he had to admit, even though Tressa was always there, he needed time out. They asked so many questions and their energy and learning levels were that of eight children. The family had provided every outlet for enjoyment. They had swing sets, teeter-toddler, racecars, DVD players, learning games, etc. By age two and one-half, they were accepted in a school for gifted children. Avery and Devan were skeptical, they felt they should be home-schooled. However, Tressa and Marcus wanted them to mingle with other kids, to learn social skills.

Once enrolled in school, they excelled far beyond Marcus and Tressa's imagination. They did need encouragement in one area; they wouldn't mingle with other children; they kept to themselves and would furiously object to being separated.

They once walked out of class holding hands because the teacher wouldn't let them spell their words together. Marcus had to leave a meeting and rush to the school. He was told they moved so fast the teacher had to stop class and run after them. When she caught up with them, Bulee kicked her and grabbed her around the leg. He told Bunne and Budde to run and wait by the door until "Great Pop" came for them. When Marcus arrived all three were in the principal's office sitting quietly, holding hands, swinging their feet and staring at the door. When they saw their dad they slid off the bench and ran to him. "Daddy, Daddy, the lady was bad." He cuddled all three children and asked them to explain what had happened. "How Bunne? How was the lady bad?"

"Daddy, we had an assignment to show the incorrect word in the block. She, pointing to the instructor, and told Bulee to read his word. Bulee said the word that was different and she said it was wrong, but it wasn't cause we all had the same words. I told her and she, pointing to the instructor, said I wasn't talking to you missy. Please be quiet, your brother can speak for himself. She hurt my feelings; I said I was sorry, and she said next time to wait until I was spoken to. She said it real mean. So Bulee said "Oh no, she cannot talk to my sister like that." Then Budde said we need to call our daddy, and we walked out. Then she came running for us, and that's when Budde grabbed her around the leg and told us to run, run for our lives. But we didn't run and leave Budde; he's our brother. So that's why she's a bad lady."

Marcus found the situation hilarious, but he had to be the adult. "Well, I see. Ok, the three of you sit on the bench and wait for Daddy." Marcus and Mrs. Anderson walked out in the hall and talked. He tried to explain the triplets' personalities and admitted they were a bit eccentric for their age. He promised he would talk with them and impress upon them the importance of being obedient and respecting the instructor. "You see, Mrs. Anderson, we often joke that they operate on one brain. They seem to think they are one, and in a way, they are." Mrs. Anderson wasn't buying it. She politely listened as she shifted from one foot to another. "Anyway, we will address the issue. I am sure this situation will not happen again." Marcus felt like a child himself. When they arrived home, Marcus explained the emergency to Tressa. "Really, Marcus they actually attacked the teacher." "No, Budde grabbed her by the leg so Bunne and Bulee could run; where I don't know."

After dinner, Marcus and Tressa sat the kids down to discuss manners and respect. Tressa tried to explain that there was a correct way and an incorrect way to do things. The triplets weren't buying it; they debated back and forth until they wore Tressa out. Marcus seeing Tressa's frustration, told them in a sterner voice, "Listen you three, it's important to respect the teacher; don't walk out of class, and the next time you feel she is unfair, tell us, your parents, and we will address Mrs. Anderson." "OK Daddy, but she is not a nice lady. We will do as you and Mommy ask, but from now on we will write down what she says and how she says it. Like if she says something in a nice voice or an angry voice, is that alright Daddy?" "That's a good idea Bunne, but you must be accurate." Les thought it was hilarious, he couldn't wait to tell the family. Tressa asked Marcus if he made the children apologize to Mrs. Anderson and promise never to walk out of class. He said he apologized for them and made them promise not to walk out of class and to respect Mrs. Anderson. From that point on, a member of the Dallas and Bower family would stop by the school periodically to check on them. Mr. Miller, the principal found their popping in a sign of support, but Mrs. Anderson found it intrusive. "I don't know what the problem is Mrs. Anderson, we should have more families support their kids; you have nothing to hide do you?" "No, I have no problem with them being supportive, but I feel that their visits are to check on me because those kids dislike me and fear I would do them harm. And there's no truth to that, none whatsoever!" As Mr. Miller walked away, she muttered, "Quite frankly, I do find them creepy to say the least."

Marcus and Tressa's work schedule was overwhelming. Though she worked from home, the firm leaned on her more and more. In addition, she had several new clients that demanded more of her time than she had contracted for, and Jazz was a handful. Marcus's new position as Director of International

Affairs and his daily commute to Washington was grueling. Les and Avery had taken on several construction jobs that made it difficult to pick up the children after school. Marcus and Tressa understood and decided to hire a nanny. She looked after Jazz in the mornings; picked the children up after school; fixed them a snack and kept them busy until dinner. Tressa was adamant she did not want anyone to stay overnight unless there was an emergency. Fortunately for them, Bridgett lived just blocks from the Dallas's and was simply a phone call away.

Marcus learning of an attempted kidnapping of a neighbor's child prompted him to institute code words or phrases to identify anyone that was not a family member or the nanny. Marcus taught the code words in French, and they changed every month. It was not a challenge for the children. Bunne assumed the responsibility of recording all code words which changed the first of every month. The system was not a challenge to the children as they grasped the importance and urgency of the situation.

This precaution proved to be a lifesaver. On a Wednesday morning, it started to snow so hard the school decided to cancel classes. Everyone in the Dallas and Bower family was either working or out of town. The principal called Tressa to come and get the children. She promised to be there within a half hour. This was convenient because she was at the office and scheduled to only work a half-day.

On her way to her car, she heard a loud cry. Her first instinct was to rush to assist, but she erred on the side of caution. She called security and asked for assistance. She told them the cry came from the back of the garage where the executives parked. She called the police and waited for their arrival. Upon investigation, they found Mr. Goode lying unconscious. Blood was spurting from his head; an ambulance was called as the police investigated the scene. Tressa called the school to inform the principal what had happened and that she would be running late. "Mrs. Bowers, we were trying to locate you; someone arrived and said you sent them to pick up the children. We heard yells and saw someone trying to take them." We called the police, and they are on their way. Apparently, the person could not identify their password or code, and the children refused to leave."

Tressa was beside herself. Who could that have been? She wondered if it had anything to do with Mr. Goode being attacked. But why would it? Whoever it was underestimated the Dallas children. When Tressa arrived the children greeted her with a big hug. "Mommy, a person tried to get us, but they didn't know the code. We yelled like Daddy told us and ran into Mr. Miller's office and told him what happened." Mr. Miller explained that the security officer had just stepped away from his post at the front door but assured her he immediately called the police. When the police arrived, they asked if the children were harmed and if they were capable of giving them a description of the perpetrator. Tressa started off by telling Budde, Bunne and Bulee how proud she was of them. "Children, Mommy and the police need to know what happened, and if you can remember anything about the person." They all agreed that it looked like a woman in man's clothes. "Mr. Policeman and Mommy, she had on dark glasses, a black coat with the collar up and black boots." "No Budde, it was brown boots that tie up the front." "No, I wrote it down; see shoes black, but I didn't say tie up." "No Bunne, they were brown, said Bulee!" "OK, OK, maybe they were brown, but we all agree they were boots. And, she had on dark gloves and a big green coat that smelled funny." "Yea, that we agree with, the coat smelled funny." "Now, can you tell me if the person was tall like me," said Officer Brown, "or shorter?" They looked at each other and shrugged their shoulders. "Honestly, we cannot tell. The person wasn't short like Mrs. Anderson, we know that, but we can't say how tall." "That's fine. Can you tell me if you could see the person's face; can you tell me the race of the person? What I mean by race is ..." "We know what race means, Officer Brown. It was a person of color, not a white person like you, sir." "OK, now we're getting somewhere. Why do you think it was a woman and not a man?" "Because she had a girl voice, not a man voice though she tried to talk like a man." "OK, is that it? Can you remember anything else?" "Yes, she was mean, very mean." Officer Brown was quite impressed with the Dallas children. He couldn't believe the details. He complimented Tressa on their cooperation and knowledge. After he finished his investigation, he promised Tressa he would get back to her as soon as possible.

Tressa called the family. Marcus hurried home from a conference in Virginia. He was horrified, who could have wanted to take the children? Thank God, they were alert and remembered the code words. In the paper the next day, the headlines read: 'Prominent Maryland Attorney Murdered.' "Oh no, Mr. Goode passed on, this can't be! Who did this?"

The murder of Mr. Goode was senseless; no one could wrap their head around such a brutal act. The garage cameras did show a person fleeing the scene, but they were completely covered. Upon close inspection, the clothing and build of the person did resemble the person that tried to kidnap the children. However, this person was on foot, which was a clue. The police concluded that the person was agile, able to run. The attack was planned well in advance, but he or she did not expect bad weather. The footprints in the snow could have been anyone's, and they had been walked over from passersby. When questioned, no one in the firm noticed anyone lurking around.

After the kidnapping attempt, the children became reserved. They didn't want to go to school. Les cancelled all contracts, and Marcus took a leave of absence. They took turns taking the children to school, and they stayed all day. They actually became an asset. Mr. Miller felt their visibility not only calmed their children but the other children as well. Devan assigned a police car to patrol the school as much as possible. Marcus dismissed Avery's suggestion of hiring a security officer to be with the children. He wanted someone that had the authority to shoot if necessary. "Shoot? Marcus really?!" "Yes, Dad, if need be." "Marcus, I concur. I believe no one can watch the children better than us. There are only a few more weeks before holiday break, and hopefully, this mess will be over."

Several weeks later, the children told the family they were afraid of the lady in the wall. They said the lady with the blue hair stopped her from getting them. Tressa wondered if this was fact or fable. Did they overhear Marcus and Tressa talking about the lady with the blue hair? They knew who she was, but how did they know her? And who was the other lady?

Les asked them about the other lady and the magic door. Where is the door that opens? Budde anxiously ran to the wall. "Here it is, Granddaddy; here is the magic wall. It's not a door Granddaddy; it's a wall. See it opens when the lady pushes it; sometimes she pushes the button." "Pushes what button Budde?" "The magic button, when she pushes it the wall opens." "Bunne and Bulee, can you help granddaddy find the magic button?" "No, Granddaddy. I don't know how the button works, only Budde knows."

The family pushed and probed; they examined the door, and they found no button or trick knob, nothing. They believed the children, they were not the type to make up stories. Jazz gave them a clue. When he saw them patting on the door, kicking and hitting, he started laughing. "Granddaddy, that's not the way; you're doing it wrong." They forgot all about Jazz; he was in the room as well. "Ok, Jazz, show us." Jazz raised his arms, "Lift me up." Les lifted jazz, "Right here, Granddaddy," Jazz quickly flicked the light switch three times, and there was a rumble, the door scraping the floor. Now excited, "Yes, Granddaddy, that's the sound it makes when it opens," the family stood around observing. They were amazed. When the doors opened, they asked the children to step back. One by one, they ventured down the stairs. "What, oh my God," Marcus hurriedly walked over to a pile of clothes. He picked them up and examined them. "Dad, I believe these are the clothes the children described." "But how did they get down here?" Les banged and kicked on every wall. He noticed sunlight streaming from beneath an opening.

"Come, come over here Avery; here's an opening." "Dad this is nailed shut, there's no way anyone could use this entrance!" "There's an entrance here somewhere, I know it. I know, let's go up and get the blueprints, this time we'll take our time and study them. We need to get to the bottom of this."

While the men reviewed the blue prints, Jesse gathered the children around the kitchen table. "Kids, I need your attention, this is very serious. Grandma and all the family want to protect you from anyone that would do you harm. What I am asking you to do is very important. I want you to carefully look at these pictures and tell me if you recognize anyone." They moved their chairs close together and slowly turned the pages taking their time to look at each person. Jazz quickly identified the family. "That's Great Pop and Granddad, and that's Aunt Simone and that's ..." "We know who they are Jazz, Grandma wants us to find someone different." They looked and looked and suddenly, Bunne recognized someone. 'Here she is, the lady with the blue hair, there she is!

Jesse and Tressa rushed over to see. She was pointing to Jesse's mother, Tressa's grandmother. "That's Grandma Keys; I remember her from the ride. What a dear lady, she's has been protecting us from hurt, harm and evil. Perhaps now she will find rest."

Jesse and Tressa told the guys that Jazz had identified the lady with the blue hair. However, they were perplexed because they still didn't know the identity of the other woman. Marcus felt Jazz knew more than he was telling. He sat beside him and cupped his face in his hands. "Son, I want you to think, concentrate; can you describe the lady that the lady with the blue hair was fighting?" Jazz said he would try. They once again showed him the photo album. After an hour, he came up with nothing. "This is useless; he's just a child, a baby. You can't expect him to remember ..." "Daddy, here she is here is the lady!" "You have got to be kidding, are you sure that's the lady Jazz?" They were shocked, "Are you really sure this is she?" "Yes, Mommy and Daddy, that's her." "Yep, that's her," said the triplets in unison. Everyone was surprised, it can't be; it just can't be and why, why would she be lurking around peeping in on our children?" "Not only that, how did she find this passage in the house?" "What is her motive?" "Daddy, the lady said we better not tell she comes to visit or she will stop giving us toys and money." "What toys and money, Bunne?"

They ran to their secret box and opened it. There were about three hundred dollars in small bills in the box, and out of fear of being punished, they cautiously showed them the toys that were hidden in the closet. Tressa called Devan and asked him to come over as soon as he could. Devan told them to call the police, he was on an important case but would be there as soon as possible. When the police arrived, they took fingerprints, searched the house and gathered as much information about the products as possible. It was hopeless, the toys had been played with, and the packaging had been discarded. The family decided to bring in a child therapist in hopes of obtaining more information. This proved to be fruitless. Jazz cried and Bunne, Bulee and Budde wouldn't talk to him. This was strange, they were usually so forthcoming. They eyed him; half-listened and whispered among themselves. The therapist had to admit he was getting nowhere.

Jesse took a shot at it; after all, she was a psychologist. She bundled them up and took them to the park. The ground was still covered with a little snow. She let them play until they were tired and then took them to their favorite restaurant. As they were eating, she laid the picture in the center of the table. "Budde started talking about the lady; he offered up an excellent clue. "Grandma, is today Tuesday?" "Yes, today is Tuesday. What's so important about the day of the week?" Budde interrupted, "Because the lady comes to our house on a T-day, a Tuesday or Thursday, but she probably won't come today because she sees cars outside." "Wow, she's a clever lady. Why do you think she won't come around when she sees cars?" "That's easy because she don't want the babysitter lady or Mom and Dad to see her.

If they see her, we won't get our money or toys. She says she gives them to us because we are very good children. And you know what else, Grandma? She said one day she would take us to see Santa, and Superman and the Wizard because Jazz loves the Wizard of Oz, I don't like him, he's scary. Me and Budde, we like Santa and his elves, and Bulee likes Superman." Jesse thought she has all her bases covered. Wait until I get my hands on that crazy woman." "And, Grandma, she takes things from the house." "That's right, we forgot that, and she takes Mommy and Daddy's stuff. Then Daddy asks us where his things are. We tell him the lady took them, but he says he thinks we are the ones, and we're not," said Bunne. "What kind of things?" "Like ties, and socks, and sometimes a shirt. And Grandma, she takes Mommy's stuff too. She takes her hairpins and some makeup, all kinds of things.

But Grandma Jesse she is very nice, she read to us and sings to us. You won't hurt her will you?" "No, we'll try not to." "Grandma Jesse, Bunne don't like her, only the boys like her." "Bunne, why don't you like her?" Anxious to express her opinion, she said, "Because she steals and she lets us little children take the blame; that's not nice, I don't think." When Jesse got home, she told the family to hang onto their hats, she had vital clues to find out who the person was.

Chapter fifteen

Just as the police were on their way to the house, Maximillian called Marcus in a panic. "Marcus this is Max; I don't have time to explain; but you need to protect Tressa and the kids, that crazy woman is after your family. She'll do anything to destroy them." "Max who are you talking about? What crazy woman?" the phone went dead. "Max!" Marcus called him back but no answer. "This mess is crazy. Why do I need to protect Tressa, and who is trying to harm us? Lord, we need your help!"

In the background, Marcus heard sirens; it sounded like thousands of them. "Are they headed towards my house? Marcus frantically ran to get Tressa and the kids. He told the family what Max said. The police told Marcus they had an idea who the person was and received a tip from ..."

Suddenly, there was a rumble in the back of the house. Devan's car door opened, and he ran chasing someone dressed in black. The entire family had emerged on the front porch. "Get back in the house!" yelled Devan, "She has a gun!" "Who, who has the gun?"

Devan tackled the mysterious stranger to the ground and subdued her. He slowly pulled the scarf from off her face. "You crazy fool, I knew you were off, but this?! You tried to kill ..." "Yea that's right; I tried to kill your sister, the incomparable Tressa Dallas. And, I tried to kill that stupid Simone. I hit her across the head with a hammer, but she survived, just my luck." Not knowing the situation, Simone and Jesse ran down the stairs to confront Ciera. When they approached her, they realized she was the person menacing the family. "It can't be! Ciera, you're my best friend!" cried Simone. "What would make you do such a horrible thing? You wanted me dead!"

Rising to her feet and brushing the dirt off her clothes, subdued by Devan, she threw back her head and with a yell that could be heard blocks away she screamed, "Yes, Yes, Yes, dead, dead and dead! But not as much as I wanted that prima donna Tressa taken out! I hate her! With my whole heart I hate her! I've been trying to destroy her for years, but she must have a covering over her, some type of voodoo. I declare, I did everything I could to make her life miserable. Of course, you want to know why, I'll tell you ... because I've been in love with Gregory Montgomery for years! I might say all my life if that's possible! When he was dating Tressa, he was with me, and my dear girl when he was with you he was with me. When he married Tressa that broke my heart; he was mine. We pledged ourselves to each other, and then he ran off and married Tressa. He betrayed me with his love for her." "Ciera, you and Gregg were together. You have been romantically involved with Gregg all this time?" "That surprises you, Simone? I don't know why; he wanted everything he saw. He convinced me that I was the fairest one of all. He often bragged about how he manipulated the two of you and played one against the other; I loved it. Let me let you in on a little secret," She said, pointing to herself with pride, "I was the one who instigated the car thief and tried to convince Taylor to kill Tressa." "I knew he didn't love you Simone; you were so needy

Mildred K. Simpson

282

and jealous of Tressa, he knew he could play you, and that was fine with me. He wined and dined me using your money Simone. I had hoped he would get you pregnant; that would really hurt Tressa. What friction, what joy! And the lies, Jessica Bowers covered lie after lie after lie, and you all thought you were one big happy family. What a joke. "And then I had to hear about Tressa's engagement and wedding plans. It sickened me. All I heard from Gregory was 'Tressa isn't happy, I can tell, I know her. She always looks sad; that clown is no good for her.' He would come to me, hold me and love me; take me out to fancy restaurants and buy me flowers, and before the night ended I would hear her name. Then it dawned on me, "he must think we're just buddies." Why else would he feel like he could talk to me about her? But he loved me, he told me so. The truth is he was blinded by his feelings for Tressa. Remember the wedding when he made a mockery of himself? Do you know that weak wimp actually laid his head on my chest and cried the day she was married."

Stomping her feet and squirming, trying to break away from Devan, she wanted it known he betrayed her, and she had made it her mission to destroy the two women that held a place in his heart. "Tressa will never admit that she enjoyed his mooning over her, but that's over; I took care of him. "I encouraged the crush she had on Gregg. She was just like you Simone—stupid. All these years, you thought of me as "nothing." I was just your stupid little sidekick. Now, what do you say, hotshot? I pulled the wool over your eyes. But so did Gregg. I guess you're wondering what brought this to a head; I'll tell you. Do you believe that Gregory Montgomery in his will bequeathed half of everything he owned to none other than Tressa Bowers-Dallas? Ciera paced, disgusted. "Do you know what he left me? He left me NOTHING! NOTHING! But that wasn't the killer, the last straw was the song he recorded on a CD and played in his car and on his phone. I hated it, Cherish the Love. And after all these years, he still had a picture of her by his bed. You know by that old group. Whose love was he cherishing but hers?" No one was surprised to learn Gregory kept a picture of Tressa by his bed. However, they were shocked to learn he had left everything to her. He truly loved that woman. Devan tried to console Ciera, but she was beyond comforting. She was angry, cursing and swearing. "Ciera, what did you mean when you said you took care of him?" "Just what I said, I took care of him; he's probably trying to make a deal with the Devil about now, and so be it—the bastard!" "Ciera are you saying Gregg is dead? Did you kill him?" "I left him gasping for his last breath, lying on the floor, calling for Tressa; so to hell with him." Ciera smiled, looked around at the crowd and said, "Like I said, you all have always thought of me as stupid; I'm admitting nothing. Devan Bowers, I plead the fifth." She stuck her hands out to be handcuffed. "Wait, I need to say something to Ms. Jessica." Devan didn't think it was a good idea, but Ciera insisted. Jesse walked up to her and waited for Ciera's revelation. Miss Tootie Fruity, I want you to know that your best friend (Ms. Vye) knew about Gregg's escapades. I hope this hurt your heart like Gregg hurt mine." "Ciera, this is discouraging news but not devastating. If Vye kept this from me, she was trying to protect me. Maybe it was misguided, but I believe it was done in love. So dear girl, I refuse to give you what you're looking for." "That's special, a real friend, I never had one." Simone scoffed. "That's a lie Ciera; I loved you like a sister, and I still love you. Look at me Ciera; I'm Simone, your best friend." Simone reached out to embrace Ciera, but she yanked away. "Don't you get it, Simone, how many ways can I say "I hate your guts? Do me a favor and never contact me again." With that, she beckoned the officer to open the car door. She showed no emotion; she was cold and indifferent. Who was this woman? Simone had lost a lifelong friend. "Mom, I didn't see this coming, what am I to do? She needs someone." "Simone, if and when she needs you, she will let you know, but for now, leave it."

Devan knew he had to find out if Ciera had harmed Gregory. He phoned him, and the answering service came on; he called his cell, nothing. In a flash, Devan and a stream of officers rushed to Boney Lane. Devan knocked repeatedly, no one answered. The officers looked in the back windows and saw someone lying on the floor. They broke down the door and rushed to see who it was. It was Gregg: he was deceased. Devan couldn't believe what he was seeing; he excused himself, sat in his car and cried. Gregg was a cad, but he did didn't deserve this. He regained his composure and did his job.

He found a note written to Gregg asking him if he was coming over, signed Rena. Who was Rena, perhaps one of his girlfriends? He played his answering machine and found a treasure trove of information. There were numerous calls from a Doctor Spiegel asking Gregg to return his call. He had not kept any of his appointments, and he checked with the pharmacy and discovered he had not refilled any of his prescriptions.

Devan discovered this was his primary care doctor. This was going to be hard; he dreaded calling Vye to give her the news.

Learning that Vye was aware of Gregory's affair with Ciera was a bit unnerving, but Jesse took it in stride and felt Vye had her reasons. Tressa wasn't as understanding; she was furious with her. In Tressa's mind, this was an awful deception; however when she heard about Gregg's death, she was horrified. "Did Ciera do it, do they know? Lord Mom, we need to get to Ms. Vye. Regardless of what she knew, she needed them." Marcus was not surprised to hear those comforting words. That's why he loved Tressa; she was kind and forgiving.

Devan had his hands full. He arranged for a senior detective to investigate the mysterious goings on at the "Dallas Estate." They needed to locate the secret doors and identify these mysterious people that were coming in and out. Avery and Les had already begun investigating. They took the children to Avery's home to be safe.

The detectives, with the assistance of Les and Avery, familiarized themselves with the blueprints and found the stairway that led to the children's room. Clicking the switch three times as directed by Jazz, the door opened. When the door opened, they smelled a familiar odor. "This smells just like that witch's perfume," said Avery. "She must have been hiding or sleeping in here." They slowly crept down the stairs, feeling the presence of someone. "Simone is that you?" "No, it's Les Dallas." They reached out to grab whoever it was, but she threw a can in their way and quickly escaped through an open door that led to the outside guest house. "Dad,

call the officers that are stationed outside, I'll get her."
Just as they had decided to go to Ms. Vye's, the phone
rang. All Tressa could hear were wails, screaming and
wailing. "Vye, we're on our way!" "No don't come; you
don't understand, it's dangerous. She is out to kill him;
forgive me, I should have told you. But I just thought it
was the plans of a silly woman." "What do you mean
Vye, tell me?" "No, Marcus move out of the way!" Tressa
turned to see Avery running with all his might. A
woman was behind the wheel of a big black SUV with
her high beams on, driving straight towards Marcus.
She was laughing and crying, and could hear her
yelling, "My love, my love. You told me you loved me,
and now this, no more." Just as Avery snatched Marcus
out of the way, they watched in horror as Tressa slip-
ped, and the car smashed into her. The driver quickly
turned and sped away. Police cars chased her; she was
driving about 100 miles an hour. It was a high-speed
chase, and she was making headway. Tressa was covered
in blood, bleeding profusely from her head. "Tressa,
speak to me, who am I? Tressa, can you open your
eyes?" She did not respond. Marcus kissed her forehead
as Avery called for an ambulance, and within minutes,
they arrived. Hearing the sound of the ambulance,
Jesse and Les hurried to see who was hurt.

She saw Marcus and Avery kneeling over
Tressa. "My God, my baby, my baby; did anyone see
who it was?!" "Yes, Jesse, it was Ma Lizzy! She was
trying to kill Marcus but hit Tressa instead." Simone
was in shock; first Gregg and now her sister. What
had they done to deserve this? Simone wanted to
make a bargain with God but prayed instead; she begged
God to save her sister's life.

Marcus rode with Tressa in the ambulance, and the family followed. Jesse felt so guilty. She wanted to comfort her best friend, and now she needed comforting. She thanked God for the warm and loving arms of Avery and the comfort of Les and Simone. This was going to be a long night.

Tressa was wheeled into the emergency room at record speed. The family gathered in the waiting area; they prayed until they felt prayed out; the only thing they could do now was wait.

After what seemed like an eternity, Dr. Wheeler came out to speak to the family. "Sorry, it took so long; we had to wait for the results of her tests." He explained Tressa's condition. "Mr. Dallas, your wife has sustained multiple injuries. She has cracked ribs; serious injuries to the brain; her right arm is broken, and there may be damage to her spinal cord. It does not look good. We are going to take her up for surgery. The surgeries are extensive and will probably take many hours." Marcus was all over the place; he could not wrap his head around this. Not Tressa, his jewel.

Dr. Wheeler paged Detra. When she appeared, she saw the family in the hallway. "What's going on? Did something happen to the children? Who's hurt? Tell me!" Marcus held her for a few minutes before telling her; he needed to get himself together. "Detra, Tressa is in a critical condition. She was trying to protect me from Ma Lizzy." "Ma Lizzy? What did she have to do with this?" "We're not sure. It seems she and Ciera had made some type of pact to ..." Marcus broke down; he couldn't go on. Avery filled Detra in on the rest. "That sly two faced ... I knew she was up to something!" "Detra, you haven't heard the rest. Gregg is dead; they believe Ciera killed him. We know what drove Ciera to do what she did, but, Ma Lizzy, we haven't a clue." Jesse realized Devan did not know about Tressa. He was dealing with the death of Gregg and assisting in the capture of Ma Lizzy, and now, his sister was critical. Simone took the lead. "Mom, you've had enough; I'll call Devan." "Hello." "Devan, you need to come to Community Lifeline Hospital; it's Tressa. I'll fill you in once you get here." "No, tell me now; is my sister dead?" "No, Devan, she's alive, hurry." Just as they were taking Tressa up for surgery, Devan burst through the doors. He was frantic, "Where's Tressa?" "Devan, they're taking her up now for surgery." Jesse took Devan aside and explained what had happened. "Here I am trying to solve the death of that creep, and my sister's life is in limbo. Lord, please don't let Tressa die, please!" "Devan, what happened to Ciera, is she locked up? Have they caught Ma Lizzy?" "Yes, Mom. Ciera is locked up, and depending on the charges, she may be in there for a lifetime or at least, I hope so. She is being questioned; however, she has not confessed to killing Gregg. And no, we haven't caught Ma Lizzy." "Have you talked to Vye?" "Yes, I have, she is devastated. She kept asking me if I thought you would forgive her." "There's nothing to forgive. I never told her everything about my children; I didn't feel the need." Devan smiled at his mother. "Mom, I know Ms. Vye is your best friend, but there's more to the story. That's why she's hoping you will forgive her." "That may be, Son, but right now she needs a shoulder to cry on, not someone contributing to her pain." Devan nodded. "OK, Mom, you're right."

As the family waited, local programming was interrupted. "This is Duncan Townsley of WDDE News, reporting on a high-speed chase of the woman responsible for the attempted murder of a leading citizen. The woman is being identified as Mazzie Lee, known to everyone as "Ma Lizzy." She's driving at least 90 miles per hour. Police say there's possibly someone who is in the car with her. The police are trying to contact her family. This woman is a danger to the public. The police are asking the public to avoid expressway 222. Spikes are being laid across the road to stop the car." Just before Mr. Townsley signed off, the cameras focused on the car hitting the spikes, it overturned and caught fire. The door jammed, preventing the police from rescuing Miss Lee. She could be seen trying to open the door, and it was confirmed that there was a dog in the passenger seat. The police ran with fire extinguishers to extinguish the fire. They smashed the window, released the lock and pulled her out of the van. "This is Duncan Townsley returning to local programming." What the newsman didn't want the public to see was Ms. Lee's badly burned body. Ma Lizzy grabbed one of the policemen and pulled him close to her. Barely breathing, she asked him to tell Marcus she loved him! No, tell him I love him too! Please promise me you will tell him I love him. I know he's been waiting to hear this from me." "Yes, miss, I promise to tell him." She was carefully placed in the ambulance, and with the assistance of the same police that had just chased her, they escorted the ambulance to the hospital.

The fire department was on the scene in minutes. Flames from the car could be seen for miles. "This is incredible; all in one night. I am happy that crazy demon has finally been stopped. I pray they don't bring her here; I'll kill her," cried Les, "I'll kill her! She hurt my Tressa!" Les was shaking uncontrollably. Detra asked that he be given a sedative to quiet his nerves. Marcus had settled in a corner with his head down, praying and weeping. Avery was the rock. He did his best to comfort everyone. He reassured Jesse that the family would be celebrating anniversaries and more Christmases together. He asked everyone to have faith, believe that Tressa will be healed and that she would pull through this. Marcus's faith was at an all-time low; he was scared. Per Detra's request, the hospital chaplain visited the family and offered hope and prayers.

Ma Lizzy survived the explosion. With every breath, she asked to speak to Marcus. Les and Avery were appalled that he had consented to see her. Marcus agreed to see her because he needed answers. Les and Avery accompanied him; they wanted to hear her explanations and to keep Marcus from knocking her head from her shoulders.

Ma Lizzy was taken to Memorial Hospital across town. When they entered her room, she was covered from top to bottom, wrapped like a mummy. Her eyes, nose, and mouth, were exposed. The nurse whispered to Ma Lizzy to let her know she had company. She spoke slow, careful words; Marcus had to lean in close to hear her. "Is it Marcus, my beloved Marcus?" Marcus knew he had to act concerned, but he hated every minute. "Yea, Lizzy it's me, Marcus." "Come closer." Marcus leaned in closer. "Darling, I love you more; she could never love you like I do. I have every card, every note you've ever written me. I know you were miserable with her. The way she spoke to you; I overheard her tell you to get out. She wanted you to sleep on the streets, and she spent your money like it was water and had all those babies and then got another one. What was she trying to do to you? Not my love; how dare she? If she loved you, she ..." Ma Lizzy drifted off, perhaps it was the pain medicine. "Is she dead Marcus?" "No, Dad, that kind never dies. She'll live for another 100 years. What a sad, misguided woman." "How and why did she get the impression I cared for her. I never gave her any cards or notes, and how did she hear ...?" Marcus stopped ... "She was sneaking in the house through the secret doors. But how did she know how to get in the house?" Les knew, "I bet it was Mr. Crenshaw. She probably bribed him."

When Marcus, Les and Avery returned to the hospital, Dr. Wheeler was talking to Jesse and Devan. Marcus searched the doctor's face for good news. "Dr. Wheeler, how did it go?" "We repaired the bleeding artery in her head; she's on a breathing machine. Only time will tell if she will walk or regain her memory. She's going to need a lot of prayers." "Can we see her?" Marcus asked anxiously. "She's sedated, and I must warn you she's swollen; be gentle with her." "Yes, one at a time and for no more than five minutes." They were given protective gear to guard against infection. Marcus was horrified; this was not his wife. She had tubes running everywhere. Her eyes were closed; she looked like she was in a coma. He sat beside her; gently holding her hands. "Hi, my love, it's Marcus. Can you hear me? Tressa, can you hear me?"

He kissed her hands and laid his head beside her face. "Baby, please, don't leave me; I can't make it without you! Tressa, I love you, everything will be alright. You have to fight; fight your way back to us. Don't let the enemy win. The children have been asking for you, and I told them you'll be home soon. Babe, my five minutes are up; your momma wants to see you. I am not going to leave you; I'm just a few steps away, I promise." "Mr. Dallas, your five minutes are up." "Yes, I was just leaving." The nurse told the other family, per the doctor's request; she wasn't able to see anyone else today, perhaps tomorrow. They camped out at the hospital. Dr. Wheeler said the next 48 hours were crucial to her recovery. No one left; the children were with the babysitter, who assured Marcus they were safe and being taken care of. Devan assigned a police car to sit in front of the house.

Rev. Rayford visited the family daily. He was vigilant; whenever they needed him, he was there. When allowed to enter the room, he anointed Tressa.

After two days, they saw no progress; miraculously, on the third day she had regained consciousness, and her breathing had improved. She responded to the doctor's questions and began to receive therapy. Prayerfully, she was on the mend. Dr. Wheeler cautioned the family that Tressa was a long way from going home. She would need months of therapy, her speech was slurred, and she would have to learn to walk again. Marcus didn't care; she was alive.

Les made a recording of the children to play for Tressa, and Avery brought pictures to display. It was apparent that Tressa was well thought of—her friends, church members, co-workers, and neighbors sent so many cards, balloons and tokens of love that her room looked like a shrine.

As she gradually improved and things started to seem somewhat normal again, the family was allowed to visit longer. The children drew pictures of them and sent daily drawings. Jazz cried for his mother; he missed her and wanted to see her. Because Tressa was in critical care, no children under 12 were allowed to see her. However, they were allowed to talk to her on the phone. Tressa never tired hearing their voices. "Mommy call your children, they are listening; you are on speaker phone." "When are you coming home, we miss you so much. It's not the same without you. Just in case you forgot, this is Bulee." "My sweet baby, I know who you are; I haven't been gone that long. I hope to be home soon; Mommy is doing much better. When I come home, I'll need your support. Now, you be good for Daddy. Love you, hugs and kisses." "Hugs and kisses, Mommy."

Tressa had been in the hospital for three weeks and was beginning to get restless. She tried to get out of the bed on her own and fell. When Marcus entered the room, he heard her moaning. He hurried around the side of the bed and saw her. "My Lord." He tried to lift her, but Tressa cried out in pain. The assigned nurse had just entered the room and saw him trying to lift Tressa. She buzzed the nurse's desk for assistance. Dr. Wheeler was paged, but he was in surgery. Marcus was furious. "Why wasn't someone watching my wife? Why were the rails down? I want answers dammit!" "Mr. Dallas, I will get to the bottom of that, but right now, we need to attend to your wife. Please leave us to do our job." "And you are?" "I am Dr. Phillips; Dr. Wheeler is in surgery." "Yea, yea, yea; just take care of my wife." "She will need an MRI a stat." The results were not good. The area in which she had previously had surgery was bleeding. Dr. Phillips assembled a team of surgeons and operated. Dr. Phillips told Marcus it was unfortunate they had to operate on the same injury and told him the recovery time had obviously changed. "Dr. Phillips, be honest with me; if she's going to recover from this, what are her chances? I need to know." The doctor shook his head. "Mr. Dallas, I don't know; she hit her head twice in the same area. I truly don't know what to tell you." There were no more tears, no prayers. "Lord, I can't pray anymore, and I can't cry, forgive me." Les and Avery had made up their minds to ask Marcus to move Tressa to a better hospital, a private facility.

They didn't think the care she was receiving was up to par, Marcus agreed. They chose Mt. Saint Williams Hospital across town. The day of the transfer, Tressa took a turn for the worst. She began to slip in and out of consciousness. Detra made her as comfortable as possible; they cancelled the move until she was more stable. Sometime during the midnight hour, Tressa awoke and asked for Marcus. He had just stepped out of the room. "Marcus, babe, where are you?" "I'm right here Tressa." "Marcus, come lie beside me. Let me feel your body next to mine." Marcus threw caution to the wind and lay beside her. She asked him to put more covers on her; she was cold. "Marcus." "Yes, babe." "I need to talk to you." Marcus took her hand. "I am here."

She struggled for breath and the right words. In a weak voice, struggling for her next breath, she said "Marcus Daye Dallas, we have lived life's greatest love story. I don't know two people that have devoted themselves so completely to each other. Other than God, I don't think I have shared my heart with anyone else to the point of pain. I asked God to forgive me for thinking of you so much and neglecting my children in thought. My heart still beats a thousand times a minute when I see you enter a room. The way you move still thrills me. You are the best father a child could have and a man that was born to be a husband. You are an awesome provider, a man of God; funny, kind, and patient. No woman could have asked for more. My soul longs for you when you are out of my sight, and when I miss you the most, you always appear. Do you know what I cherish the most? The day you told me you loved me. Do you remember Marcus?" Marcus smiled. "Yes, Tressa I remember. I played 'Betcha by Golly Why' and when they got to the part 'forever will my love for you be growing strong,' I sang long and loud. And you joined in—we sang to each other on a cold and rainy night." "You sure did, making all that noise." "That was the second time I told you I loved you." "It was?" "Yes, it was." Tressa took his hand and played with his wedding ring. "My man." She laid her head on his chest and said, "Tell the children I love them," and passed away. "Tressa, Tressa," Marcus looked down to see Tressa's closed eyes; just then, out of the corner of his eye he saw a cloud slowly moving across the sky until he could no longer see it. He lay there holding his wife, stroking her face. Detra walked in to make her rounds thinking Tressa had fallen asleep. "Marcus is she OK? Let me check the chart to see if she's due more pain medicine?" "No Detra, she's in no more pain; Tressa just passed away." Detra checked her pulse and dropped her head. "Yes, she's gone." Marcus's eyes widened, and his heart began to beat a thousand times a minutes. NO, NO, NO, NO! TRESSA! DEAR GOD, NOT MY WIFE. NO, NO, NO, JESUS YOU CAN DO ANYTHING, PLEASE BREATHE LIFE BACK INTO MY WIFE!"

With her warm body still in his arms, the doctor

came in to pronounce Tressa dead. Marcus stayed with her until family arrived. When Jesse arrived, she went to see her child. She buried her head into Tressa's stomach, begging her to come back. Jesse clung to Tressa with all her might. It took Detra and four nurses to lift Jesse off of her. "Jesse, come with me to the waiting area, the family is waiting for you."

It was pandemonium in the family. No one could believe she had passed. They didn't understand; she was recovering. What was Marcus to do? He was now alone with four children to raise. How was he going to tell his children their mother was not coming home? Avery gathered his son in his arms and held him for hours as he sobbed.

Marcus dreaded going home to tell the children their mother wasn't coming home. Les and Avery accompanied him for support, but Marcus insisted he tell them. When he entered their bedroom, he found them wide-awake. "What are you doing up so late?" "Waiting for you Daddy. We knew you were on your way home." "Really, how did you know that? I didn't call." "Jazz said because Mommy said you were on your way home and to be good children." Marcus called Les and Avery to the kids' room. He wanted them to hear what Jazz had just said. "Jazz, repeat to granddad and great-granddad what you just told me." "I'll tell you, Daddy," said Bulee. "Mommy was just here, and she told us to take care of Daddy until she comes back. She said she was happy to see us and that she loved us with all her heart. Then she threw us a kiss and walked out the door. We were so happy to see Mommy." "Yes, but Daddy, when is Mommy coming home?" Marcus explained that Mommy was in a different home, and that she would be with them forever, but not in the same way. He said she was happy because she was in heaven. "We know, Daddy, with the lady with the blue hair."

Over the next week, Marcus lost weight; he couldn't eat or sleep. Making funeral arrangements was one of the hardest things he had ever done. The day of the funeral, he sat in the limo until it was time to march into the church. He gathered up the courage to perform the service; it had to be performed with dignity with class. That's what Tressa would have wanted.

Rev. Rayford honored his wishes by allowing Marcus to perform the eulogy. Marcus walked in ahead of the casket and stood at the podium. The church was packed. Marcus talked for an hour, often taking long pauses. He talked about the early years, Tressa's pregnancy, their wedding, anything that came to his mind. He had nothing written down; he just spoke from his heart. The obituary was designed in the form of a letter. It sweetly told the story of a woman that was kind, loving, and cherished. Marcus's tribute to Tressa was like none other. Rev. Rayford said a few uplifting words, and Marcus allowed members of the family to speak.

Just before the benediction, Marcus requested the string quartet play a tune by the Righteous Brothers, and on the count of three, Marcus sang: "Oh, my love my darling, I hunger for your touch." He sang these precious words between tears. "I need your love." Avery couldn't stand it anymore, he escorted Marcus from the podium, and Rev. Rayford gave the benediction. Marcus wasn't sure he wanted to go to the cemetery.

At first he fought it, but Devan encouraged him to go. He promised him he would be there for him. "I don't think I can stand anymore Brother; I don't think I can. Please forgive me." "We understand Marcus, your family is here. This is the last leg of the journey." Marcus gathered up enough courage to attend the burial but refused to get out of the car and also declined attending the repast. He went home and climbed the stairs to the bedroom he had shared with his beloved Tressa. "Jesus, this has been the worst day of my life. Please grant me a good night's sleep."

Weeks later, Ciera was charged with second-degree murder of Mr. Goode. She confessed she had only wanted to frighten him, not kill him. Why, because he was responsible for executing Gregg's will, knowing how she felt about him. That was the last straw, a slap in the face. She had stood by him through thick and thin, and he left everything he owned except a small policy to his mother. Why? She was happily married and rich. The coroner concluded that Gregg died of heart failure. He had terminal cancer and chose not to take his medicine, but Vye believes he died of a broken heart. Ma Lizzy was placed in an insane asylum for the criminally insane for the rest of her life.

Simone received a fifteen-page letter from Ciera. She said she wanted her to try and understand why she felt the way she did and why she did such horrible things. She talked about how her mother had neglected and mistreated her. How every man she loved eventually loved someone else. The fact that she longed to be married and have children but realized that the only man she wanted was Gregory. Simone shared the letter with Marcus who in turn gave a copy to Devan to be used as evidence against Ciera. "Mom, listen to this: 'Simone (page 5): I've been planning and plotting for years as you very well know by now. Let me let you in on a few mysteries. I found out that Sheila, the Sheila that worked at Benton and Lewis, was the person sending Marcus those emails. The email warned him to "Watch Out, stay away from my girl!" This will floor you conservatives; Sheila was in love with Tressa. After getting to know her, Sheila knew that Tressa would adamantly reject any advances from the church girl. But that didn't stop her from taunting Marcus. And, I was the person that encouraged Tia to meet with Tressa, to pour out her heart to her. I blackmailed her into it; yes, blackmailed her. How, I found out that Tia was on drugs when her baby died, the pressures of motherhood, I guess. No, she didn't kill the baby, but the guilt and shame ate her up.

She couldn't imagine Marcus knowing she had smoked weed around their son; he hated drugs of any kind. She was another one that was searching for God, but unlike Simone, she wasn't sure she really wanted to find him. Quite frankly, I didn't care if she found him or not; I had ammunition to hurt Tressa by hurting Marcus. Did you wonder how she got that limp? She and I actually got into a fight; she fell and hurt her poor little leg and had to come to the meeting on a cane. Simone, you would say I'm sick, maybe crazy, but I say I used what I knew. I caused hurt and pain because others hurt me. The sad thing is, I'm not sorry. Now the ironic thing is both Tressa and Gregg are gone, and I can't do anything more to hurt either one of them except write letters. This is not a cry for prayers; I don't want them. The only thing is I want Gregg back! Please do not respond to this letter, I have no desire to communicate with you. Ciera.'" "She's lying Simone, the very fact that she wrote the letter in the first place says she wants you to respond; she definitely wants feedback. I suggest you avoid her but pray for her soul. One day, she may write to say she accepted the Lord Jesus Christ as her savior."

Ma Lizzy's daughter contacted the family and shared what they had found hidden behind a wall in her bedroom. It was a shrine. She had six-foot photos of her and Marcus, obviously imposed. There were boxes of cards and love letters supposedly signed by Marcus to her. One card looked original. It was a birthday card that was signed with only Marcus' signature. All over the card were kisses with red lipstick. They found neckties and cologne and pajama bottoms all belonging to Marcus. It was a treasure trove of tokens. In a diary, she wrote poems to him. And, disturbing items; hair brushes, locks of hair, upside down crosses, and pictures of the children and Tressa with Xs across their faces. It was awful, totally demonic. Devan had the articles boxed for evidence.

No one had a clue that those two women were so diabolical. Now, all secrets had been revealed, some at the loss of friendships, some at the loss of family, and others at the loss of past lives. Now, prayerfully, there would be peace.

Les remarked that it seemed they were living between heaven and hell. They were surrounded by good and evil. But in the end, the good prevailed.

Epilogue

The stress of the past few months since Tressa's death had taken a toll on Marcus. Sleep was a luxury. It was as if his prayers for peace and rest went unanswered. His father's words rang in his head. "Marcus, pray even when it seems God has ignored your cries." Lord, I've cried out in anguish, why have you chosen to ignore me. When Marcus shared these feelings with Avery, his heart sank. "Don't feel that way Son, we all loved Tressa and miss her terribly. You have four children to take care of and a family that would be lost without you. I am not going to lie and say I know how you feel. However I believe, in time your pain will subside, and you will find peace."

Marcus had fallen asleep, and he thought he felt the presence of someone by his bed. When he opened his eyes, he saw a beautiful misty figure. It was loving and comforting. His voice was like none other he had ever heard. "Marcus, I have heard your cries. Do my will, rest in my promises and trust in my word. I will never leave you nor forsake you Son. I took a precious jewel and left behind a man among men. I have a mighty work for you to do. It will not be easy. There are times you will grow tired and weary, but I'll be there to strengthen and encourage you. Now, rest and be blessed."

The following morning Marcus remembered every word. He had heard the voice of Jesus. He was happy and encouraged. He knew that the loneliness and longing for Tressa in time would be less painful. A knock came on the door. "Who is it?" "It's your children's daddy, can we come in?" Marcus closed his eyes and took a deep breath. "Yes, come in." The door flung open and they ran grabbing and squeezing him. "Daddy did you get a good night's sleep?" Marcus looked astonished, "How do you know I've been tossing and turning?" Budde answered, "Because mommy told us. She and the lady with the blue hair came for a visit last night. She told us to be patient and nice to you." Bunne spoke, "Daddy mommy also said to tell you not to wear that horrible pink tie with that plaid shirt." Marcus flinched, "She did, did she really tell you that?" "Yes, daddy, she did." They had no way of knowing that this was the outfit he had selected. Marcus knew Tressa was there; his heart was full of joy. Marcus looked lovingly in the eyes of each child; he saw a little of Tressa in all their faces.

**"Lord I am encouraged, your servant,
Marcus Daye Dallas."**

From the author

Mildred K. Simpson is a retired administrator of the Baltimore City Health Department and a proud graduate of Towson University.

Mildred is also a world traveler who currently resides in Baltimore, Maryland.

Contact: simpson540@comcast.net

CPSIA information can be obtained
at www.ICGtesting.com
Printed in the USA
BVOW06s1813271216
471947BV00001B/52/P